AF570675

UNSEEN
ELVIS

UNSEEN ELVIS

Candids of the King

From the Collection of Jim Curtin

A Bulfinch Press Book
Little, Brown and Company
Boston Toronto London

First Edition

Library of Congress Cataloging-in-Publication Data

Curtin, Jim.
Unseen Elvis: candids of the king from the collection of Jim Curtin.—1st ed.
p. cm.
"A Bulfinch Press book."
ISBN 0-8212-1912-X
1. Presley, Elvis, 1935–1977—Portraits. 2. Rock musicians—United States—Portraits. I. Title.
ML88.P76C87 1992
782.42166'092—dc20
[B] 91-30712

Bulfinch Press is an imprint and trademark of Little, Brown and Company (Inc.)
Published simultaneously in Canada by Little, Brown & Company (Canada) Limited

PRINTED IN THE UNITED STATES OF AMERICA

In memory of my parents

My mother, Louise M. Curtin (1921–1991), who stood by and supported me,
and who also tolerated my outrageous hobby—Elvis

My father, James J. Curtin, Jr. (1925–1988), who first turned me on to Elvis
(with the *Ed Sullivan Show*) and bought me my first
Elvis record (a 45 of "Return to Sender")

CONTENTS

Elvis has been an important part of my life since the first time I saw him. It was 1956, and he was performing on the Ed Sullivan show. His style just captivated me—the movements, look, voice, mannerisms, talent. This guy's wild, I thought. I was seven years old, and I was hooked forever.

So was America. We grew up with him, and so did our cameras. We started snapping him with our Brownies in the '50s, went on to give him Instamatic red eyes in the '60s, pointed and shot in the '70s. If Elvis had lived into the '80s and '90s, he would have become America's favorite home video.

Don't judge the photographs in this book on technical considerations. They're not professional—they're family pictures, clumsily captured records of important events. The people who shot them were overcome by emotion. This was the moment they'd long dreamed of: they were meeting Elvis.

I'm sure most of the unknown photographers represented here lovingly tucked their snapshots into picture albums next to all the other people they cherished. "The trip to Graceland" probably shared space with "Christmas '58" and "Graduation Day."

Look how young everybody is in the photos shown in the first chapter. Elvis' first fans were teenagers—girls, mostly. He shook 'em up with the way he moved on stage. Girls came to Memphis from all over, and waited outside the gates for a glimpse of Elvis. Look at the proud expressions on their faces. They got Elvis to pose with them! To smile just for them! They'll be able to show everybody they know!

And Elvis loved his fans. He knew his success depended on them, and he never took them for granted.

Once he got out of the Army, he'd grown up somewhat, and so had his audience. "It's Now or Never" was played on stations that catered to the parents of the kids who swooned to "Heartbreak Hotel." They became fans, too.

I didn't have much money growing up; summers would go by without an ice cream cone. I did a lot of odd jobs even as a young boy—returning used soda bottles for the refund, shoveling snow, painting addresses on houses, shining shoes. I'd hit every bar as far as 52nd and Market in Philadelphia shining shoes for a quarter, and practically every place I went into had Elvis Presley playing on the jukebox.

In 1962, my dad bought me my first record player for $38. Of course, I bought an Elvis record, "Return to Sender," to play on it. Then I bought my first album, "Elvis' Golden Records Volume I." The more I looked at the picture of him on the cover, the more intrigued I was. I decided I wanted every one of his records.

That's how I became a collector. I called every record shop in the Delaware Valley, all 116 of them, and drove to each one. By 1966, I owned every LP, album, and 45 Elvis had recorded.

Then I got in deeper. I wanted every 78. I wanted his foreign releases. When I got involved with the foreign fan clubs, I discovered that every foreign country had different covers. From 1966 to 1971, I went international. I was intrigued by any little differences in the releases—the cover art, the lyrics. I accumulated 5,000 records—652 songs — from 57 different countries.

My dad first turned me on to Elvis on screen. He took me see *King Creole*. Then I went back and saw it six times in one day. My favorite movie, though, is *Jailhouse Rock,* which I've seen about 50 times. I have every one of Elvis' films on both 16 millimeter and video.

Still, it wasn't until 1971 that I got to see Elvis in person for the first time. I paid $50 for a fifteenth row seat on the floor that sold for $15 at the Philadelphia Spectrum. From seeing the documentary *Elvis: That's The Way It Is,* I had a basic idea of the jumpsuits he wore and how he began a concert. But actually being there was different. When the lights went down and "2001: A Space Odyssey" came up, I got a supernatural feeling. I'd idolized this man since I was a little boy, and here he was in front of me.

After that, my passion to collect Elvis material took off. I didn't just want records but photos (I now have 25,000 of them, organized chronologically) and everything else Elvis related. That was a tall order; Elvis Presley Enterprise Products began manufacturing in 1956 and cranked out a lot of different products—menus, tour books of Graceland, buttons, lipstick, wallets, toy guitars, handkerchiefs, you name it. Things slowed down when he went into the Army in 1958, then built up again in the early '60s. The new products still came with a 1956 copyright.

Starting to collect this stuff more than a decade later put me far behind the game, which was frustrating and expensive. Elvis lipstick was a dollar in 1956. Today, if you can find one on the original card, you'll pay $1,000. Still, I managed to develop a collection which has made me an Elvis authority and a resource for numerous projects, including the best-selling Elvis poster in history and eight calendars.

I had several face-to-face encounters with Elvis. After seeing *Elvis: Aloha from Hawaii* in 1973, I decided I had to meet him. But how? Millionaires have tried to bribe their way into Graceland without success. I knew I'd need something different. The closest thing to Elvis is his music, so I designed a custom guitar and commissioned the Gibson Corporation to build it—a black acoustic instrument with Elvis' name on the finger board and two crowns inlaid in mother of pearl. With the case it cost $2,000 and took almost a year to make. Gibson shipped it to me in June 1974, a few days late to try to get it to him during his Philadelphia tour.

So I set my sights on Las Vegas, three months away. At the time, I was working at a supermarket in South Philadelphia, making $122 a week. I saved every nickel for a year to put together the money for my scheme to meet Elvis. When I flew to Vegas, I was afraid to put the guitar in luggage, so I bought another seat for the guitar.

Once I got out there, I managed to meet

Vernon Presley at the Hilton, by the dollar one-armed bandits. I explained that I had this $2,000 guitar that I wanted to give to Elvis. He said, "I'll see what I can do." I saw 29 shows in Las Vegas, paying $150 per show to sit right up front so I could shake his hand. It was worth it, though. I got 32 handshakes.

A lot of people used to take my picture, too, in Vegas, because I'd started dressing like Elvis. I think he got a kick out of it; he'd come right over to me on stage during his show.

Still, after a few days with no word from Vernon, I almost gave up. Then one night, I was watching the show and Vernon found me and said, "Elvis wants to meet you. Go back to your suite and I'll call you. Then you can come up to see Elvis." At 5:00 A.M., he finally did, and I asked him over the phone if I could take a picture of Elvis, and he said no. Then he softened a little and said to bring my camera, but he couldn't promise anything. At 5:10 I went upstairs, past the guards on the 30th floor and into Elvis' suite.

Charlie Hodge offered me a Coke and said, "Hand me the guitar, I'll put it in tune." Soon Elvis walked in, dressed in black, sunglasses on. He smiled at me and walked past, through a beaded curtain. After a while, Vernon waved me in through that curtain, and I entered Elvis' living quarters. Everything was white and gold French Provincial, and there was a portrait of Elvis in his Army uniform with his parents hanging over the couch. I sat on the couch with his girlfriend, Sheila Ryan. Elvis walked out and said hello. I said, "Elvis, I've waited all my life to meet you." He gave me that little smile, then introduced me to Sheila Ryan, and sat on the couch with his arm around her. He was super-polite, and very down to earth.

I got the guitar, and leaned it in its case, upright against the coffee table in front of Elvis and sat down next to Elvis. I made sure my knee touched his, I couldn't believe that Elvis was sitting right next to me. Without touching the guitar, Elvis tilted his head and read the inscription on the fingerboard, then he asked me why did I put the crowns on the guitar. I said that I saw his movie *That's the Way It Is* and that he had a tan guitar with stars on it. I told him that I thought he was bigger than a star, that he was the King. Then he stood up and said, "Come here, you," and gave me a big hug. He picked up my guitar, put his leg up on the coffee table, and played and sang "Baby, What Do You Want Me to Do?"

Here I am holding the guitar I had made for Elvis.

After Elvis hugged me, I asked him if I could take a couple of pictures, and he said okay. Joe Esposito shot them, but the pictures didn't come out. I called Vernon at his office, and he said he'd try to help me if I came back to Las Vegas again. I got there in March 1975 with another $2,000 in gifts—a hand made leather karate belt with tigers carved into it, a 14K gold and turquoise ring shaped like a king's crown, and

18 hardback books on karate and other martial arts. Then I found out that Vernon had had a heart attack. I told my story to Joe Esposito, but I could tell he didn't believe me about my pictures not coming out and thought I just wanted to meet Elvis again. He said he couldn't promise anything, that Elvis had gained a lot of weight and wouldn't want any pictures.

Joe did call me to come to Elvis' dressing room. As soon as I walked in, Elvis said to Diane Goodman, his new girlfriend, "This is the fellow who gave me a beautiful guitar the last time I was here." After I gave Elvis the gifts I asked him, "Elvis, could I take a picture with you?" He lowered his head and wouldn't say a word. Joe jumped in: "Didn't I tell you not to ask him for pictures?" I said, "I know you hear a million stories, but the pictures I took didn't come out. I thought I'd ask the man personally."

It was Elvis who broke the tension. He promised me if I came to Memphis he would take the photos with the guitar again, because the guitar was in his home in Memphis. I then asked Elvis for a memento, something to bring back to Philadelphia to show a million people. He went into his dressing room and brought out one of his jumpsuits and handed it to me. Redd Foxx was there, and he said, "Now hug each other," and we did. I said, "I love you, Elvis," and he said, "I love you too."

That was the year I started impersonating Elvis. Fans seemed to like what I was doing. Then a friend of my mother's got me an audition at a hotel in Philadelphia. I got a band and an agent and on May 28, 1977—the same night Elvis was appearing at the Philadelphia Spectrum—I performed in public for the first time, at a Philadelphia club. Our next gig was the Great Gorge Playboy Club; then it was somewhere new every week, all around New Jersey, Pennsylvania, Maryland, Delaware, and New York. Finally, after 400 shows, I cut back.

I have spiritual feelings for Elvis, a closeness that I can't explain. That's why I do what I do. Something's making me do it. You know, my mother's due date for my birth was January 8, 1949, the same day as Elvis' birthday, but I was born six weeks earlier.

By the end, Elvis was a legend. He'd achieved more than any other entertainer in the world, and he rested on that. After 24 years of entertaining, including 1,100 concerts, he was burned out. His life just kind of crumbled: Recordings were slowing down, and the choice of material wasn't as good as in the old days. He and his wife had split up, he was estranged from the Colonel, and he'd lost a lot of his best friends. He was overweight and had a lot of health problems, and all his medications were taking their toll.

I'm proud of the photos on the following pages, and happy to share them with other Elvis fans. Cynics may wonder if the world really needs another book about Elvis, but unlike so many others, this book was created with love. It's a communal family photo album from his fans.

Any photo of Elvis that hasn't been published before is worth its weight in gold. It's like bringing him back to life for a split second. These photos tell the human side of Elvis, not just the superstar but the down-to-earth, regular guy, willing to give of himself to his friends and fans. Elvis gave away cars, houses, jewelry. He supported over 50 charities. He gave away millions of dollars. From 1961 to 1971, Elvis was the biggest single taxpayer in the U.S.—the I.R.S would come in and he'd say, "What do I owe you?" and write them a check.

The day after Elvis died, every store in the country ran out of his records. "Suspicious Minds," which was recorded in 1969, still sells one million copies a year. Over 700,000 people visit Graceland annually—the only residence that draws more is the White House.

Elvis' fans miss him, and even a lot of people who once put him down now realize he was a great person. He was a spiritual man, a generous man, a family man. He was someone I really admired, and I'll always be his fan. Elvis, we love you.

UNSEEN ELVIS

THE

He broke upon the world like your mother's worst fears, strutting on stage with long hair and black leather, singing songs from the wrong side of town. If the squeaky-clean '50s was the nation's most conforming decade of the century, Elvis was its flip side. Wearing enough grease in his dirty blond hair to turn it black, Elvis made love to his microphone and rasped a hybrid of southern gospel, rhythm and blues, and that new beat soon to be known as rock 'n roll. He was just expressing himself, but his idiom would be adopted by a generation.

Elvis was an original, who came in the nick of time to rescue a generation stifling in suburban complacency. As Sun Records' owner Sam Phillips said, "I knew if I could find a white man who had the Negro sound and the Negro feel, I could make a billion dollars." The throne was ready; the ticket was bought for the ride to the top of the charts. To his fans, even Elvis' death wouldn't interrupt his reign.

His beginnings were humble. The Presleys—Vernon, Gladys, and Elvis—were a poor family struggling to make ends meet in early-'50s Memphis, where they'd moved from Mississippi. They lived in public housing for a few years until Gladys' $4 a day nurse's aide job pushed them over the eligibility ceiling. When the Memphis Housing Authority evicted them, the Presleys moved from their small but well-maintained apartment in the public Lauderdale Courts to a dingy, $52 a month apartment on downtown Cypress Street.

Music had a powerful hold on Elvis from childhood. Gladys bought him his first guitar for $12.95—ironically, it was something she did just to distract him from the $55 bicycle he'd really been asking for. He soon figured out how to pick out a few chords, pestering a couple of guitar-playing uncles for help. Living along the Mississippi, the young boy grew up with musical influences as rich as the soil. Every Sunday and Wednesday, Elvis joined his mother for revivals at the Pentecostal Assembly of God Church, where he learned to sing spirituals. As a teenager, one of his favorite forms of entertainment was to attend all-night sings, where he was spellbound by the full lineup of top gospel quartets and quintets. Gospel provided the lyrics, but the beat usually ranged from swing to soul. These shows transformed church events into fast-paced entertainment complete with patter, full bands, choreography, costumes, and fancy hairdos.

From the nearby black part of town, Elvis was exposed to the black gospel tradition that was slowly evolving into R&B, and he probably tuned in often to WDIA, the South's first black radio station and a key factor in popularizing the blues.

Elvis graduated from high school in 1953 and soon began contributing wages to the family's income, which allowed them to move again, this time to their own frame house on Alabama Street. It was in their old neighborhood, near Lauderdale Courts, where many of their friends stilled lived. It was pretty crowded inside, with Elvis on the couch, grandmother Minnie Mae on a cot in the dining room, and Vernon and Gladys in the house's only bedroom. Elvis worked the summer of 1953 at Precision Tools, making shells for the Army. His $66 weekly paycheck outstripped his father's, but monotony and hassles with the foreman over the length of his hair soon prompted Elvis to look for other work. At summer's end, he began a year's stint driving a truck and working in the warehouse at Crown Electric. Even though Elvis took a pay cut down to about $41 a week after taxes, he enjoyed the job more.

During this period, Elvis was considering a musical career as a gospel singer, although he hadn't taken any formal steps in that direction. Gospel was his lifelong favorite type of music. He'd befriended members of a popular Memphis gospel group, the Blackwoods, and hung around with their younger, feeder group called the Songfellows. Elvis joined both groups for occasional rehearsals, and the Blackwoods sang backup for Elvis at all-night sings where, as James Blackwood observed, Elvis liked to sing with his eyes closed and hips moving. Elvis did occasionally sing solo on the secular stage, covering Dean Martin hits between big band sets at the Eagle's Nest, a motel and nightclub complex on the outskirts of Memphis. His dearest hope, though, was that one day he'd be asked to fill in an opening with either the Blackwoods or the Songfellows.

On June 30, 1954, the day after winning first place on "Arthur Godfrey's Talent Scouts" show, R.W. Blackwood was killed in a plane crash. When Cecil Blackwood left the Songfellows to take R.W.'s place in the Blackwoods, the Songfellows invited Elvis to join them. But by then it was too late for him to take advantage of what would once have seemed a golden opportunity. Declining the Songfellows, Elvis told them, somewhat sadly, that he'd already signed a contract to sing the blues.

Actually, he was about to help invent a new kind of music—rock 'n roll. He would do it in the service of Memphis' Sun Records. How Sun found, signed, and promoted the young truck driver with a sexy sound is familiar to every Elvis fan and is the stuff of recording-industry legends. He stopped into the record-your-own-record sideline at Sun Studios and plunked down $2 to cut a record for Gladys' birthday gift. When office manager and former radio personality Marion Keisker heard him sing, she remembered her boss' perennial search for a white man with a black sound and rolled her own tape recorder. Sam Phillips wasn't too impressed by what he heard first time around, but sometime later Elvis went in and recorded "Without You" and "I'll Never Stand in Your Way." Marion tracked him down for an audition based on that recording.

Phillips introduced Elvis to musicians Scotty Moore, who also would sign on a few weeks later as Elvis' first manager, and Bill Black, and several difficult weeks of rehearsal began. The magic was still missing the night they came into Sun to record, so the boys took a break after a few hours' earnest practice and started cutting up in the studio, singing a "race" song with a funky beat. Phillips ran in and told them to do it again on tape.

"That's All Right (Mama)," released in 1954, had its first airplay on WHBQ, a white station that played songs by black bluesmen. The night it was scheduled to air, Elvis tuned in the station so his folks could hear it. Then, overcome with shyness and stage fright, he ducked out to the movies.

Gladys and Vernon walked the aisles to find him: The song had been received with so much enthusiasm deejay Dewey Phillips (no relation to Sam) was playing it over and over again and wanted to get Elvis into the studio for an interview.

Selling 20,000 copies, "That's All Right (Mama)" was a respectable regional hit for about six months. It earned Elvis a few hundred dollars, a few more local singing gigs, and a slot on two of the nation's most venerable country music shows, radio's "Grand Ole Opry" and television's "Louisiana Hayride."

Elvis' debut at the Opry on September 25, 1954 gave him a rude introduction to show business. With a few hours to fill before the show, Sam took the group into a nearby juke-joint to hear a piano player. Elvis went in briefly, seemed uncomfortable, then said he'd just wait outside. When Sam asked why, he told him, "My mama wouldn't want me in a place like this."

Showtime only made things worse. Jim Denny, the Opry's talent booker, accused Elvis of violating their deal by not bringing the entire band heard on the single—he couldn't believe Sam had produced such a big sound from just Elvis, Scotty, and Bill. Emcee Hank Snow was snide about Elvis' name, unnerving him just as he went on stage. Their reception was cool from the hidebound Opry audience. Finally, Denny snapped at Elvis as he was leaving, "We don't play that kind of music around here. If I were you, I'd go back to driving a truck." Elvis cried all the way back to Memphis. Reporting to Crown Electric the next morning must have been a bitter disappointment.

Only three weeks after the Opry, "Louisiana Hayride" proved far more receptive to Elvis and the Blue Moon Boys, as Scotty and Bill were now called, offering them a year's contract. They took it—and spent weekends driving the 800 miles roundtrip from Memphis for a total of $42 each time for the band. On the plus side, they greatly expanded their audience over the airwaves and soon were completely wearing out Scotty's '54 Chevy Bel Air with steady tours throughout Louisiana, Arkansas, and Texas.

During this time, Scotty was Elvis' manager, collecting 10 percent of Elvis' share of any bookings he made. But Scotty preferred playing to booking, and all the road trips sleeping in the back of the car were wearing him down. He figured it would help to be able to concentrate on music instead of marketing. So after just six months, he handed the manager's hat over to Bob Neal, a Memphis deejay, and went back to being a full-time Blue Moon Boy. Bob drew up a simple contract that gave him 15 percent of the gross on any bookings he made, and the still-underage Elvis and his parents signed.

At first, it was Bob Neal's fame that drew people to the concerts he lined up in schoolhouses and advertised on his radio show and with fliers posted around town. His wife collected the cash—about $300 a night—in a cigar box. But soon enough it was Elvis who attracted the crowds. Word of his magnetism on stage plus the songs people were hearing on Bob Neal's radio program built a local following. The Blue Moon Boys played 200 gigs in 1955 alone.

Bob pushed the boys hard for strategic reasons as well as monetary ones. Beyond his own enthusiastic spinning, he was getting rebuffed in his radio-play promotional efforts. Elvis was rejected by country stations as too bluesy, by blues stations as too country, and Bob realized that it wasn't going to be the airwaves but personal appearances that would build his client's momentum.

His next managerial act was to change the terms of Scotty and Bill's membership in the Elvis juggernaut. They'd each been getting 25 percent and Elvis, 50 percent. But Elvis was the star, and Bob informed the boys that he was taking away their share and paying them a salary instead. Despite grumbles, they stayed.

Somehow, the boys also managed to pack in some Sun studio time among all the touring. Many consider these Sun recordings the height of Elvis' creative powers. He had a lot of fun, preferring long studio jam sessions to hours of rehearsal. His phrasing and delivery were inventive and playful; experimenting with songs by various artists, he would syncopate and jazz up the beat until the sound was his own. When he toured, Elvis the wild technician became Elvis the unfettered performer. The hip thrusts, splits, and amorous touch on the microphone were no affectations, no additions urged by his managers. Elvis was the Pelvis right from the start.

This sizzling new talent that was Elvis Presley caught Colonel Tom Parker's eye as early as 1954. Parker had heard about him from several of his talent scouts, and in February 1955 he helped Bob Neal book Elvis onto a two-week tour of Nevada. In May, he signed Elvis up with Hank Snow's southern tour. The Colonel must have gotten quite a jolt watching Elvis ignite a virtual riot in a crowd of 14,000 in Jacksonville, Florida, as he was recovering from a heart attack.

One month after being rejected in his audition for "Arthur Godfrey's Talent Scouts" television show, Elvis scored with an entire stadium. He was nearly smothered to death by a female crowd whipped to a feverish pitch by his performance and concluding whisper to the microphone, "Girls, I'll see you backstage." Several hundred took him at his word, and stadium security had to rescue him. Soon other artists on Snow's circuit refused to perform in the slot following Elvis. He was too tough an act to follow.

Late in 1955, Colonel Parker started moving in on the position of Elvis' manager, laying the groundwork to take over from Bob Neal when his contract expired on March 15, 1956. One of his first acts was to get Elvis airplay north of the Mason-Dixon line, over radio station WERE in Cleveland, where deejay Bill Randle set the same clamor spinning as Dewey Phillips had in Memphis. Next, after long negotiations, he got RCA Records to purchase Elvis' contract from Sun Records for the then hefty price of $40,000 plus a bonus to cover future royalties Elvis would have received from Sun.

Sam Phillips probably regretted the deal for the rest of his life, but at the time he needed the cash, and Elvis was still purely a "live" phenomenon. His concerts were a lot more powerful than his record sales. Besides, Phillips' attention was elsewhere, focused on a new artist, Carl Perkins. Only with hindsight would Phillips see that he'd put his money on the wrong pair of blue suede shoes.

Just 21 years old, Elvis was jittery when he entered his first recording session for RCA on July 2, 1956. He paced the room as the musicians set up (his fine studio band included guitarist Chet Atkins), then sat down at the piano and unwound a little by crooning a few gospel tunes—a ritual with which Elvis would begin recording sessions for the rest of his life. Harmonizing behind him were members of the Jordanaires, a quartet from the "Grand Ole Opry," who would become Elvis' regular backup group.

Ray Charles' "I Got a Woman" was the first song recorded that day. During the first take, Elvis didn't just sing, he performed—moving around so much that the mike missed half of his vocals. Producer Steve Sholes ordered him to stand still. Meekly, Elvis complied, but during the second try the spark was missing. "Mr. Sholes, please don't make me stand still!" Elvis said. "If I can't move, I can't sing!" The magic returned with a solution that let Elvis shake it up: extra mikes suspended from the ceiling to catch the singer wherever he was. Elvis performed with passion, landing from a jump into a kneedrop that split the seam of his pants and whacking the guitar so hard his fingers bled.

He then recorded the song that would deepen his image by hitting the heart of any teenager who had ever lost in love. The eerie, despairing tone of "Heartbreak Hotel" came from the echo chamber in which it was recorded, the "ooohs" and "aaahs" of the Jordanaires, and Sholes' minimalist instrumentation. Combined, the elements provided the perfect backdrop for Elvis' bluesy, woebegone lament. With this 45, Elvis became the first artist to hit number one on all three *Billboard* charts—Hot 100, country, and rhythm and blues.

The day after the January release of "Heartbreak Hotel," Elvis, Scotty, and Bill made their first national television appearance on the Dorsey Brothers' "Stage Show." It would be the first of five performances, which sent "Heartbreak Hotel" up the charts with a bullet and landed Elvis appearances on the Milton Berle show, the Steve Allen show, and the Ed Sullivan show.

None of those shows gave fans the real Elvis. Steve Allen had him perform "Hound Dog" as part of a cutesy sketch with a live basset hound, while Sullivan dictated his musical selections and eventually, of course, shot his guest from the waist up—a phenomenon witnessed by an estimated 54 million Americans.

While the nation was won over, the critics were not. "Elvis," wrote Jack Gould of *The New York Times,* "might possibly be classified as an entertainer. Or, perhaps quite as easily, as an assignment for a sociologist." A week later, Gould elaborated. "When Presley executes his bumps and grinds," he wrote, "it must be remembered by the Columbia Broadcasting System that even the 12-year-old's curiosity may be overstimulated."

All the controversy got Elvis his first screen test, on April 1, 1956, with Paramount. His audition of a scene from *The Rainmaker* was amateurish but good enough to land him a three-picture deal worth about a half-million dollars.

Three weeks later, Elvis made his first Las Vegas foray. Ironically, this glitzy town that would nurture Elvis' comeback a decade later was disheartening the first time around. Instead of the screaming teens that were Elvis' adoring supporters, the New Frontier Hotel was filled with their blue-haired moms and disapproving dads. Curiosity was probably the most positive emotion they felt toward the long-haired, hip-thrusting performer. Their response was so lackluster, even hostile, that Elvis' name was quietly dropped lower and smaller on the marquee, until Colonel Parker and hotel management agreed to tear up the two-week contract halfway through.

For consolation, Elvis had his booming record sales and two months later another hard-driving session at RCA studios, where he sailed happily into pure pop terrain with "Don't Be Cruel," backed by "Hound Dog." The disk was a huge success, although putting two potential smashes on one record cost Elvis a lot in lost sales. Fans could thank RCA's inexperience with the pop world and its attitude of "grab-it-while-he's-hot" for the bargain of two hits for the price of one.

In the studio, Elvis was as original and natural as he was on stage. His musical talents included grasping a song's melody and often the lyrics as well, after just one hearing. He pioneered an instinctive approach to music that the pop world uses now as a matter of course and was the first pop star to really produce his own material. Elvis improvised arrangements as he went, then performed up to 60 takes on a given song until it had just the right feel.

By summer's end, Elvis was in Hollywood to film *Love Me Tender.* Paramount turned it into a musical by adding four songs, including the title one, after Elvis was added to the cast. RCA couldn't fail with this record release: The company received 856,327 orders before shipping a single one.

The young country boy brought a lot of enthusiasm and hope with him to Hollywood, and it comes through in his first film. Although teenagers were disappointed that *Love Me Tender* was a Western, not a rock 'n roll vehicle, they came in droves, enabling it to recoup its million-dollar costs within three weeks—a record at the time. Every theater in the land filled with screams as Elvis poured on his wonderfully sweet, unself-conscious smile. Elvis was very much himself: affectionate, handsome, shy, and sexy to the core. Although he didn't play the starring role in *Love Me Tender,* it was arguably his most compelling acting turn in more than two dozen leading screen roles. He gave the kind of natural performance that lent credibility to his dream, often expressed, of becoming the next James Dean.

Elvis longed to be a movie star, to use the rock 'n roll fame as the vehicle to bring him there. In those heady days, anything seemed possible. Serious acting wasn't the only desire about which Elvis spoke openly. He made no secret about his first Hollywood crush, on leading lady Debra Paget. He confided his unrequited affections to a few Tinsel Town reporters and in long conversations with Gladys, his lifelong confidante. He even asked Debra to marry him, by long-distance telephone from Texas.

But Debbie Paget—who rejected the newcomer as a hayseed—was just the first in a long line of starlets whose names would be linked with Elvis', from Natalie Wood to Nancy Sinatra to Ann-Margret.

There was one girl who did have Elvis' heart, and gave him hers, too. Memphis native Anita Wood met the town's leading citizen in 1957, and they stayed a steady item until Priscilla appeared on the scene five years later. Anita was petite, curvaceous, and talented, a pop singer and dancer struggling through the local stage-and-television circuit to break into big-time show business.

Anita was the Girl Back Home, both to Elvis and to the fan magazines. Yet she was forbidden to be candid about her role in Elvis' life. Marriage, deemed Colonel Parker, was out of the question. "We could not publicly admit that we liked one another or were going together," Anita says. "I always had to say that we were just friends because otherwise the publicity would hurt his image. He had to be free so that all the girls, the fans, could love him."

Once his national career began, success came fast and with a big, big bang. From August to December 1956, Elvis monopolized the airwaves with three number one hits. "All Shook Up" spent eight weeks at the top of *Billboard's* Hot 100 chart. His next two movies, *Loving You* and *Jailhouse Rock,* were produced and released within a year of the distribution of *Love Me Tender,* and Elvis was back in Hollywood to begin work on *King Creole.* He toured Canada and made a third appearance on Ed Sullivan. The income rolling in enabled him to give Gladys a pink Cadillac and to buy Graceland, where he established the Presley family compound.

He purchased the estate in March 1957 from a local Memphis family for $100,000, and he made it his home for the next 20 years. It became a Mecca for the King's millions of fans. Many photographs on these pages were snapped outside the estate's wrought-iron music gates, where admirers congregated for hours in the hope of getting a glimpse, a photo, or maybe even a word with Elvis. Such was the King's drawing power that when police anywhere in the United States were alerted of a female teenage runaway, they contacted Memphis first to check the throng outside the gate. Elvis was on top of the world, both personally and professionally.

Then, on December 20, 1957, he received a personal visit from the chairman of the Memphis draft board. He'd brought an induction notice for Elvis. Of all the boys in Memphis, why him? Why then?

Some suspect that powerful people wanted to get him out of the way: the forces of suburban complacency reasserting themselves. After all, Elvis was doing much more than inventing an art form: He had unleashed the passion of a generation and had redefined its relationship to music and dance, its attitude toward fashion and most of all, toward propriety. It was too late to push all that back in the box, but timid, conservative America was prepared to try. A draft certainly would get Elvis out of the way, at least for a couple of years, giving things a chance to settle down.

It worked. The meteor would shortly flame out, halfway across the sky. And a Memphis boy whose only crime was an uncontrollable wiggle on stage would pass many sleepless nights wondering when he'd have to go and whether his fans would remember him in his absence.

Opposite page: Elvis, age 9, at Lauderdale Courts, where the Presleys lived until Gladys' $4-a-day nurse's aide job meant eviction from public housing. The photo at right was Gladys' favorite.

Elvis had to borrow a bicycle—his parents had bought him a guitar instead.

Elvis is in the top-right corner, wearing overalls. He attended sixth grade in Milam School, Tupelo, Mississippi, after moving from East Tupelo, where he went to Lawhon Elementary.

Fifteen-year-old Elvis with friends.

With his fellow school library workers, Elvis is in the top-right corner.

Hanging out with friends, Elvis has already adopted a pompadour and jive style of dress.

Humes High School, Memphis, Class of 1953.

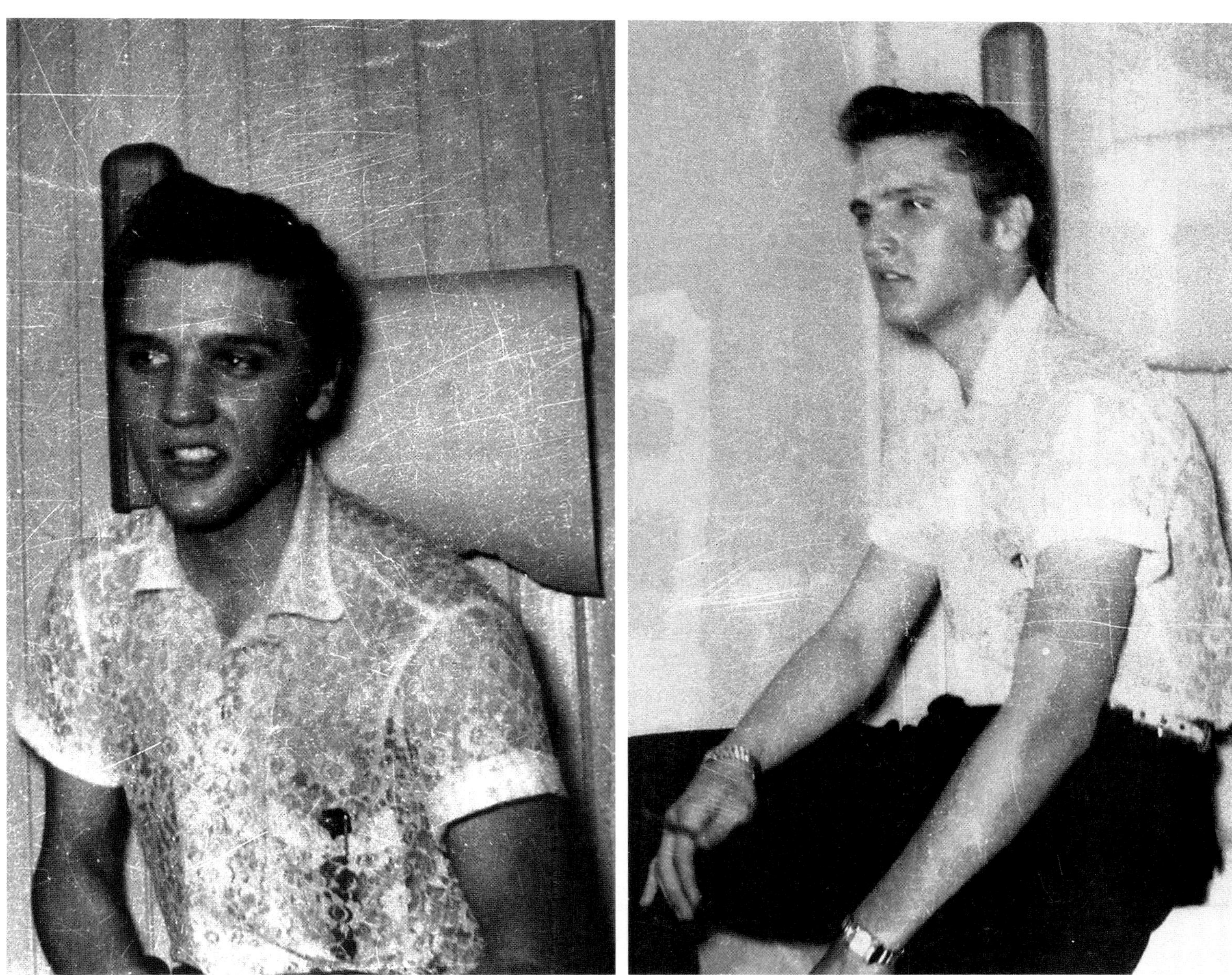

"I just relaxed and sang in my own style," said Elvis after his first recording session. The result was "That's All Right (Mama)," released in 1954, which had its first airplay on WHBQ, a white station that played songs by black bluesmen.

Opposite page: These photos were taken during Elvis' earliest barn-storming years. Clockwise from upper left: posing with a fan; outside the Eagle's Nest Club, where Elvis covered Dean Martin hits between big band sets; with a fan while on tour with Bill Haley and the Comets; snapped at the time Elvis was recording on the Sun label.

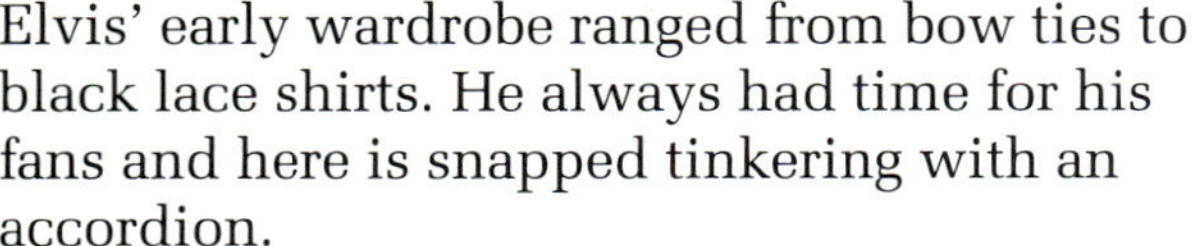

Elvis' early wardrobe ranged from bow ties to black lace shirts. He always had time for his fans and here is snapped tinkering with an accordion.

Opposite page: Elvis hugging super fan Jan Edwards, backstage, Richmond, Virginia, during the Hank Snow tour 1955.

All shot in 1955, a pivotal year for Elvis. He played 200 gigs with the Blue Moon Boys, including tours of Nevada and numerous states through the South.

July 1956. Elvis was vacationing at the Gulf Hills Dude Ranch in Biloxi, Mississippi, when fans recognized him and asked for autographs.

These rare photos were taken in Tupelo, Mississippi, when Elvis returned for the 1956 centennial of his birthplace. Memphis contributed police officers to guard its adopted son.

Opposite page: Elvis taking a break from a grueling schedule at the Gulf Hills Dude Ranch in Biloxi, Mississippi, in July 1956.

Elvis with fans.

With his pink Cadillac in Shreveport, Louisiana, in 1956.

In front of Lansky's Men's Store, where Elvis bought his clothes for "a dollar down and a dollar paid every week." (1956)

All taken in
Memphis in 1956.

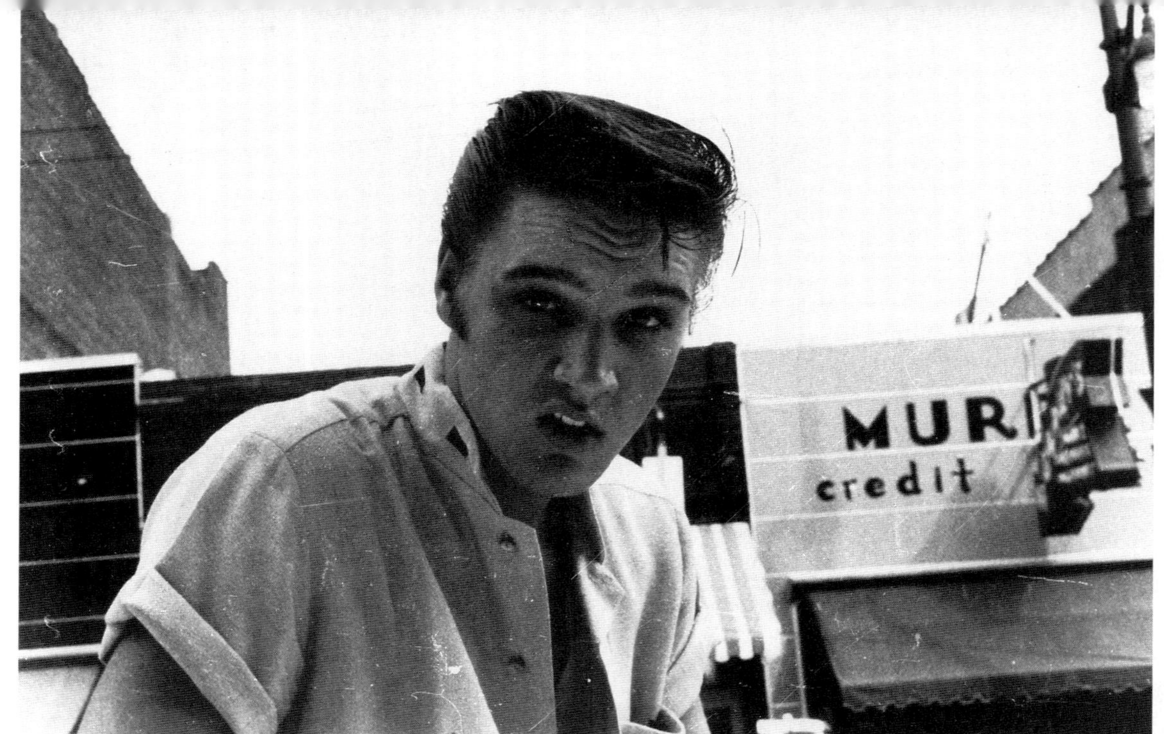

Elvis at home.

Elvis and his mom share a moment with an Elvis Presley fan magazine.

With three waitresses in Dallas.

With fans.

Backstage with fans following a 1956 performance.

Opposite page: Posing in front of the Presleys' new home on Audubon Drive, Memphis.

Posing outside WHBQ where the George Klein Radio Show was broadcast. (Memphis 1956)

April 1956 press conference at the Philadelphia Arena.

Left, outside the house on Audubon Drive, Memphis. Below left, with Scotty Moore, stopping for gas while on tour. Below, outside Ellis Auditorium in February. (All photos 1956)

Arriving at Graceland. (1956)

Opposite page: Two photos at top, "Win A I
With Elvis" Contest winner—Andrea June
Stephens from Atlanta, Georgia 1956.

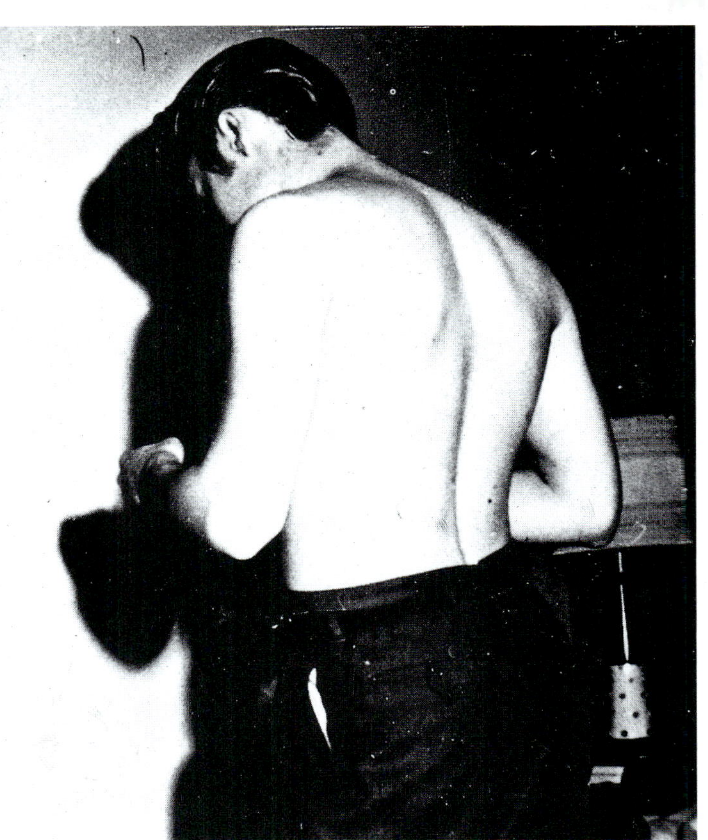

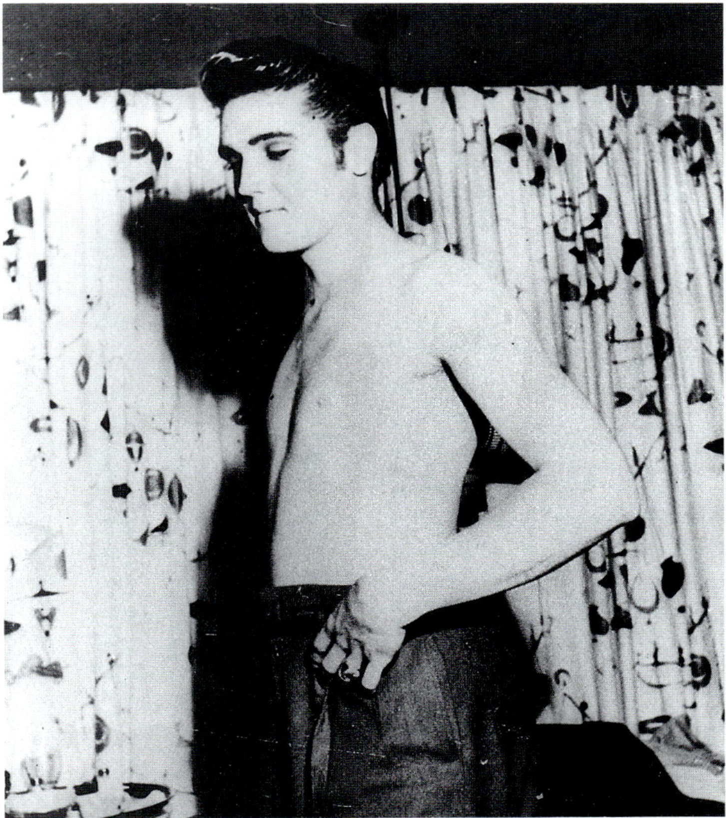

All of these shots were taken in Elvis' private suite at the Frontier Hotel, Las Vegas. After breakfast, he would read fan mail while playing records. (1956)

Opposite page: Taking a break during a "Love Me Tender" recording session. (1956)

The photos on these pages were taken in April 1956 at the Frontier Hotel, Las Vegas. Unfortunately, Elvis didn't get to perform for these fans but put on his show for their stodgy parents, who did not swoon for the entertainer that the hotel billed as "atomic-powered."

Mingling with the fans at the Frontier Hotel.

Elvis plays the piano for fan Judy Spreckles.

1956 mug shots.

At the end of the Frontier Hotel gig.

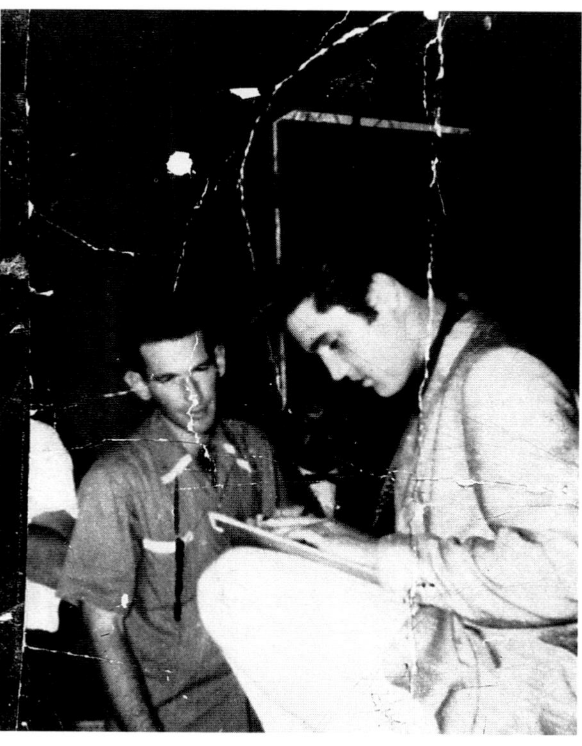

With fans in 1956. Upper left, Elvis autographs a shoe. Bottom left, with bodyguards.

With fans.

With Anita Wood.

A fan kisses Elvis for winning his court case alleging assault of a gas station attendant. (1956)

Elvis makes a personal appearance at a record store in San Diego, California the day after the Milton Berle Show.

The King relaxes. (1956)

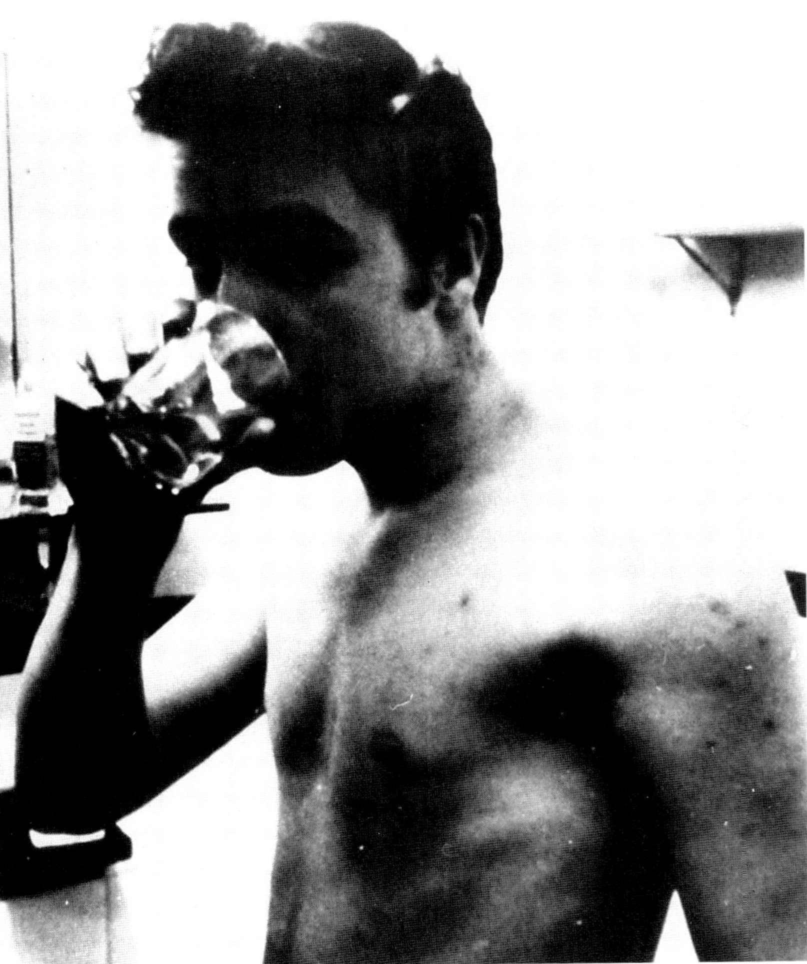

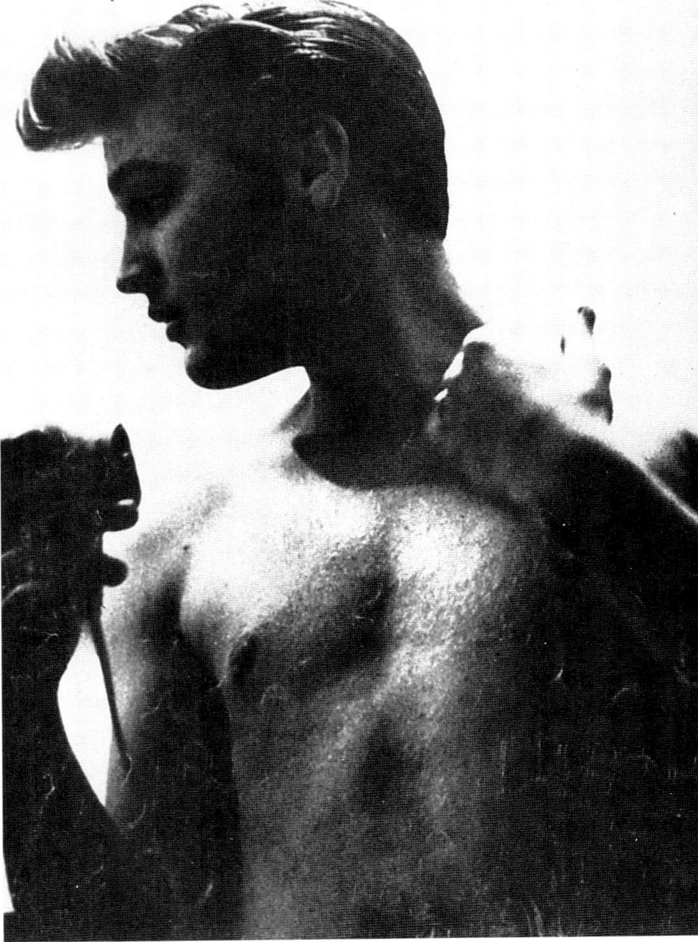

Morning ablutions. (1956)

With girlfriend Kate Wheeler in Dallas.

Captured after
a business meeting.
(1956)

Elvis already owns his horseshoe ring, one of his favorites.

Opposite page: In his '56 convertible.

Aboard the *Matsonia* en route to Hawaii. Elvis took a liking to these children and spent the whole day with them. (1957)

MEN'S
SHOP

All the photos on these pages were taken in 1957, about the time Elvis was making *Loving You*.

Autographing an Elvis Presley skirt.

Opposite page: Standing in an empty room inside Graceland. (1957)

Elvis with fans outside the gates of Graceland. (1957)

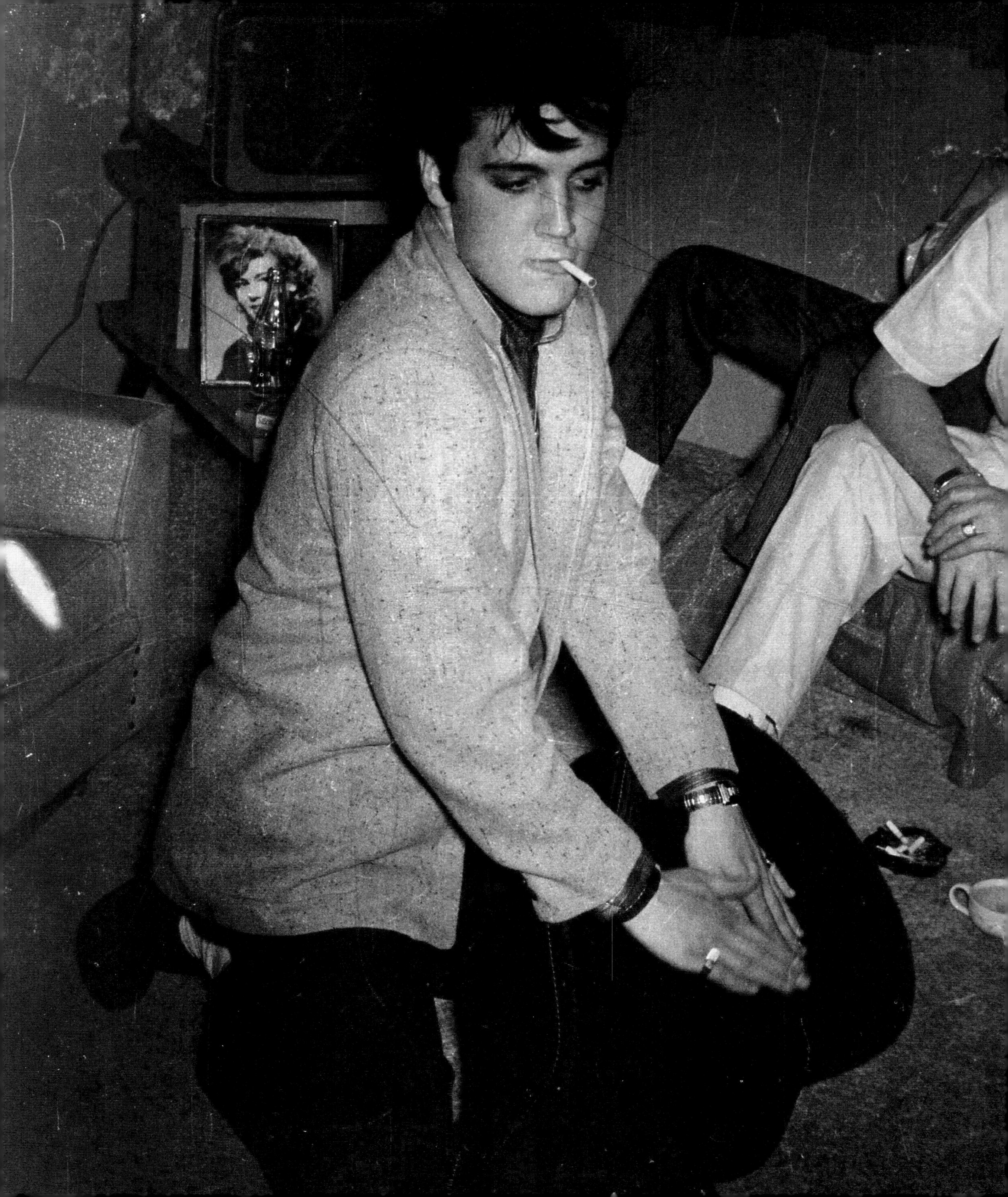

These two photos capture Elvis with fans during his only Canadian tour. The one at the bottom shows him with a fan in Ottawa after the April 3 concert. He's wearing his $10,000 gold lamé suit. (1957)

Opposite page: Elvis jokingly stole a cigarette from a fan before posing for this picture. (1957)

Opposite page: Upper left, Elvis relaxes. Upper right, with a fan in Tupelo, Mississippi, on October 3. Below, back in Memphis, driving one of his many cars. Elvis had a special fondness for convertibles. (All photos 1957)

Elvis and best friend George Klein, escorted by police while touring Canada. (1957)

Horseback riding at Graceland. (1957)

Meeting with fans on the New Orleans set of *King Creole*. (1958)

Opposite page: On the back steps at Graceland. Elvis' rock 'n roll years are drawing to a close with the decade. (1958)

While in New Orleans for the filming of *King Creole*, Elvis accepted an invitation to the home of some fans. (1958)

The Presleys plus a friendly fan on a family fishing trip on the *Aunt Jennie*. (1958)

Shortly before putting down his microphone to pick up a gun as a private in the U.S. Army. (1958)

THE

The visit from Memphis draft board president Milton Bowers was not unexpected. Nearly a year before, on January 4, 1957, Elvis had reported for his preinduction physical at a Memphis veterans' hospital. Unlike the usual recruit, who moves through the day with about 40 others, Elvis went it alone—relatively speaking, that is, given the hordes of fans, journalists, and photographers trying to grab a shot of the King with his robes off.

On January 8, Elvis' 22nd birthday, the Army recruiters held a press conference to pronounce Elvis "A-profile," the highest physical category. The Army spokesman declined to release either his actual score or the date Elvis might be drafted. That would depend, he said, on such factors as the Memphis quota and the number of local volunteers. Once he was called up, Elvis would get to select the branch of service he would like to enter.

The nation's teenagers bit their nails, awaiting word of Elvis' draft. But there could be no doldrums where the King was concerned. A tempest was still swirling around a published story that quoted unnamed Army sources as assuring that Private Presley would receive preferential treatment: hair left long, time off to record and make films, an abbreviated basic training period. The hint had surfaced first in *Billboard,* dateline Fort Dix, New Jersey, around the time of Elvis' physical, but other publications picked it up over time, including the *Associated Press.*

"Relax, girls!" was the AP piece's jovial beginning. Many readers did not. The notion of star treatment for Elvis unleashed an immediate uproar, particularly from veterans. Some even complained to their Senator, who made a formal inquiry to the Pentagon. The Pentagon issued an immediate response denying the article and blaming its allegations on the circus that had surrounded Elvis' physical: "Many were present and it is possible that numerous conjecturable remarks and off-the-cuff comments were expressed by military personnel, cameramen and reporters. It must be emphasized that these remarks, if made, do not represent the official position of the Department of the Army."

If drafted, Elvis would be inducted at Fort Chaffee, Arkansas. Post spokesman Captain John Mawn further squashed any lingering rumors. "No one gets preferential treatment at Chaffee. All recruits get a military haircut the day they arrive." It was not unlike, he added, "a peeled onion."

The storm continued to rage. On one side, groups like the Veterans of Foreign Wars raised a ruckus in the press and with their legislators. Kentucky state representative Nick Johnson resigned from his draft board, saying, "I cannot conscientiously ask any mountain boy to serve the same country unless afforded the same treatment as Presley." On the other side, fans were furious with the Memphis draft board, calling Milton Bowers around the clock, even threatening him. "I'm fed to the teeth," he said. "I talk Elvis Presley more than I sleep. With all due respect to Elvis, who's a nice boy, we've drafted people who are far, far more important than he is. After all, when you take him out of the entertainment business, what have you got left? A truck driver."

When you reflect upon it, why *shouldn't* Elvis have been funneled into Special Services? There was no war in the late '50s. Elvis' talents would have been much better used to burnish Uncle Sam's image for potential volunteers; revving up the troops and selling bonds with his songs and smile would have been more effective and more fun than plugging along as just plain serial number US53310761. But the articles made such an assignment politically impossible.

Who planted the story? The Pentagon denied it. So did the Memphis draft board. An ambitious reporter? *Billboard* attributed its information to unnamed business associates of Elvis. For many, that points the finger squarely at Colonel Parker. But if so, why? One school of thought holds that he wanted to cut Elvis down to size, to make him remember who had put him in the spotlight and that, furthermore, the Colonel couldn't stomach the concept of Elvis performing free—even for Uncle Sam. Another school believes it wasn't malice, just bad advice on how Elvis should change his black-leather image to that of red-blooded All-American. Whether Parker engineered Elvis' having been drafted in the first place or not, he did see Elvis' service as a public relations plus and milked it for all it was worth. Unfortunately, it was no game for Elvis: He was the one who had to live through the experience. The very prospect of Army service terrified him, and the reality would prove both personally debilitating and damaging to his career.

By the time the induction notice came, Elvis was, if nothing else, resigned. "I'm kinda proud of it," he told reporters. "It's a duty I've got to fill and I'm gonna do it."

Paramount Pictures, however, felt differently. Filming on *King Creole* was supposed to begin the same week as Elvis' basic training, and the studio stood to lose as much as $350,000 if their star didn't show. Elvis requested a deferment, which the Memphis draft board unanimously granted. With a new induction date of March 20, 1958, Elvis thanked the board and headed to Los Angeles to make his last pre-Army film.

King Creole was Elvis' fourth and favorite movie. It was also his first to be shot on location—the French Quarter of New Orleans. Cast, crew, and entourage relocated there after finishing the studio work in Hollywood, struggling with the screaming presence of the hundreds of fans who thronged the set. In the film, Elvis plays a busboy-singer in a New Orleans cabaret, where he falls in with small-time hoodlums and agrees to help them rob his father's store. Luckily, he meets a sweet store clerk (Dolores Hart) who helps him back to the straight and narrow and a reconciliation with his father. Along the way, he sings 11 songs, which RCA promptly released as singles, EPs, and LPs, a number of which sold over a million.

It was raining at 6:30 A.M. on March 24, 1958 when Elvis arrived at the Memphis draft board, straight from an all-night send-off at Graceland. A crowd of at least 50 journalists and photographers were waiting, along with swarms of fans and even Colonel Parker, who was handing out "See *King Creole*" balloons. The swarm from the media bulged to around 200 by midday. Elvis and a hapless dozen other recruits endured the poking and prodding that constitutes induction day illuminated by a thousand popping flashbulbs.

The circus went on all day. In the afternoon, the Colonel announced an impromptu news conference and got the cameras to roll as Elvis read telegrams, such as Tennessee Governor Frank Clement's: "You have shown that you are an American citizen first, a Tennessee volunteer, and a young man willing to serve his country when called upon to do so." The following day, young fans followed the bus that took Elvis to Fort Chaffee, and even sneaked into the barracks. The media trailed Elvis into the long-anticipated barbershop, where he wanly joked, "Hair today, gone tomorrow" as thousands of photos captured every angle of the most famous haircut in modern history.

Elvis paid his 65 cents, then dashed to a phone booth to call Graceland, but Gladys was unable to come to the phone. She was in bed, "grieving," he was told. It made Elvis' induction the first life experience that he—a sensitive only child—had been unable to share with his mother. The day also marked the start of Gladys' physical and emotional decline. We can imagine Elvis' pang of loneliness as he stood in a phone booth, only the smudged glass affording him a moment's privacy from the hordes of hungry photographers.

Elvis was looking at another potential abyss from that phone booth—the one he feared might swallow up his professional success. There's no time off for good behavior in the Army, which meant Elvis stood on the threshold of a two-year interruption in a career that had been powered by astonishing momentum. Two years is a long time in the pop world. And while Elvis might have helped invent rock 'n roll and remained its acknowledged king, a slew of pretenders would launch plenty of product in their battle to unseat him. With no new movies, records, or concert tours, Elvis would be helpless to defend his title.

From Fort Chaffee it was on to Fort Hood, Texas. Elvis was assigned to A Company, Second Medium Tank Battalion, Third Armored Division. He did well on all his aptitude tests, though not well enough to qualify for the Officers Candidate Exam. He rose promptly, and his zealous participation in the competitive training exercises won him praise from his drill instructor and an appointment as assistant squadron leader. When his efforts on the pistol range fell below standard, he took a remedial course in his time off.

In short, Elvis was a perfectly average G.I.—no ordinary feat given his constant scrutiny by the world media, Army brass, and fellow soldiers. Elvis was bravely swimming Army circles in a fishbowl, and a lot of people licked their whiskers as they waited to pounce on any blunder or sign of goldbricking.

Elvis gave no one that opportunity. Determination helped, as did a support system he built of Master Sergeant Bill Norwood, in whose home Elvis was a frequent guest; Eddie Fadal, a Waco cinema operator; and steady girlfriend Anita Wood, who traveled to Fort Hood nearly every weekend. After the first eight weeks, the clan arrived to add their reassuring presence, and Elvis installed Vernon, Gladys, and grandmother Minnie Mae in a three-bedroom house near the base. As they were technically his dependents, Army regulations permitted Elvis to sleep off-base with them. The family also planned to follow Elvis to Germany, which must have set his mind further at ease.

The summer began well in other ways, too. Elvis had lost 12 pounds in basic training and had hardened up. On June 10, he went to Nashville to record, just as a song from *King*

Creole, "Hard-Headed Woman," zipped to the top of three *Billboard* charts. *King Creole,* released at the same time, garnered the best reviews of any Elvis vehicle. *Billboard* gave kudos to Elvis' "best acting performance to date"; *Hollywood Reporter* said Elvis showed real promise; and longstanding critic Howard Thompson of *The New York Times* wrote, "Elvis Presley can act . . . [that's] his assignment in this shrewdly upholstered showcase, and he does it."

But things changed. Gladys' health must have been troubling her long before she told anyone about it, but by August she looked and felt poor. She was having trouble walking and concentrating and was slipping into a constant gloom enlivened only by bursts of temper. She was also drinking. Elvis and Vernon finally insisted she return home to Memphis to see the family doctor, who immediately admitted her to a private room in the brand-new Methodist Hospital. The diagnosis: hepatitis.

Her condition was serious. Elvis, frantic, stayed in constant touch with her doctors from Fort Hood while he fought for an emergency leave. Gladys' life was fading away. Finally granted leave, Elvis contradicted his mother's wishes and boarded a plane to her bedside, where he and Vernon kept a constant vigil.

Her death several days later—officially listed as a heart attack, although the family refused an autopsy—devastated Elvis. He sobbed for days, putting any energy that wasn't absorbed by his wracking grief into preparing an elaborate funeral. Arrangements were made to fly in the Blackwoods, Gladys' favorite gospel group. Vernon wanted a huge funeral at Graceland, with loudspeakers on the lawn to allow everyone to hear the singing and preaching. Soon, though, the crowd of well-wishers grew out of hand. They ranged from distant Presley relatives up from Mississippi to fans to women bringing covered dishes of food, in the rural southern tradition. Some women probably even thought of attracting Vernon's eye.

When Colonel Parker arrived, he saw Graceland virtually under siege by the crowd and stepped in to rescue the grounds. He insisted the funeral be moved to a funeral parlor and fought with Vernon for hours to convince him. Vernon finally agreed and scheduled services for the next day. Over 400 people attended the funeral, which ran long, with the Blackwoods honoring request after request from Elvis and Vernon. As the cortege wound its way afterward to Forest Hill Cemetery, thousands of fans stood in respectful silence, lining a route patrolled by 150 uniformed police officers.

Elvis' emergency leave was extended one more week. Then, on August 24, 1958, he made his way back to Fort Hood in preparation for embarking with his unit to Germany. In Dallas, he spoke to reporters: "One of the last things Mom said was that Dad and I should always be together," he told them. "I'll report back to Fort Hood in the morning. Wherever they send me, Dad will go, too."

Elvis landed with his unit in Bremerhaven, Germany, on October 1 and immediately boarded a train to an Army base outside Friedberg, near Frankfurt in central Germany. Large numbers of photographs exist from this period, thanks to Army photographers. The post also allowed a large international press corps free run of the place to chronicle Elvis' first days. Elvis' role in the NATO defense was driving a jeep. It was described by the Army as a job with greater responsibility than his original tank assignment, but the hours were long and the task pretty unexciting. One of the week's high points, no doubt, was mail call, which brought Private Presley as many as 10,000 pieces at a time.

If that wasn't enough to reassure Elvis that his fans still remembered and loved him, there were his record sales. With very little unreleased material around, RCA was reduced to reissuing old songs. By February 1959, there wasn't one Elvis single on the *Billboard* Hot 100—the first time there had been such an omission since 1956. Then in March, RCA dug up and released "A Fool Such As I" and "I Need Your Love Tonight." Together they sold a million records (Elvis' 19th consecutive one) and hit the number two and four spots on the pop chart. The last nuggets of unreleased material went out in June: "A Big Hunk o' Love" and "My Wish Came True." This record, too, sold over a million copies and flew to number one. "It's a tribute to his staying power that he continues on such a powerful level," producer Steve Sholes told reporters a month later. "And we don't sell his records on a guarantee basis, you know." He meant that, counter to the usual industry policy, record-store owners couldn't return unsold quantities of Elvis' records.

While Elvis' fan mail included frequent love notes from his Memphis sweetheart, Anita Wood, an important new figure entered his world in 1959. Priscilla Beaulieu would eventually edge out Anita and all other contenders to become the most important woman in his life since Gladys. Elvis met her through Airman Currie Grant, who bumped into the 14-year-old Priscilla in the Eagles Club for American service families in Wiesbaden and invited her to join him and his wife on a visit to Elvis.

Imagine how sweet Priscilla must have looked at that first meeting, wearing a sailor suit and practically too shy to speak. Elvis, enchanted, spent time chatting with her, and when he sat down at the piano, he addressed his songs to her.

Priscilla arrived in Elvis' life at just the right time. He was very lonely after losing Gladys, who had always been his trusted confidante. His universe had shifted into one that was all male, from the Army by day to his evenings with Vernon and the good ol' boys he'd imported and installed in the house in Bad Nauheim. Young as she was, Priscilla wasn't in any way threatening. She was a beautiful young lady offering unconditional admiration and eventually, love. As a genuine American teenager, Priscilla could even provide reassurance of his continuing popularity back home, thus helping to ease Elvis' constant worry about losing his fans while overseas.

The two saw a great deal of each other. Priscilla wasn't intimidated by their 10-year age difference, but comported herself as Elvis' peer. One of the things he must have shared with her was his unhappiness over his father's short-lived mourning period. Vernon was seeing Dee Stanley, a young mother divorcing her Army sergeant husband, who moved into the Presley home before the divorce was complete. Considering how public Elvis' life was already and the risk of scandal he was courting by being involved with an underage girl, he couldn't have been happy about this added threat. Elvis did not attend their July 3, 1960 wedding in Huntsville, Alabama, claiming to be tied up in the filming of *G.I. Blues*.

On March 2, 1960, Elvis put this anxious, boring period behind him. He'd passed his last inspection, done his last drill, signed his last autographs outside the white picket fence at Goethestrasse 14. Elvis was going home.

His homecoming was grand. From the landing at McGuire Field in New Jersey to the 48-hour train ride in a private car to Memphis, thousands of loyal fans waited patiently to glimpse the King and add their joyous screams to his homecoming. There were other signs that Elvis' place as King of Rock 'n Roll had been preserved. RCA rang up one million orders for his new record—"Stuck on You" and "Fame and Fortune"—which had yet to be recorded. Frank Sinatra handed Elvis a $125,000 check to commit him to sing two songs on Sinatra's upcoming musical television special, one in a series sponsored by Timex. *Life* magazine wanted to splash his portrait on the cover, but scrapped the plan when Colonel Parker requested $25,000 for the privilege (he *did* offer to refund it if *Life's* newsstand sales that week didn't go up at least 35 percent).

Easing Elvis back into place, too, was the vacuum at the top of the pops. Richie Valens, Buddy Holly, and the Big Bopper had died the year before in a plane crash. Chuck Berry faced a jail sentence for transporting a minor across state lines for immoral purposes, and Jerry Lee Lewis had fallen from grace for much the same thing—with his underage cousin. Little Richard was a tax exile, and fellow former-Sun-artist Carl Perkins' career had derailed after a bad car accident. The rock world was all shook up by the payola scandal: Deejay Alan Freed resigned on-air from New York radio station WABC in November, 1959, one step ahead of public charges that he had accepted money from record labels to play their artists. The remaining performers still out there, attempting to fill Elvis' blue suede shoes, were the likes of Fabian, Frankie Avalon, Bobby Darin, and Ricky Nelson—pale imitations all.

Elvis surely breathed a sigh of relief once he realized the kingdom was still his. He had great things to look forward to: live performances, recording sessions, his acting career. The Army was safely behind him. If he had any thoughts on the era he was leaving behind, it was probably only one. It may only have been an image, that of a beautiful face in a crowd, a teenage girl with a grown-up's maturity, waving to Elvis as he boarded the DC-7 in Frankfurt. Priscilla had captured Elvis' heart, but their goodbye didn't break it. Her beau was used to getting what he wanted, and in the case of Priscilla, it was just a matter of time.

At 6:35 A.M. on March 24, 1958, Elvis was sworn in at Local Board No. 86.

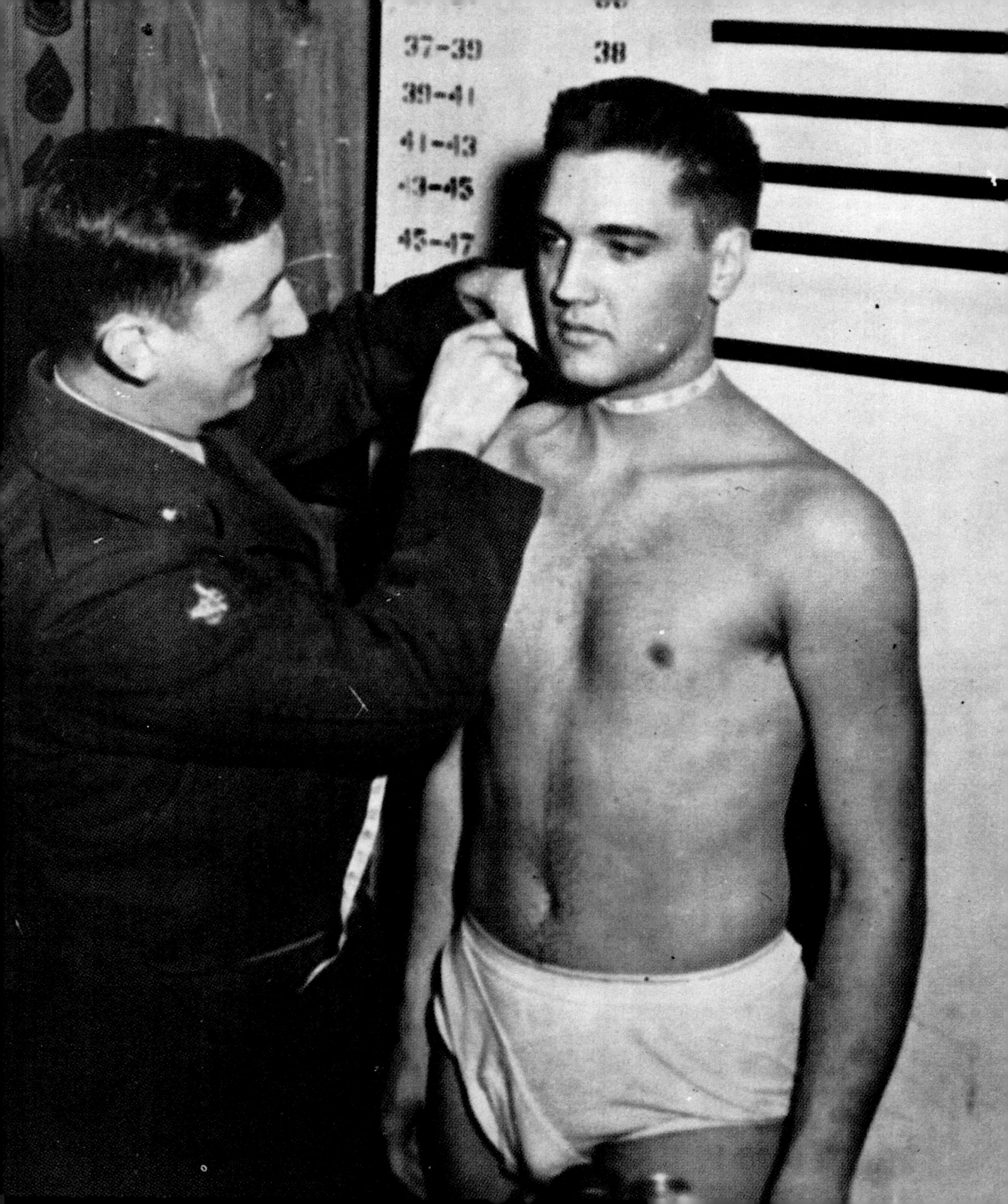
37-39
38
39-41
41-43
45-47

On January 4, 1957, Elvis reported for his preinduction physical, given by Dr. Leonard Glick at the Kennedy Veterans Hospital, Memphis.

Elvis' first Army dinner—spaghetti, salad, crackers, and two Cokes.

Opposite page: August 14, 1958, the day Gladys died. Her devoted son told friends he felt that everything he had was gone.

“Hell On Wheels” tank battalion, the Third Armor Division. Elvis is in the top row, third from left. In the close-up on the opposite page, the number 3 on his shoulder stood for the Third Armor Division. (1958)

Elvis had been made an acting assistant squad leader early in his basic training.

Upper left, with a young fan whose adoring letter so touched him that Elvis gave the boy a ring and had the boy spend the day with him.

Elvis was promoted to specialist 4th class on June 1, 1959. The honor also brought a raise, to $135.30 a month.

At the piano Elvis had installed in his house in Germany.

Opposite page: Priscilla Beaulieu was the daughter of a career U.S. Army officer living in Germany when she met Elvis.

In and around the house Elvis rented at 14 Goethestrasse in Bad Nauheim, Germany. A sign out front said, in German, "Autographs between 7 and 8 P.M. only!"

Surprised by some German fans, who said they learned English just for him.

Opposite page: Elvis at play and relaxing at his home off-base in Germany.

Taking a local young woman for a spin in his German sports car.

Elvis was frequently the center of attention during military parades and maneuvers.

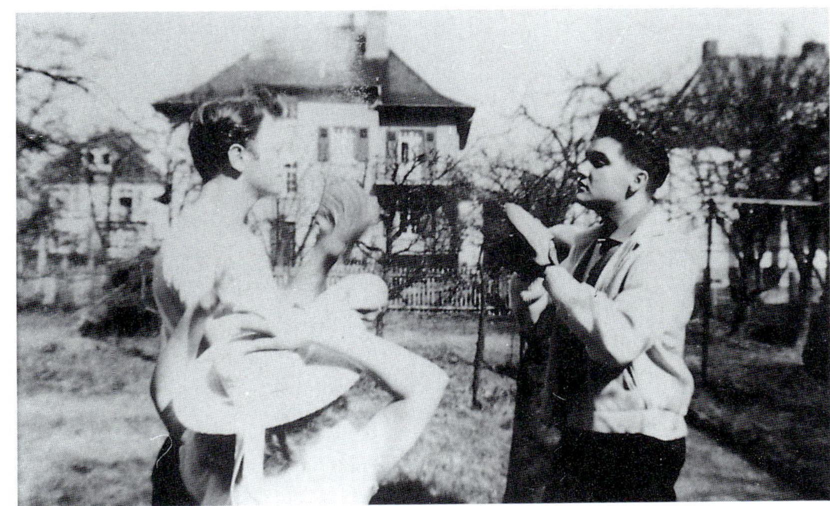

Elvis at the home of the German "Win A Date" contest winners.

Opposite page: January 1958, the month Elvis was supposed to have entered the Army. The date was delayed until March, however, to allow Elvis to finish *King Creole*.

The good-natured star of the "Win a Date with Elvis" contest.

On January 20, 1960, Elvis was promoted to sergeant during winter field maneuvers in Grafenwohr, Germany.

On the way home to trade in his army cap for the crown he left behind.

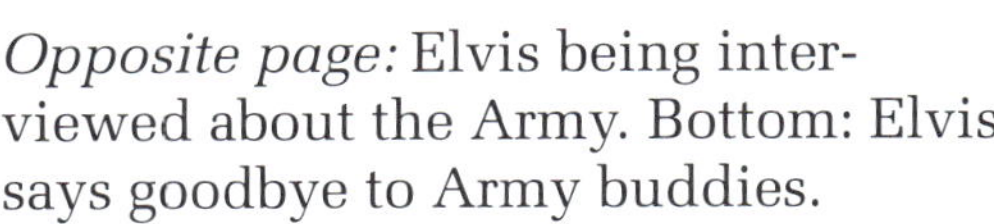

Opposite page: Elvis being interviewed about the Army. Bottom: Elvis says goodbye to Army buddies.

HOLLYWOOD

The time Elvis spent fretting over his fans' loyalty proved groundless. His first week in America told him all he needed to know and set his mind at ease. Elvis was greeted like a king returning from exile.

While that must have been very gratifying in the short term, the long term effect is darker. The fans' kindness—their unconditional adoration—seems cruel or at least stifling, in retrospect. It seduced Elvis and corrupted him from his path of musical originality. After all, if the old formula worked so well, where was the motivation to try anything new?

It might have been good for Elvis to have had to fight his way back to the top—to prove himself once more. If the old crown hadn't been popped so quickly over his crewcut, he might have been forced to stretch himself in his film parts, to be more inventive in the recording studio, to woo his fans face to face once more on the concert circuit. At the same time, he would gain the greatest reward of all: inner satisfaction.

A long, luxurious train ride brought Elvis home from New Jersey to Memphis, with hundreds of fans screaming their welcomes at every whistle stop along the way. Once back at Graceland, he took two weeks out of the public eye to call old friends, reassemble the gang, consider some redecorating ideas, and just pad around the rooms and grounds he hadn't seen for 18 months.

On March 20, 1960, Elvis piled part of his entourage in the car and drove to Nashville for his first post-Army recording session. Many familiar faces were there: the Jordanaires, original band members Scotty Moore and D. J. Fontana, and studio musicians Buddy Harmon, Floyd Cramer, and Hank Garland. The only missing person was Bill Black, who had abandoned his spot in Elvis' band to become the leader of his own combo.

"Stuck on You," backed by "Fame and Fortune," was produced that night. RCA released the 45 rpm single before the month was out.

By April 25, it reached the top spot on *Billboard's* Hot 100 chart, where it stayed for four weeks (it also hit number six on the rhythm and blues list). The merchants who had helped the record ring up nonrefundable advance orders of more than 1,125,000 were not disappointed by their gamble. Pent-up Elvis fever ultimately generated the sale of more than two million copies.

Immediately after the recording session, Elvis boarded another train, this time to Miami, for the filming of Frank Sinatra's fourth and final Timex television special. In the history of people having to eat their words, Frank Sinatra earned a spot at the head of the table. Three years earlier, he had dismissed rock 'n roll as "phony and false, and sung, written and played for the most part by cretinous goons." Now, in an effort to boost his specials' lackluster ratings, he was hosting a rock singer—to the tune of $125,000—for three songs.

"Welcome Elvis" was an exercise in politeness. The two American entertainment kings got on like old friends. Despite his star billing, Elvis was his respectful self, donning a tux and calling his host Mr. Sinatra. He agreeably sang not only his two new singles but Sinatra's signature "Witchcraft." For his part, Sinatra seemed gracious about having passed on the role of teen heartthrob. Ol' Blue Eyes crooned his usual repertoire, plus "Love Me Tender." In the studio audience, two generations of idol worshippers swooned (the critics were less enthusiastic). Home viewers gave ABC a 41.5 share when it aired the special on May 12—nearly twice the ratings of its nearest competitor.

By April, RCA and Paramount were in a heated tug of war over who got the star first. Production had begun on *G.I. Blues,* cried Paramount's Hal Wallis, but record company executives were equally anxious to "fill the can" with fresh material. Elvis answered the musical call first, promising a speedy arrival in Hollywood as he headed back to Nashville.

One marathon, 12-hour session on April 4 produced enough material for an album, "Elvis Is Back," released one week later. On its heels, Elvis changed his musical direction with the single "It's Now or Never," released in July 1960.

"It's Now or Never," far more "romance" than rock, became Elvis' second post-Army hit. It stayed at number one for five weeks, thanks in part to airplay on a much broader spectrum of stations than usually played Elvis songs. In England, the cut stayed number one for eight solid weeks—setting the record for any Presley single in the United Kingdom.

Within three weeks of its U.S. release, "It's Now or Never" sold over 1,125,000 copies. The final tally was a phenomenal 22 million copies worldwide.

Into the can went "Are You Lonesome Tonight?" which RCA held to release in November 1960. By November 28, that single hit the top of *Billboard's* Hot 100 chart, where it stayed for six weeks, as well as numbers 22 and 3 on the country and rhythm and blues charts, respectively. Total sales exceeded four million copies.

In late June 1960, Elvis, with nine buddies, boarded a luxurious, private railroad car to Hollywood. In every sense, he left Nashville behind.

G.I. Blues disappointed everyone, except, probably, Colonel Parker, whose eyes rarely wandered from the bottom line. Indeed, the flick quickly grossed $4.3 million in North America alone, and its 11 songs comprised the Elvis LP album that spent the longest time on *Billboard's* Hot LP chart (111 weeks). Ten of those weeks were at number one.

The story centered on one Tulsa McLean, an Army tank gunner stationed in Germany. Tulsa accepts a $300 bet with a fellow G.I. over who can score first with a sophisticated nightclub dancer (Juliet Prowse). Compared with the old, wildcat Elvis, this one—no sideburns, short hair, a uniform instead of black leather—wasn't much of a temptation. The filmmakers domesticate this denatured creature even further with a silly baby-tending scene. Who was this new Elvis?

The fans wanted to know, and so did the critics. "When they took the boy out of the country, they apparently took the country out of the boy," wrote the *Hollywood Reporter's* critic, Jim Powers. The picture, he concluded, would "have to depend on the loyalty of Presley fans to bail it out at the box office."

Elvis wanted to know himself. He hated *G.I. Blues* and came down hard on the Colonel to get him meatier film roles. He didn't want to become a cinematic cliché; he wanted to stretch himself as an actor. Many believe that serious cinema was Elvis' deepest desire. Rock 'n roll was merely to open Hollywood's door.

Dutifully, the Colonel wrangled with Twentieth Century Fox, Elvis' current studio. The next movie, *Flaming Star,* was set to begin filming in October. A compromise was reached. Elvis would sing four songs. That was down from the normal near-dozen, plus he'd play a dramatic role, that of a half-breed son of an Indian mother and white rancher in frontier America. There would be lots of gun slinging, horseback riding, emotional confronting.

The film that followed was another dramatic attempt, *Wild in the Country.* Writer Clifford Odets demonstrated that his reputation was, at that juncture, bigger than his talent. Fans and critics alike decried this turkey as a steamy, southern *Peyton Place.*

Unfortunately for Elvis' dramatic aspirations, neither film showed him off as a great acting talent, nor was either a box office smash. That fact especially gave strong ammunition to the Colonel, whose arguments for a shift to light comedy were backed by a Greek chorus of producers Hal Wallis and Hal Kanter and William Morris Agency president Abe Lastfogel. Many see the same forces at work here as those that drafted Elvis, then kept him out of Special Services. Forcing Elvis to abandon his dreams of being a dramatic actor was part of the same calculated effort to change his radical, dangerously sexual image. It was an attempt to have Elvis taken less seriously.

The Colonel's part in this also had to do with his having a hard time believing that rock 'n roll would last. He wanted Elvis to have a cleaner-cut image that would broaden his appeal beyond the fickle tastes of rebellious, libidinous teenage girls.

Outgunned, Elvis agreed to make *Blue Hawaii.* It furthers the sanitization of Elvis that *G.I. Blues'* lost sideburns and black leather had begun. In it, his love interest, played by Joan Blackman, has all the sexual sizzle of a summer-camp volleyball game. At one point, Elvis paternally spanks a sassy teen. If that isn't enough taming, the fatherly hero ends the movie at the wedding altar.

Blue Hawaii premiered in November 1961 and became Elvis' greatest commercial film success. If Elvis hadn't been pushed to do so many movies, one after the other, he might have waited for roles that made him push himself instead of playing the same character over and over again. He might have found the time to study acting, much as Marilyn Monroe did. Perhaps if he'd been surrounded by a genuine support system, he'd have gotten the encouragement at least to get a drama coach.

Meanwhile, the recording studio was quiet. "It's Now or Never" and "Are You Lonesome Tonight?" marked the end of Elvis' hit singles for 1960, at least in the United States. A few cuts off his albums were released in Europe, including "Wooden Heart," from *G.I. Blues,* which he sang partially in German and which sold a million copies there despite a government ban on its radio play.

Blue Hawaii set up the new formula: Elvis as beefcake, surrounded by sex kittens at a beautiful, lush, or otherwise arresting locale. Each plot offered some limp excuse to hang a guitar around Elvis' neck and get him to burst into song, backed by an unseen orchestra. Throughout the '60s, he produced an average of three films a year. Yet as the decade moved on, rousing seemingly everything in America, the only evidence of the revolution outside the Elvis film studio was the increasing raciness of the camera angles and the skimpiness of the costumes they captured.

A select roster of Elvis movie titles includes *Girls! Girls! Girls!*, *Fun in Acapulco,* and *Tickle Me* (this last described by *The New York Times* as "the silliest, feeblest, and dullest vehicle for the Memphis Wonder in a long time"). It must have been galling for a man who'd once hoped to inherit James Dean's dramatic, bad-boy mantle. Yet how could a man who began life as poor white trash walk away from a salary of a million dollars per picture? As he would sing years later in "Suspicious Minds," Elvis was "caught in a trap." He had neither the external support or the "right stuff" inside himself to walk out.

In a way, the pictures weren't the worst part of Elvis' Hollywood years. The music was. "Good Luck Charm," released in February 1962, stood as Elvis' last number one single until the end of the decade. Ever attentive to quantity, not quality, the Colonel decreed in 1964 that his star wasn't going to compete with himself any more and from that point forward would record nothing but movie soundtrack albums. Elvis Presley's marvelous two-and-a-third octave range, soulful feeling, and great skills, not only at phrasing and emoting a song but at arranging it, were now reduced to such throwaways as "One Boy, Two Little Girls" *(Kissin' Cousins)* and "Wheels on My Heels" *(Roustabout).*

Gone were the earnest blues of the Sun sessions, the intensity of *Jailhouse Rock,* the soulful ache of "Heartbreak Hotel"—in short, all the original stuff inside Elvis that he'd poured out during the earliest days and that had caused him to rise so swiftly to the top of the charts. Now, more than the music was different. Elvis-Gone-Hollywood *looked* much the same as the Man from Tennessee. The flashy clothes, erotic gestures, twisted grin, all were long familiar and hadn't changed, but they were growing somewhat practiced, premeditated. Underneath, the essence of Elvis was slipping away.

The Hollywood years were gravely disappointing professionally, but Elvis' life had its compensations. There was the money, for one thing. His fee eventually reached about a million dollars per picture, which was to say about half the film's budget. By the mid-'60s, his fee alone made him the best-paid actor in Hollywood. When you add to that number 50 percent of the movie's profits, Elvis was pulling in five or six million dollars a year. Even minus the Colonel's 25 percent, there was enough to let Elvis live comfortably in the style to which he had become accustomed—he and the small piece of the Memphis economy he supported. Elvis always kept quite a few people on salary, from Vernon and the uncles who'd once taught him a few guitar chords, now employed guarding the music gates, to employees, related and not, working in his office, home, and grounds. There were also always members of the "Memphis Mafia" around, who were also known collectively as "the Guys." A partial list includes Joe Esposito, Lamar Fike, Marty Lasker, Charlie Hodge, Sonny West, Red West, Gene Smith, Billy Smith, Jerry Schilling, Alan Fortas, George Klein, Ray Sitton, Marvin Gamble, Jimmy Kingsley, Bitsy Mott, Patsy Gamble, and Cliff Gleaves. They were his 24-hour-a-day cronies whose tasks ranged from bodyguard to driver to companion. At one point, in 1965, Elvis' payroll included ten "Guys," three maids/cooks, two secretaries, three gatekeepers, and two yard men.

Another compensation was feminine attention. Never mind the adoring throngs—consider Elvis' leading ladies. Debra Paget, Nancy Sinatra, Natalie Wood, Ann-Margret—these were just some of the names linked with his during his many years in Hollywood. Which rumors were true? Elvis inspired discretion in his women.

Romantically, there was always the home-front. Elvis' relationship with Anita Wood continued on and off until 1961. The pert, loyal girl-next-door who often put aside her own show biz aspirations to be there for Elvis finally quit believing his promises of marriage "someday." With his next love interest already in the wings, Elvis had no reason to be too upset by Anita's departure.

That heartthrob, of course, was Priscilla. Since he left Germany in March 1960, Elvis telephoned her many times and received many letters, scrawled in her adolescent hand. Once Anita left the picture, Elvis wasted no time revving his engines for a full-speed assault on the Priscilla's parents. His first act was to convince them to let him fly their 14-year-old daughter to Graceland for the Christmas holidays that year.

For Priscilla, the visit was a dream. Elvis was openly devoted to her, and they spent long, lazy hours together. In a delicious change from the Bad Nauheim days, there was no rushing off at night in a car driven by one of the Guys to make her father's curfew. In fact, she ignored her promise to her parents that she would stay with Vernon and Dee and slept each night with Elvis at Graceland. Nonetheless, Elvis honored his private commitment to keep Priscilla a virgin. She remained so until their wedding night.

No sooner had Priscilla been returned safely to Germany than the lovers began plotting a permanent reunion. As any parent knows, the word "sullen" perfectly defines an adolescent denied. Priscilla sulked, refused to leave her room, and generally made Beaulieu family life miserable as she pressured her parents to let her move to Graceland.

Finally, they caved in. At the time Priscilla had neither educational nor career goals for her post-high school existence, and in a generation when most women were married by 21, the idea of a 16-year-old "encouraging" a fabulously wealthy entertainer who adored her—and with whom she was deeply in love—probably seemed more shrewd than strange. Priscilla moved to Memphis in the spring of 1962, scattered enough possessions at Vernon and Dee's home to maintain appearances, and settled quietly into her classes at Immaculate Conception High School and long, social nights with the permanent hangers-on at Graceland.

Throughout the middle and late '60s, Elvis probably spent less time at Graceland than at his homes in Bel Air and Palm Springs. There he presided over endless parties involving him, the Guys, and dozens upon dozens of pretty girls. The Guys and Elvis played football without helmets and other games with an occasional violent twist, and there were assuredly some kinky scenes with the hordes of women willing to do anything for a night with or at least near Elvis. There may not have been open alcohol consumption, but Elvis was already caught up in the drug use that ultimately would contribute to his death.

Elvis made no public appearances from 1961 to 1967 and, following the Colonel's 1964 edict, cut songs only from his movies. He loathed these records and came to hate the movies, too. They were unreal, cookie-cutter vehicles, with 17-day shooting schedules that left no time to rehearse musical numbers or take pains to get anything else right.

Nobody else seemed to care. Producer Hal Wallis, whose 1964 work on *Becket* makes it clear that he was capable of quality, regarded Elvis as little more than leverage when he went to finance less commercial projects. The Colonel's fortunes rose with Elvis'—and he wasn't too interested in cultural enrichment. Priscilla, who was completely dependent on Elvis, rarely risked saying anything that might upset him. Nor did the Memphis Mafia.

Had Gladys lived, she might have talked to her boy and helped him find the strength to fight for better scripts or the time to make the ones he had better. But nobody ever replaced Gladys in Elvis' life, and the lessons she'd taught him—be polite, don't rock the boat, take care of the people who are financially dependent on you—blocked any stirrings he might have felt to fight for his growth as a performer.

Elvis was by now miles from his rock 'n roll roots. But something else had changed, too, something even deeper and more essential. His image and his inner self had reversed. He had begun public life as a teenage idol, with the look of a greaser and image of a sexual wildman, while underneath, he was safe—a gentle, courteous mama's boy. By the late '60s, his clean-cut looks and squeaky image had lost lots of teens but gained their blue-haired moms and even grand-moms. Behind closed doors, however, Elvis was not the wholesome guy he appeared. He had become the womanizing, rough-playing, drug-using tyrant he'd once portrayed. He no longer looked like a bad boy. He was one.

Elvis typically brought dates to the movies.

Regrowing the pompadour now that he's out of the Army.

Above and opposite page, top, returning to Union Station, Memphis from shooting Frank Sinatra's Timex Special. (April 18, 1960)

Opposite page: Bottom left, at the Rainbow Skating Rink that Elvis rented for a party from 12 A.M. to 5 A.M. Bottom right: taking Anita Wood for a spin in "Dodgem Cars," Elvis' favorite ride at the Memphis Fairgrounds. (1960)

On the set of *G.I. Blues*, where the winner of the third contest to meet Elvis was announced.

Top, in a Memphis official's office. Above, greeting a fan while filming *Wild in the Country*.

Opposite page: A lunch break—all the milks are Elvis'—between shooting scenes of *Flaming Star*. Elvis played an Indian and wore brown contact lenses to match his darkened skin. (All 1960)

CALIFORNIA
MPW 832

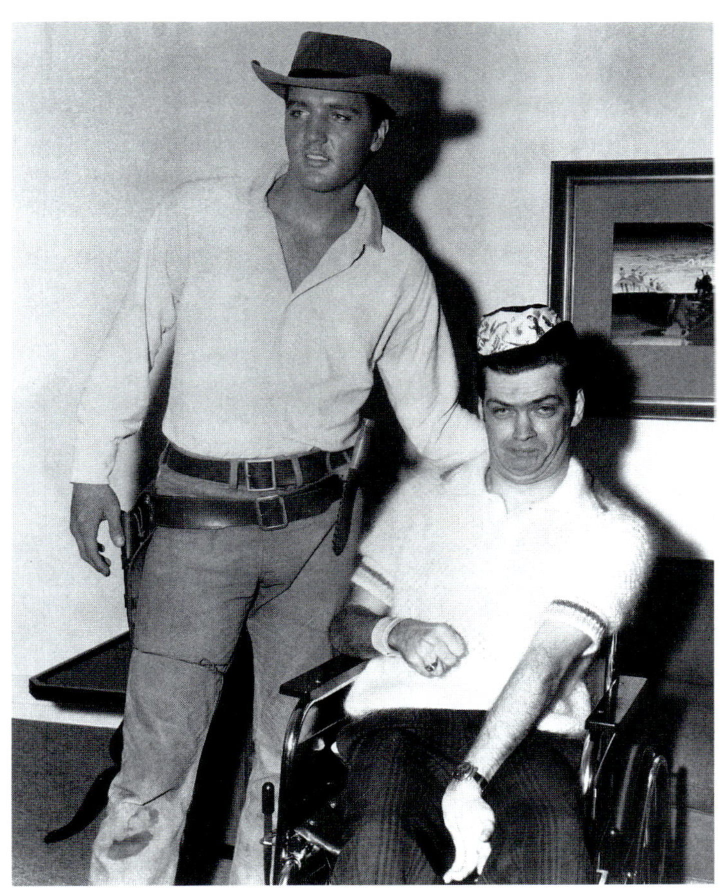

Above, with a fan on the set of *Girls, Girls, Girls*. Left, with Tankers fan club president, Gary Pepper on the set of *Flaming Star*.

Though Elvis loved the water and would swim and dive for hours, he was also hydrophobic, and insisted on having lots of people with him whenever he entered any body of water.

Elvis enjoyed football during the early '60s and sponsored a team, the E. P. Enterprises. Players included his friends and bodyguards Sonny West (middle row, left) and Red West (middle row, second from right). Elvis is in the top row, second from left.

Near the end of filming *Follow That Dream.* Elvis is shown with Colonel Parker and swarms of fans. (1961)

Opposite page: Displaying a "wrist lock"—a judo/karate move that can break an arm—on the set of *Follow That Dream.*

With stagehands on the Florida set of *Follow That Dream.* (1961)

Elvis virtually commuted between Memphis and Hollywood. Here he is shown on the set of of *Kid Galahad* and, below, taking time to thrill this young fan. (All 1962)

Opposite page: The top four photos were shot at the Memphis Fairgrounds. Bottom photos were taken on the set of *Girls, Girls, Girls.* (1962)

Right, getting off his custom-made bus (his right hand in a cast because of a broken finger); below right, greeting superfan Jimmy Velvet (center) with musician Bill Lynn looking on.

Opposite page: Elvis frequently rented Memphis movie theaters for all-night private viewings of numerous films. Here, with different fans and friends invited to watch the show. (1964)

Greeting fans, signing autographs and relaxing in the Memphis area between movies in the early 1960s.

Elvis practices karate techniques in his stocking feet.

Elvis with some of his youngest fans in 1966 (left, with Priscilla in the background), 1967 (above), and below, with a young Priscilla and stagehands on the set of *Roustabout.*

Pictured far from the movie set. Top left, sporting his new hairstyle, bangs instead of a curl; top right, in front of Graceland in his $50,000 Rolls Royce, which Elvis gave away one day because he scratched it; left, with Priscilla and one of the animals they both loved; above, with grandmother Minnie Mae Presley and Priscilla.

On the set of *Paradise Hawaiian Style.*

With Priscilla, her hair dyed blonde, Jerry Schilling and girlfriend, at Graceland's meditation gardens. (1966)

Inside the gates of Graceland during 1966. Top left, astride his motorcycle; top right, with Tom Diskin, once Elvis' road manager; above left, with Priscilla, Christmas 1967, backed by the life-size Nativity scene Elvis commissioned; above right, a very rare photo of Elvis standing on the grounds with a fan.

May 1, 1967. The song that was played for the bride was "Love Me Tender," but neither Presley had much to say about the rest of their Las Vegas wedding. Elvis didn't like Priscilla's gown, which he considered too plain.

Top left and right, the newlyweds in Palm Springs. Left and right above, water sports on their honeymoon.

Opposite page: With Priscilla on the third day of their Hawaiian honeymoon.

Above left, Christmas 1967 at his $500,000 Circle G Ranch in Walls, Mississippi. Above right and below, on the *Speedway* set with friends, including Nancy Sinatra, Dee and Vernon Presley, and the Stanley brothers. (1967)

On February 1, 1968, nine months to the day after their wedding, Priscilla gave birth to Lisa Marie.

At home with their newborn. Above, with grandfathers Beaulieu (far left) and Presley (far right).

All photos taken at the Circle G Ranch during 1967 except for above right, on the Sedona, Arizona set of *Stay Away Joe*.

On the set of *Stay Away Joe* with co-star Old Grey Mayer.

Elvis would ride his golf carts for hours around the Graceland grounds. A few years later, he taught Lisa Marie how to operate a cart of her own. (1968)

Top left, a fan brandishes her Kodak Instamatic. Top right, deeply tanned for *Stay Away Joe.* Above left, having lunch in Hawaii. Above right, taking a spin around the neighborhood in his dunebuggy. (1967)

On the set of *Live a Little, Love a Little.* Left, with Army buddies Charlie Hodge and Joe Esposito who replaced Tom Diskin when he retired as Elvis' road manager. (1968)

With fans. Top left, drinking Nesbitt, Elvis' favorite orange soda pop. Top right and opposite page, astride his horse, "Rising Sun." (1968)

Top left, a bearded Elvis for *Charro.* Above right, with superfan Judy Palmer on right. (1968)

At his Beverly Hills home, telling fans about new his movie, *Charro.* Top left, with Blue Hawaiian Fan Club President Sue Wienhart. Below right, in Arizona, on the *Charro* set. (August, 1968)

Top right, on the *Charro* set. All others, with fans and one of the many gifts bestowed upon Elvis outside his Beverly Hills estate. (1968)

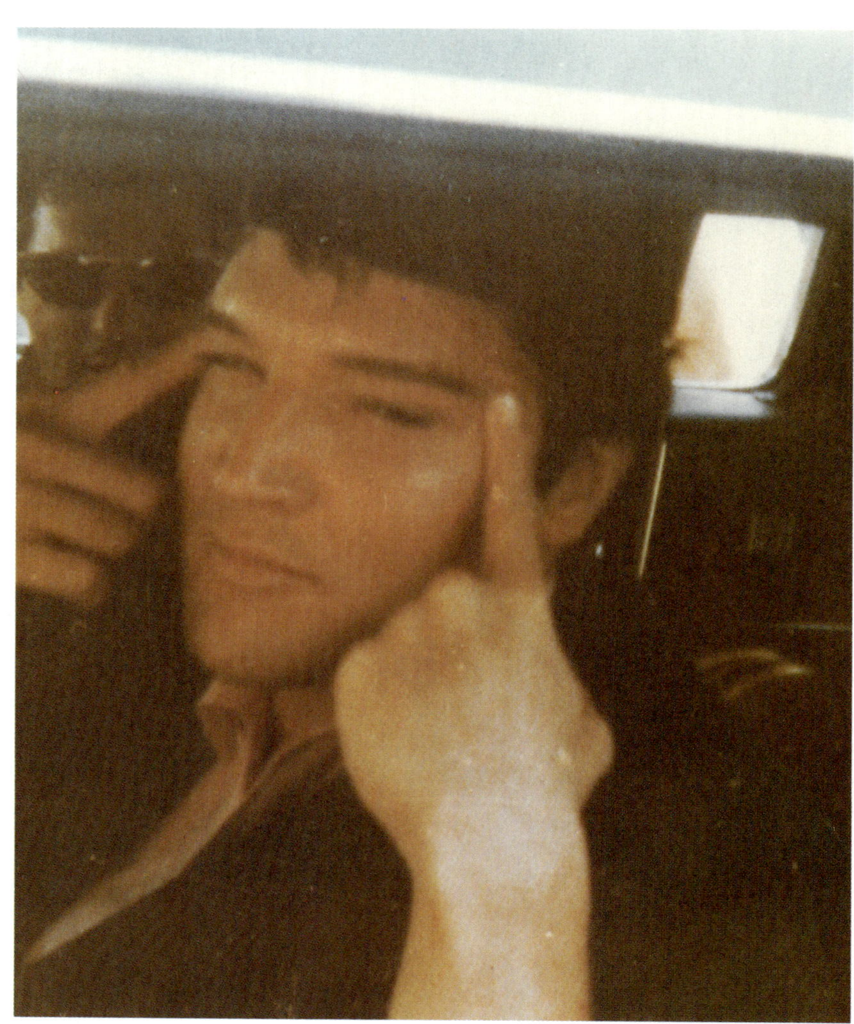

Joking around with fans outside his Beverly Hills home, Elvis slants his eyes, greets superfan Sue Wienhart, and watches a fan do some karate moves. (1968)

On the set of *Trouble with Girls.* (1969)

Top, with one member each of a set of twins outside his Beverly Hills home. Above, an early shot of Elvis wearing a scarf and preparing his lines for that day's shooting schedule. (1968)

Top left, August 1968. Top right, around the time of the 1968 television special. Above right, May 1969, after completing *Trouble with Girls*. All outside his Beverly Hills home.

Hiding a fever blister.

Top left and right, Graceland, summer 1969.

In the spring of 1969, Elvis sported a Beatle haircut for *A Change of Habit,* his last feature film.

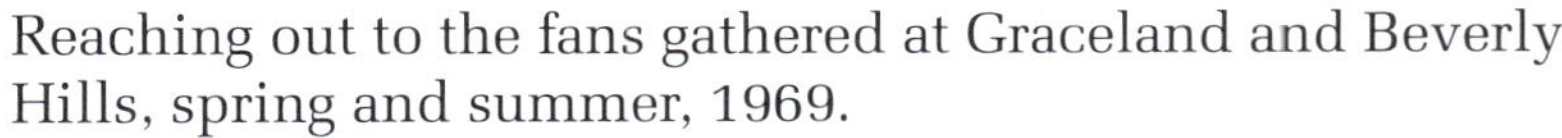

Reaching out to the fans gathered at Graceland and Beverly Hills, spring and summer, 1969.

Above, riding "Rising Sun". Below, the family with one of their dogs. Elvis bought Lisa Marie two Great Danes, "Brutus" and "Snoopy." (1969)

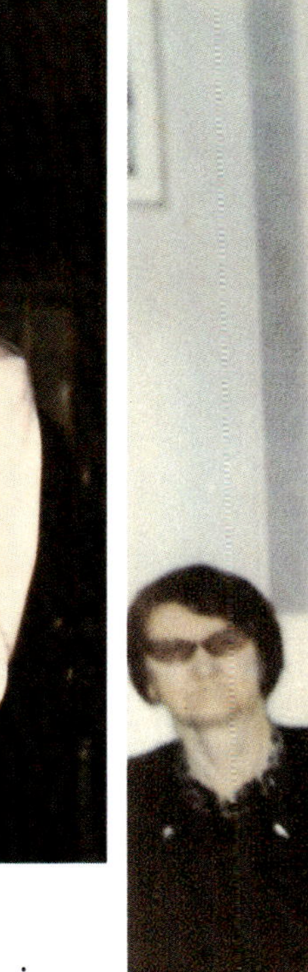

With little Lisa Marie.

LAS VEGAS

COMEBACK

Elvis turned 30 in 1965, in the midst of the massive upheaval and conflict that marked the '60s. Like many young Americans in that unsettled time, Elvis was often unsure of his proper direction.

Various contradictions characterized his life. Deep spiritual longings and ascetic quests coexisted with his impulsiveness and sexual curiosity—now expressed for real in wild parties at the Palm Springs house instead of pantomined on stage. The famous sex symbol was about to marry. A vulnerable, motherless child himself since Gladys' death, he chose a young bride to whom he could be both husband and father. He was dismayed by hippie culture, yet consumed more than his share of drugs. Though he had much cause for happiness in his life—and often was very content—he nevertheless spent many days tormented by doubt and depression.

Elvis entered his middle years at the peak of his success. His records sailed effortlessly up the charts, and his films made him Hollywood's highest-paid performer. He spent a decade proving the answer he gave to Sun Records' Marion Keisker in 1953, when asked who he sounded like: "Ma'am, I don't sound like nobody." Elvis was also beloved—not only by millions of fans worldwide but by friends, relatives, his leading ladies . . . and Priscilla. He worked hard, and played hard, too—whether riding his Harley Davidson or his horse Rising Sun, playing football or practicing karate, racing slot cars or renting an entire amusement park, roller rink, or movie house. There were always plenty of friends, relations, and hangers-on to accompany him on every adventure.

Yet depression and unhappiness darkened the spirits of Graceland's master. Elvis felt hopelessly out of control of his career. Though he was a box office smash, his success at light musicals blocked his heart's desire: to develop his talents as a serious actor. He continued to sing, but gave no concerts, he knew well that the numerous movie soundtracks he cut in the mid-'60s were largely rubbish, but the Colonel forbade him to record anything else. Elvis was in some ways his own worst enemy, since he knew what to do to make himself happier yet never managed to do it.

What made this rich and famous King helpless? One factor was his own good manners, which made a fight with either the movie studios or Colonel Parker seem impossibly rude. It would have mocked his adored mother's upbringing. Elvis was not raised to question authority but to trust, obey, and respect it.

Money also played a factor in Elvis' unhappiness. He needed it to support not just a wife but an entourage. And so he was trapped making three films and dozens of songs that disgusted him every year—because his fear of being alone made having homes filled with friends not a luxury but a requirement. It was his protection against the loneliness that threatened to undo him—and ultimately did.

Had Elvis spent his life driving a truck for Crown Electric, he might have chafed sometimes at being stuck there for the sake of his family obligations. But fate took Elvis down a different path; his talent and originality brought him to stardom, and his artistry changed the sound of American pop culture. That *he* was trapped was more than galling—it was depressing and puzzling. Elvis couldn't figure out how this had happened to him. Since childhood, he'd felt he was meant to be and do something special.

From this bewilderment and disappointment was born Elvis' spiritual search. In April 1964, Elvis met Larry Geller, a barber who came to the Bel Air house to cut his hair. Geller was a California '60s prototype, a thin, laid-back hippie, into health food, meditation, and esoteric readings. As with everything else, from horseback riding (Elvis bought horses for the entire Memphis Mafia and their wives) to food (he ate the same plateful of eggs and bacon every breakfast of his life), Elvis indulged to the hilt when he found something he liked. Geller became a key figure in his life for three years.

Under Geller's guidance, Elvis read dozens of books on the spiritual world, ranging from numerology to Rosicrucian cosmology to Far Eastern religious thought, from the 19th-century spiritualist charlatan Madame Blavatsky to the *Tibetan Book of the Dead*.

According to Priscilla, Elvis' long heart-to-hearts with Geller and discussions of these mysterious books left her feeling excluded and uncomfortable. She knew he was searching for answers to the fundamental questions that tormented him: Why was there so much pain and suffering in the world? Why had he been chosen out of the universe's multitudes of people to be so influential, and for what purpose could he best use that influence? And why, with so much in his life, wasn't he happy?

In 1965, Elvis discovered another guide in his search for enlightenment, Daya Mata (he fondly called her "Ma" for short), a California disciple of Yogi Paramahansa Yogananda. Though the yogi had died in 1952, his ashram still thrived on a serene hilltop above Pasadena. Elvis made frequent visits and financial contributions to this Self-Realization Fellowship.

Elvis' studies changed his normally playful personality. On movie sets, he no longer indulged in his famous practical jokes—he was too busy reading the spirituality books he toted back and forth each day. Back at Graceland, he remained devoted to his studies and even brought Geller home a few times. Elvis tried to involve Priscilla and the Guys in his quest for higher understanding.

Priscilla has said that he particularly pressured her, urging her to read the works that would help her to become his "soulmate." But the poor teenager could barely lift some of the thick tracts her sweetheart-mentor brought her, much less plow through them. Not only did he condemn her obvious lack of enthusiasm, but she reports that his spiritual quest also led him to periods of no physical affection. Priscilla longed for the old times listening to Elvis play music or holding court with friends, the times when they spent long days chatting and evenings taking the gang to all-night movie festivals or on outings to amusement parks.

Drugs remained one exploration they could make together. For years, Elvis had shared sleeping pills with Priscilla. During this esoteric phase, they had experimented briefly with street drugs. Marijuana, Priscilla says, was pleasant but made them so hungry that their weight gains convinced them to stay away. LSD was mind expanding, but one trip was enough for both of them.

All this spiritual exploration was part of Elvis' growing up. So was his decision to marry. For years he had armed himself against various girlfriends' pleas with what he called the Colonel's insistence that he stay single "for the fans." That line held Anita Wood at bay for a good five years until her exasperation overruled her understanding, and it held Priscilla —and her parents—for about the same length of time.

Just before Christmas of 1966, Elvis gave Priscilla a diamond ring: three carats surrounded by a detachable row of smaller ones. He proposed to Priscilla in her bedroom upstairs at Graceland, and the overjoyed couple ran downstairs at once, Priscilla clad in a terry bathrobe, to announce their engagement to Vernon and Dee and Elvis' grandmother. A few weeks later, the couple traveled to Los Angeles for the filming of *Easy Come, Easy Go*. They invited Priscilla's parents, then stationed at Travis Air Force Base near Sacramento, so they could tell them the big news in person.

On the eve of marriage, some men crave a last shot of wild behavior. Some drink, others have a sexual fling. Elvis embarked on a spending binge.

Two months after announcing the engagement, Elvis set his sights on a ranch near Horn Lake, Mississippi, featuring 160 acres, a little house, a barn, and a herd of purebred cattle. Simple though it sounds, the property's rolling hills suggested something different to everyone involved. To Priscilla, it suggested a cozy, newlywed getaway from the crowds of Graceland. To Elvis, it had the makings of a semicommunal, state-of-the-art ranch. He dubbed it Circle G for Graceland (which he put up as collateral to borrow the ranch's $500,000 asking price). To Vernon's practical eye, the peaceful spread cloaked potential financial ruin.

Naturally, Elvis' vision prevailed—but his father's forebodings threatened to come true. One small house wouldn't accommodate everyone, so Elvis arranged for six mobile homes to be mounted on concrete foundations. He had already transplanted horses from Graceland's stables for Marty Lacker, Alan Fortas, and the other Guys and their wives who were with him. Next, he decided, they all needed Cowboy Cadillacs. Elvis bought each of them an El Camino pickup truck. Still not satisfied, Elvis bought a truck for everyone involved with the ranch: for all the contractors installing the trailers, running water pipes, and laying additional electric lines. In a matter of weeks, Vernon was horrified to discover, his son had spent over $97,000 on pickups.

The spree continued. Plans were laid for a big, new house at the ranch for him and Priscilla. Tractors, huge horse trailers, expensive farm machinery, and power tools from Sears were bought. In the blink of an eye, the Circle G Ranch had drained the Presley reserves of one million dollars.

Elvis was manic in his enjoyment of the ranch. He wandered its acres and supervised every detail of construction. He puttered with his power tools and tinkered with the farm equipment. Recreation, equally crazed, was continual and involved everyone: Elvis, Priscilla, the Guys, their wives and kids. Everybody went skeet shooting, turtle hunting, and horseback riding, attended all-day picnics and all-night musical jam sessions. There was always a crowd.

The crowd's enthusiasm, however, went no deeper than that of Hollywood extras. The wives wanted to get back to their homes, the kids to their friends. Being short of cash, several of the Guys quietly sold their trucks. Priscilla longed for time alone with her fiancé.

An alarmed Vernon called the Colonel every day, begging him to find a project for Elvis before he spent every penny of his fortune. The Colonel quickly obliged, pulling *Clambake* from his sleeve like a magician's rabbit. Elvis kicked and groaned about having to make another awful movie, but Vernon told him he had no choice—they were going broke.

Reluctantly, Elvis hung up his ranch duds and headed back to Hollywood, where his overweight appearance shocked the Guys he'd left holding the fort in Bel Air. He'd been eating a steady country diet of corn pone, mashed potatoes, sausage gravy, and biscuits since leaving. He weighed in at a hefty 210 pounds (40 pounds over his normal weight) upon arrival, and showed every ounce.

For years, Elvis had been a yo-yo dieter, gaining weight between films, then shrinking down again for the next commitment with the aid of pills and crash dieting. Studio officials weren't aware of this pattern because Elvis struggled to stay under wraps until he could return to the limelight in his leaner state.

But this time Elvis wasn't so fortunate. He was spotted by a United Artists executive before he'd had a chance to slim down. The executive berated Elvis and served notice both to him and the Colonel that Elvis had better shape up or he'd be taken off the movie.

The wrangling over his appearance further depressed Elvis, who was already unhappy about having to leave the ranch to make another grade B flick. One night, groggy with sleep, he awoke to go to the bathroom and tripped on a television cord. A headfirst dive into the bathtub knocked him out cold. Priscilla sounded the alarm, and in no time the bedroom was swarming with friends, movie studio executives, and the Colonel.

Colonel Parker took charge, clearing out everyone but himself and the doctor, who diagnosed a concussion. The Colonel had his own thoughts on what else was ailing Elvis and seized the chance to cure the problem. He'd long blamed Larry Geller for making Elvis passive and muddle-headed and for changing him into a somber bookworm.

With his charge too weak to protest, the Colonel struck. Larry was not to be left alone with Elvis, he decreed, and would be permitted on the premises for nothing more than haircuts, supervised by himself or one of the Guys. In addition, the payroll would be cut back. Elvis couldn't afford all the cash that was leaking out every week. Furthermore, they all should quit bothering Elvis with their problems, he continued, and filter everything through Joe Esposito. Joe was now the group's foreman, and Marty Lacker would be in charge of special projects. His first task was the content of the Colonel's final pronouncement—Elvis' wedding. It was time for his boy to grow up and settle down.

The event took place just a few months later, on May 1, 1967, at the Aladdin Hotel in Las Vegas. Priscilla was 21 years old. Despite Marty's new title, the wedding was almost exclusively the Colonel's party. Nor did Priscilla or Elvis have much say in wedding details, including the guest list. For example, of the entire Memphis Mafia, the Colonel invited only Marty Lacker and Joe Esposito to witness the ceremony. Red West was so hurt and angry that he and his wife boycotted the larger reception.

The ceremony—conducted by a justice of the peace in a Las Vegas hotel—wasn't the sort of thing you'd expect from someone as spiritually committed as Elvis had always been. Nor was the wedding's timing particularly tailored to the Presleys. Within days after the ceremony, Elvis had to return to finish *Clambake*. Next, the Colonel dashed the couple's desire to tour

Europe, claiming it would annoy the fans there who had never gotten Elvis over for a concert. They grabbed a few days with Lamar Fike at the ranch, then honeymooned briefly in the rainy Bahamas.

Nine months later to the day—February 1, 1968—Lisa Marie Presley was born. Despite her mother's miniscule weight gain during pregnancy, the baby was a perfectly healthy six pounds, 15 ounces.

Renewed by happiness in his personal life, Elvis found the strength for a fresh approach to his work. He made plans to return to the concert stage after a seven-year absence and opted to do it on television—his first such appearance since 1960. He taped the NBC special *Elvis* in June 1968, and it aired to good reviews and ratings in December. Elvis was on the comeback trail.

In January 1969, that trail brought him back to Memphis for his first recording session there since his days at Sun, and certainly the most creative studio time he'd had in years. Next, he headed to Las Vegas—the only town where Elvis had ever bombed, in a two-week, 1956 engagement at the New Frontier on a shared bill with comedian Shecky Greene and the smooth string sounds of the Freddie Martin Orchestra. The middle-aged crowd did not respond warmly to Elvis, whose name slowly sank to the bottom of the marquee.

What enticed Elvis (really, Colonel Parker) to accept a Vegas booking 13 years later was the opening of a brand-new, grand hotel, the International. Touted as a colossus on the desert, the International Hotel was Nevada's tallest building with its largest body of water after Lake Mead, featuring a thousand slot machines and lavish entertainment. The Colonel figured Elvis could piggyback on the publicity the new hotel was sure to generate. An engagement at the International also would give "his boy" a chance to perfect his act before taking it on the road.

Although he started out unhappy about playing Las Vegas, Elvis soon changed his mind. Announcing, "I don't care if I don't make any money, as long as I give a good show," he planned the show's music, choreography, costumes, and staging, assembled 50 singers and musicians—including fine studio players from Los Angeles, a pop gospel group, a soul trio, and a 35-piece orchestra plus conductor—and pulled everything together for a two-week rehearsal.

On July 26, 1969, the curtain rose on a four-week show with a one-million-dollar contract. Two thousand guests sat enthralled (when they weren't up and screaming their ovation) that night and twice every night, seven days a week, for the next month. A newly slender Elvis careened through his rock hits first, then sank with relish into more current material, such as "In the Ghetto," released in April, and "Suspicious Minds," which was getting its first airplay on its way up the *Billboard* pop chart. In early November, it became Elvis' first number one hit since 1962.

December saw the release of *Change of Habits,* Elvis' last fictional movie. The fulfillment of his contract liberated him forever from the Hollywood travelogues he despised.

Over 101,500 people had seen Elvis at the International Hotel. The response was so strong he opted to return in January 1970 instead of waiting a year as he'd planned. The January commitment rivaled the earlier show's success.

On February 24, he opened his next large-scale show on the concert trail: six performances at the Houston Astrodome. Despite terrible acoustics, the fans came in droves. Nearly 207,500 of them filled the stands during the course of the engagement, bringing him a reported $1.2 million, even though some tickets were priced as low as a dollar to allow the poorest fans to come.

In 1971, the Jaycees gave Elvis an award as one of the "Ten Outstanding Young Men of America." The plaque hangs in Graceland's trophy room. The award capped a period of great productivity and creativity. The birth of a new, mature Elvis, now a husband and father, energized him to return to his old success. This Elvis was playing a new kind of music—much lusher and more orchestrated than those earliest R&B recordings—to a far broader audience than the teenagers who first adored him.

Unfortunately, marriage and fatherhood couldn't quell all the old conflicts nor fill the loneliness that Gladys' death had wrought. These pains would prove consuming in the coming years, just as the grueling weeks on the road would take a toll on the very family life that had enabled Elvis to resume his love affair with music and live performance. The concert circuit proved a cruel mistress.

Opposite page: Striding into a Las Vegas press conference, flanked by the Colonel, at the start of a four-week gig at the International Hotel. (July 31, 1969)

ELVIS
INTERNATIONAL
IN PERSON
ELVI
NOW
PERS

Always seeming to be surrounded by fans, even onboard an airplane, above left.

Above, Elvis with superfan Chris Trant; below, greeting fans outside his Beverly Hills home. (1969)

Top left, Elvis had the guards ask everyone to leave after a rare moment of annoyance with the fans. A group of fans had blocked the Graceland driveway, then shouted something nasty as Elvis drove in the front gate. Top right, learning about two girls from Mississippi Delta Junior College, who had had themselves shipped into Graceland in a crate marked as containing wolfhounds. Elvis, who didn't need any more dogs, had the crate shipped back. The girls kicked their way out; later, Elvis invited them to Graceland. Above, in tune with the times, Elvis wears love beads. Right, staying up all night with the fans. (1969)

Sunbathing in the backyard of his Palm Springs home. Sometimes Elvis would hook up an electric fan to cool himself while he tanned. (1969)

With fans at Graceland. (July 1970)

Opposite page: Top left, the famous musical gates of Graceland, custom built by Doors Incorporated of Memphis in 1957. All others this page, with fans who made their way backstage, Las Vegas, August 26, 1970.

Top left, around the time Elvis sold one of his California mansions to actor Telly Savalas. Top right, excited fans scream as Elvis walks back to the gate to greet them after parking his car. Above left, reaching out to give an autograph. Above right, another backstage visitor, Las Vegas, August 1970.

With superfan J. Cherry.

Around the time of Elvis' filming of *That's the Way It Is.*

Ducking so the wind won't mess up his hair, en route to the Astrodome to perform in a concert for the Houston Livestock show. (1970)

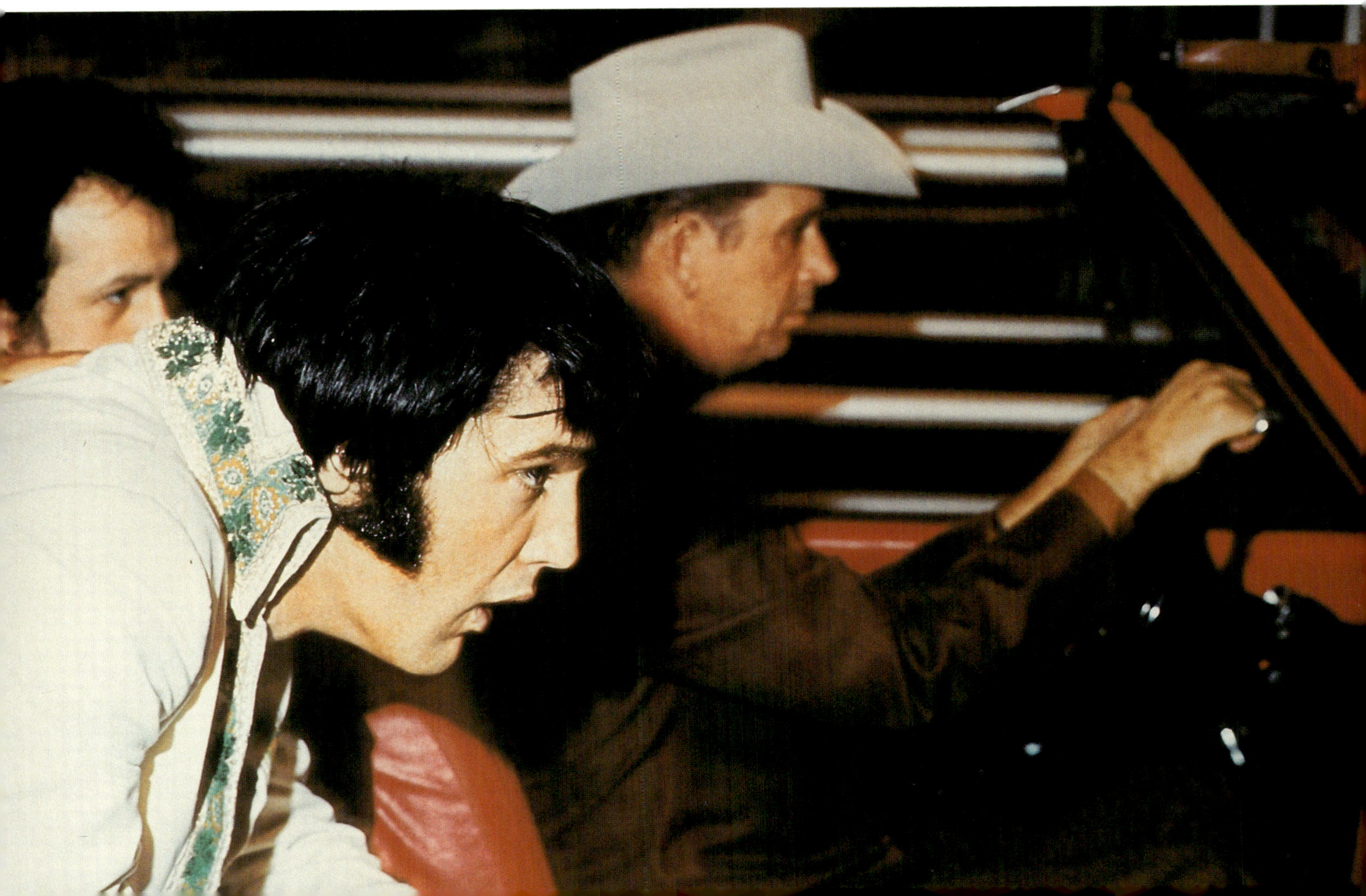

Members of the "Memphis Mafia." From left, Sonny West, Red West, Elvis, Jerry Shilling, Lamar Fike, and Joe Esposito.

Standing in a jeep just before entering the Astrodome. Sonny West is in front.

Top and bottom left, kissing super fan Mikki Malbrough—and again with her on far left with friends in Mobile, Alabama 1970.

With fans. (1970)

With fans. Right, accepting a plaque from Norwegian fans.

Top, chatting with fans through the moon roof of his limo. Below, wearing the gold belt presented to him by the *International Hotel* after setting a Las Vegas record: 101,509 paid customers and $1.5 million grossed. The heavy belt style became an Elvis trademark. (1970)

Opposite page: Showing off to friends. Elvis had 37 weapons in his Graceland gun collection, and he enjoyed target practice with his friends. (1970)

Below left, Priscilla, George Klein, Elvis, and Barbara Little at George Klein's wedding. Elvis was best man. Below right, he and Sonny West straighten each other's carnation at Sonny's December wedding. (1970)

Top left and above right, showing off his gold Jaycees medallion (1972). Above left, the theme from *2001: A Space Odyssey* was the distinctive opening music for Elvis' concerts. (Both, November 1971)

With fans, including a Las Vegas showgirl, and left, in Seattle, April 1973 with superfan Jim Borda.

Above left, President of Elvis Presley Fan Club of Italy, Livio Monari and friend (Las Vegas, Aug. 24) on their second 1972 meeting with Elvis. When Elvis heard that their first pictures didn't come out, he invited them back. Above right, in a jeep at the Honolulu Airport before doing his *Aloha from Hawaii* satellite television special. Below, gifts for Lisa Marie.

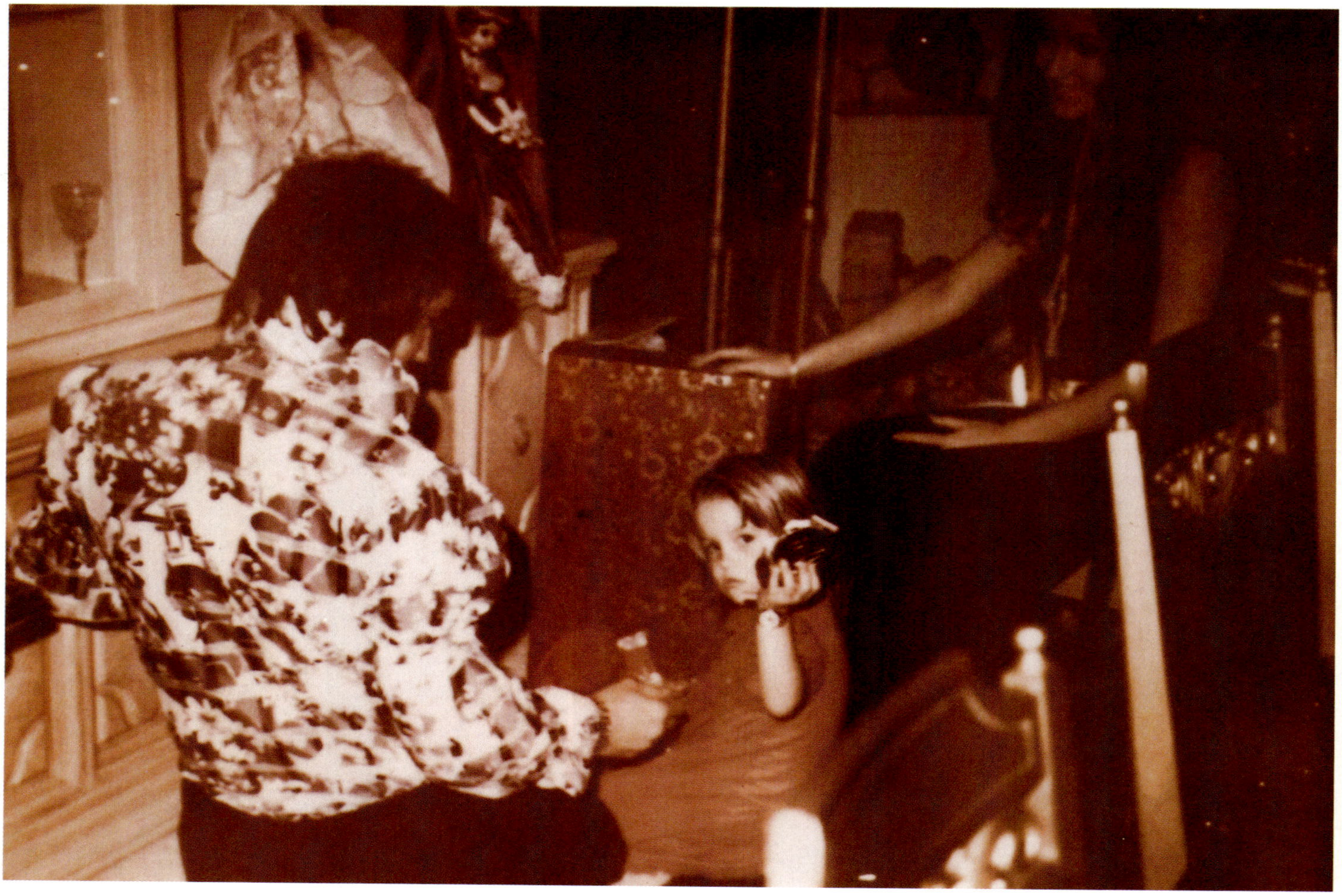

Above left, backstage at the Las Vegas Hilton with superfans Alan and Dee Bigalow. Above right, on tour in Arizona. Below left, backstage in Las Vegas, receiving an award from superfan Virginia Coons in a meeting arranged by Tom Diskin. Below right, an Asian fan presents Elvis with a gold record. (1973)

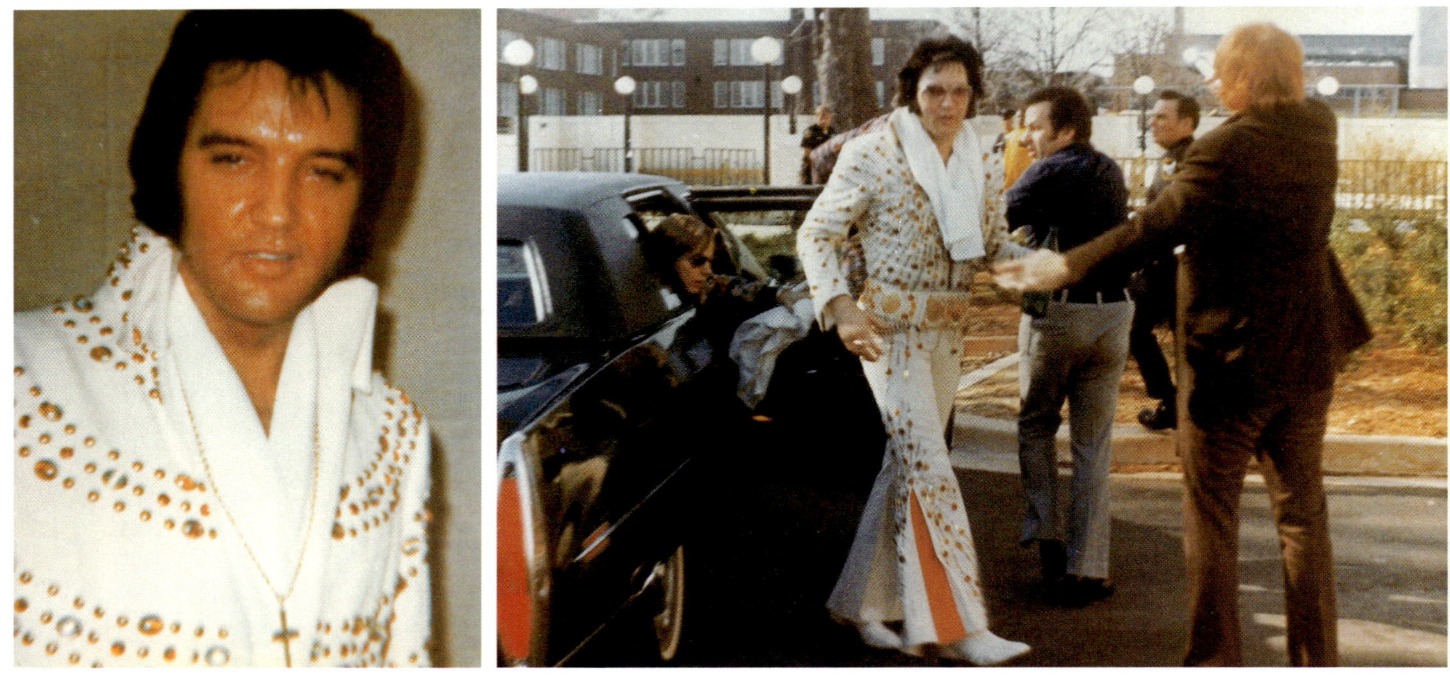

Las Vegas, March 31, 1975—the day Elvis gave me this beautiful, white-mirrored, nail-studded jumpsuit.

Above left, autographing a menu for International Elvis Presley Fan Club of Belgium (1973) in Las Vegas. Above right, receiving a new Musical Express award from members of Elvis' British fan club. Below, Elvis' March 3 return to the Houston Livestock Show at the Astrodome. Joe Esposito holds Elvis in by the the belt; bodyguards Red and Sonny West ride in back. (1974)

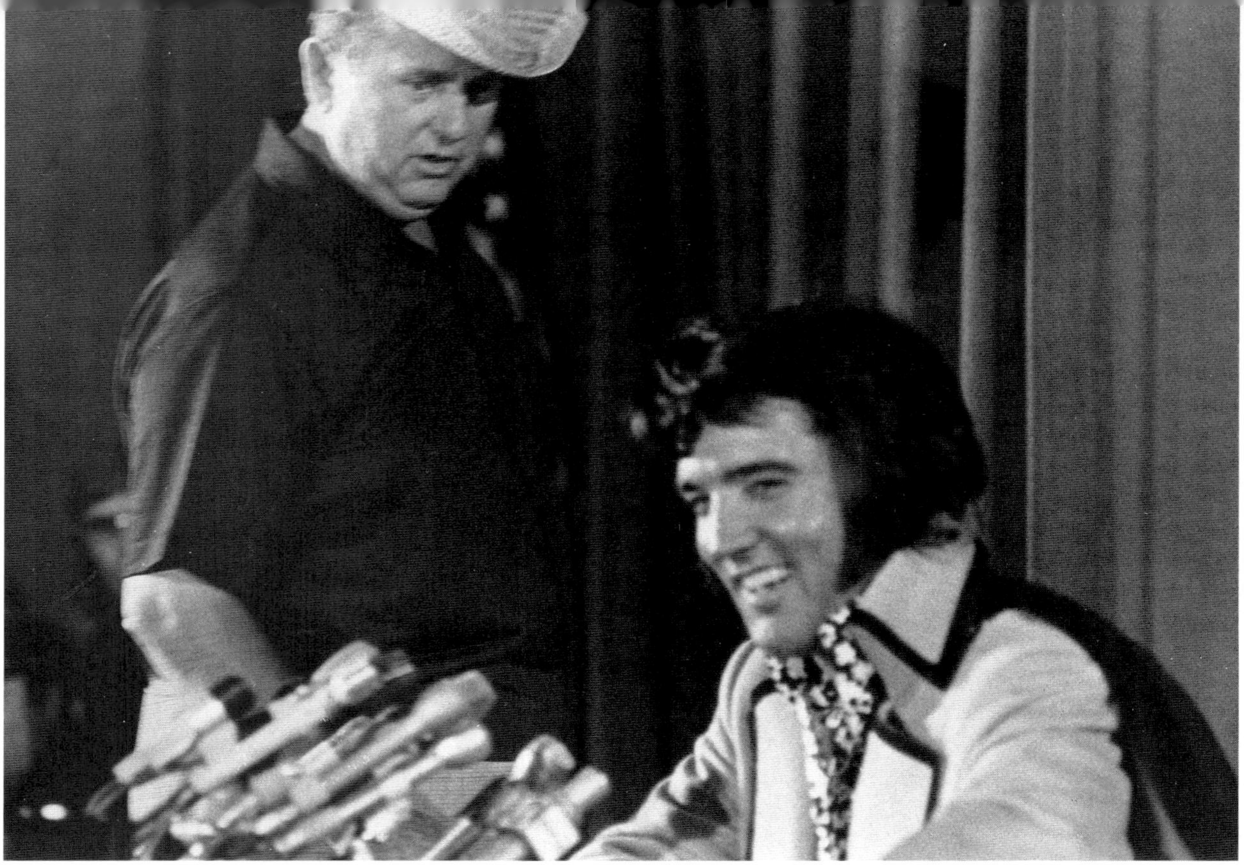

At a New York City press conference, the Colonel joked to reporters, "Let me live up to my reputation, folks," then declared the session over. (1972)

Opposite page: Relaxing with Lisa Marie after a hard karate workout. (1974)

Joe Esposito helping an exhausted Elvis after a concert.

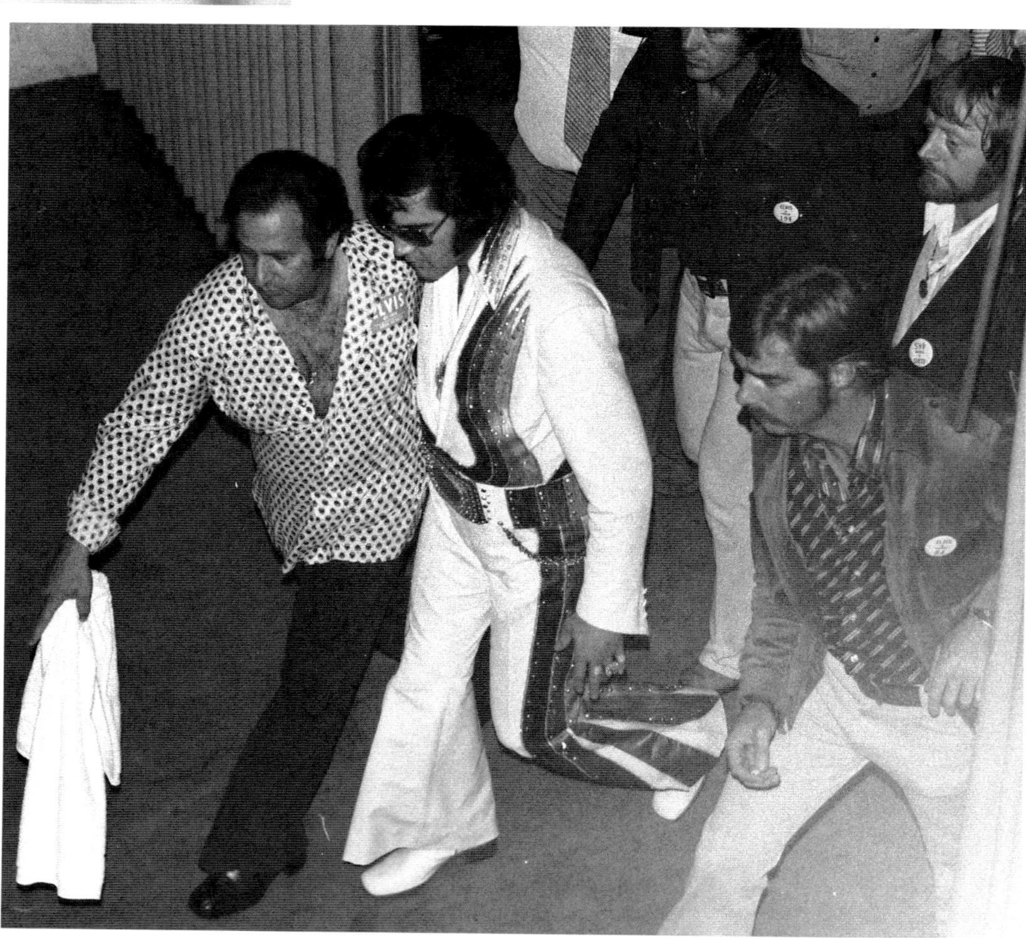

Above left, with Priscilla. Above right, acting out his lifelong fantasy of becoming a law officer in his honorary Shelby County, Tennessee, sheriff's outfit.

FINAL

DECLINE

These photos of Elvis from the '70s tell the story of his final years. To many, he would always be the King of Rock 'n Roll. He was still beloved by millions, still a financial success. In virtually every image on these pages, Elvis is surrounded by people, whether loyal fans or members of the entourage that was one of his most prized trappings of success.

But his face has lost the innocence, the unconscious sexuality of the young man the nation first swooned over. His devilish grin is gone. The pure wonder that once played over Elvis' features has been missing for a long time. What shows in his face and physique are the years of abuse: too much stodgy food, too many drugs, too little exercise. Of all the people whose task it was to look after him, he was the most negligent. Priscilla's leaving only added to his sense of isolation.

Though her departure was a long time coming, he didn't notice the warning signs until she was heading for the door. Members of the Memphis Mafia point to what might be called Elvis' benign neglect of his young wife, with whom he gradually spent less and less time. In 1971, Elvis passed a rule: No wives or girlfriends on tour. Priscilla and the other women were allowed to come to Las Vegas only for show openings and closings, and sometimes, only for openings. Sonny West says the Presleys often didn't see each other for seven weeks at a time, and Elvis' visits home with his family were brief and restless. The time apart took its toll on the Guys' marriages, too: Jerry Schilling's, Joe Esposito's, Sonny West's.

Their boss banned the wives because he didn't want them to cramp his style. Elvis valued Priscilla's loyalty and the notion of being a family man, but he wanted freedom, too. Wild parties continued in Elvis' Palm Springs house, even after Priscilla, vacationing there with one of the wives, discovered a note in the mailbox saying

"Thanks, let's do it again soon. Lizard Tongue." Priscilla was enraged, although Elvis denied any wrongdoing and laughingly insisted the note came from an unknown fan.

The house did indeed shelter some pretty kinky scenes. Sonny West, Red West, and the other Guys would scout for attractive young women to come over and surround Elvis as he held court. The women would hope to get close to the King, and many did. Others settled for one of his Guys.

Several Guys—who had the task of finding young women to spend time with Elvis in Las Vegas and Bel Air—have said in interviews and their own writings that he couldn't bear the thought of making love to a woman who had borne a child. With Lisa Marie's birth, Elvis grew more distant, and Priscilla became irrevocably shut out. He was financially generous but sexually and emotionally withdrawn. It was many months before he could bring himself to make love to her, and Priscilla felt lonely and undesirable.

There is still some dispute over exactly when, in this period, Priscilla met Mike Stone. Oddly enough, Stone was both Hawaiian and a karate champion, echoing the character of her husband's island movies and his long-time passion for karate. He was also unhappy in his marriage and on the verge of divorce.

While several Guys had guessed at Priscilla's affair, none of them told Elvis. She could have gone on leading two lives indefinitely—such was Elvis' oblivion—but she chose to tell him. On February 23, 1972, the Presleys separated. When Elvis gathered the Guys to tell them that his wife was going off with another man, they stood in embarrassed silence. Red West, who had often heard his boss complain that Priscilla should stop bugging him and should find someone else to mess around with, broke the silence with "That's what you wanted, isn't it?" He had meant to comfort Elvis.

Elvis had one more shining hour before his terrible decline—the television special *Elvis: Aloha from Hawaii.* Planned as grand entertainment of the satellite communications era, the show was announced by Colonel Parker and NBC in the fall of 1972 at the end of Elvis' season in Las Vegas. With production costs topping two-and-a-half million dollars (including one million dollars for the star), the show from Hawaii was conceived to be broadcast live around the world, until NBC realized that in doing so it would miss prime time (and top TV profits) in many countries. Instead, the January 12, 1973 show was broadcast live to Japan, where it commanded an incredible 98 percent of the viewing audience. It was taped for broadcast two days later in Europe. An expanded version was seen in the United States on April 4.

On the show, Elvis sounded great and looked fabulous: tanned, stunningly made up and costumed, and back down to fighting weight. As Colonel Parker had long forbidden overseas concert tours, the *Aloha* special struck Elvis as a chance to finally reach out to his distant fans via satellite. He roused himself from his food and drug indulgences to meet the challenge. For three months he stuck to a rigorous diet of 500 calories per day supplemented with vitamin shots.

An estimated one billion viewers in 40 countries saw the one-hour concert, beating the audience who watched the first moon landing on July 20, 1969. The show also raised $85,000 for Hawaii's Kuiokalani Lee Cancer Fund. Known for his philanthropy, it was Elvis' choice to support this charity named for the Hawaiian composer of "I'll Remember You," which he recorded in 1966 and performed on the TV special.

Four days before the show, Elvis sued Priscilla for divorce. It was his 38th birthday. By now, Elvis was already involved with former Miss Tennessee, Linda Thompson. An outgoing, motherly woman, Linda stuck by Elvis for a good four years, until she was worn out by the despair of watching him self-destruct and the hopelessness of trying to reform him. Ginger Alden, Elvis' young fiancée at the time of his death, picked up where Linda left off in 1976.

Ginger met Elvis at Graceland with her sister, the new Miss Tennessee, and nine weeks later, on January 26, 1977, Elvis asked her to marry him. Their wedding, Ginger says, was to be on Christmas Day of that year.

Unfortunately, this brief hiatus of good health vanished, to be replaced with an astonishingly abusive lifestyle. Priscilla says, not just in jest, that cooking for Elvis was simple: She would take whatever she was fixing for everybody else and burn it. He ate a great quantity of burnt bacon, eggs, sauerkraut, and cheeseburgers, the latter usually eaten just before bed and followed by up to six banana splits. The only vegetables he ate with any regularity were fried tomatoes.

One of his favorite meals away from home was the $49.95 peanut butter and banana submarine sandwich fried in bacon grease served by the Colorado Mine Company restaurant in Glendale, Colorado; the sandwich wasn't that big, but Elvis had to fly his plane over from Memphis for a late snack of them, at a cost of about $16,000.

As the photographs in this section show, Elvis was living in the adoration of his fans, which kept him walled in at Graceland. The one form of exercise he got on a regular basis was karate. Elvis practiced this martial art for 18 years and held an eighth-degree black belt. It was he who inadvertently opened the door to Priscilla's affair with Mike Stone by urging her to get involved in the sport.

Except when locked into a Hollywood shooting schedule, Elvis maintained a life rhythm all his own that was permanently out of sync with the rest of the world's. He stayed up until the early hours of the morning, then slept as late as 4 P.M. The windows in his bedroom at Graceland, and in any of the other houses or hotels he called home while out of Memphis, were kept tightly shaded. No ray of sun contradicted Elvis' definition of morning.

But Elvis' health problems went far beyond a lack of leafy green vegetables and a normal sleep schedule. Though he rarely used street drugs, he relied on sympathetic doctors and pharmacists in many cities to stock his demand for prescription drugs like codeine, morphine, Quaalude, Valium, and Demerol. Among Elvis' daunting bedtime reading stack was always the *Physician's Desk Reference*, which he consulted to avoid overdoing his doses or making lethal combinations.

He didn't always get it right. Elvis was saved from overdoses on several occasions by his girlfriends and the Guys, and his autopsy would reveal severe heart disease, clogged arteries, and a badly distended liver.

Toward the end, Elvis worked a punishing schedule of as many as 150 concert and nightclub dates a year. Their format never varied, and he found this boredom a torture equal to that inflicted by the formulaic Hollywood travelogues in the '60s.

For many years Elvis had felt out of control of his life and destiny. Gladys' death had opened a chasm of loneliness that none of the Guys nor dozens of women were able to close. His alienation and disappointment grew over time until it overcame him. The career that the Colonel had crafted for Elvis was not the one his star had craved of musical creativity, serious acting, and overseas travel. He appreciated his fans and was always gracious to them, but their eyes constantly upon him imprisoned him behind guards and wrought iron.

In the end, all Elvis wanted was oblivion, which came on August 16, 1977. But he will never be forgotten by his millions of fans. He came and changed our lives, leaving a legacy of photographs like these, lasting music, and memories. The images on these pages show something of Elvis and how he endeared himself to us. They certainly are a poignant testament to how much we adored him. On these pages, at least—and in fans' private scrapbooks—his smile will endure, like our memories, forever.

Above left, with girlfriend Linda Thompson, whom Elvis met through George Klein on July 5, 1972. Above right, backstage in Las Vegas. Left, aboard Elvis' airplane, *Lisa Marie.* (1975)

Opposite page: Elvis first learned karate in the Army. He was faithful to its study for 18 years, ultimately reaching the rank of 8th degree black belt, or senior master of the tae kwan do arts. Bottom, meditating before a tournament.

Top left, Vernon, Dee, Linda, and Elvis at a karate demonstration. Top right, Elvis stopped his limo to help an accident victim. Left, Mr. and Mrs. Sam Thompson (Linda's brother and sister-in-law), Elvis, Lisa, and Linda. Above, with Vernon, who accompanied his son on his concert tours until 1976, when he became ill. He made one final trip with Elvis, the last TV concert for CBS.

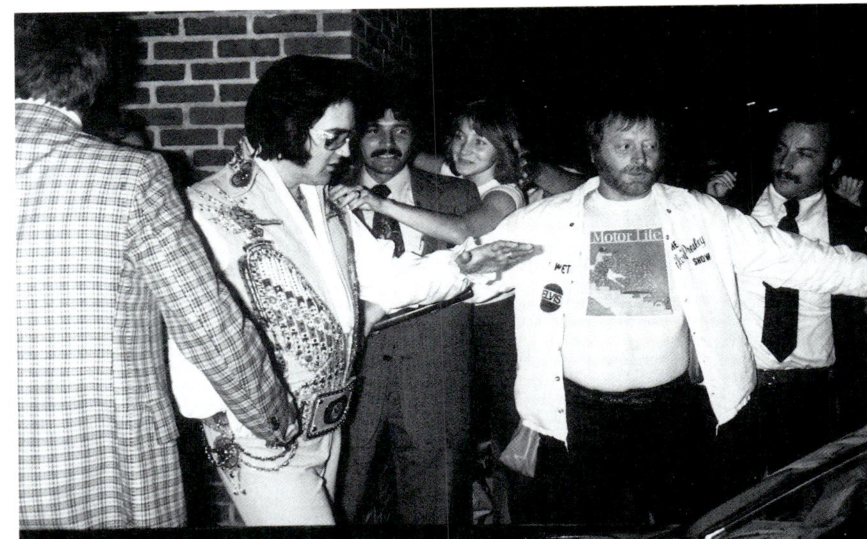

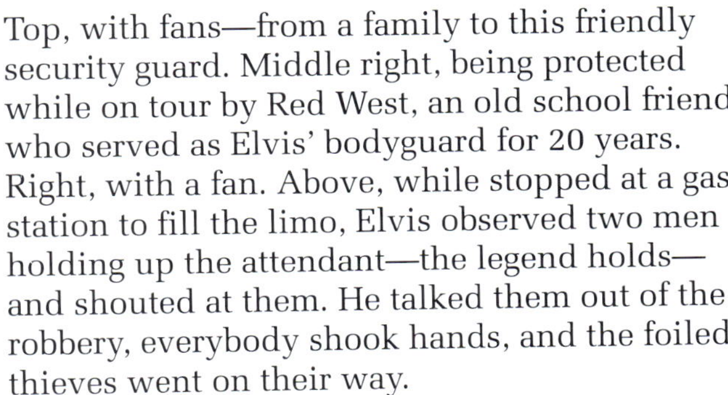

Top, with fans—from a family to this friendly security guard. Middle right, being protected while on tour by Red West, an old school friend who served as Elvis' bodyguard for 20 years. Right, with a fan. Above, while stopped at a gas station to fill the limo, Elvis observed two men holding up the attendant—the legend holds—and shouted at them. He talked them out of the robbery, everybody shook hands, and the foiled thieves went on their way.

Top right, with pal Ed Parker, a friend who was never on the payroll, but who taught Elvis karate and guarded him on tours. Middle right, on his last snowmobiling trip in Vail, Colorado, January 1976. Above left, with Diane Goodman, Miss Georgia, whom Elvis briefly dated. Above right, with Ginger Alden at Mt. Sherman, Arkansas, for her grandmother's funeral on January 3, 1977.

Opposite page: In Hawaii on Elvis' last vacation later the same year.

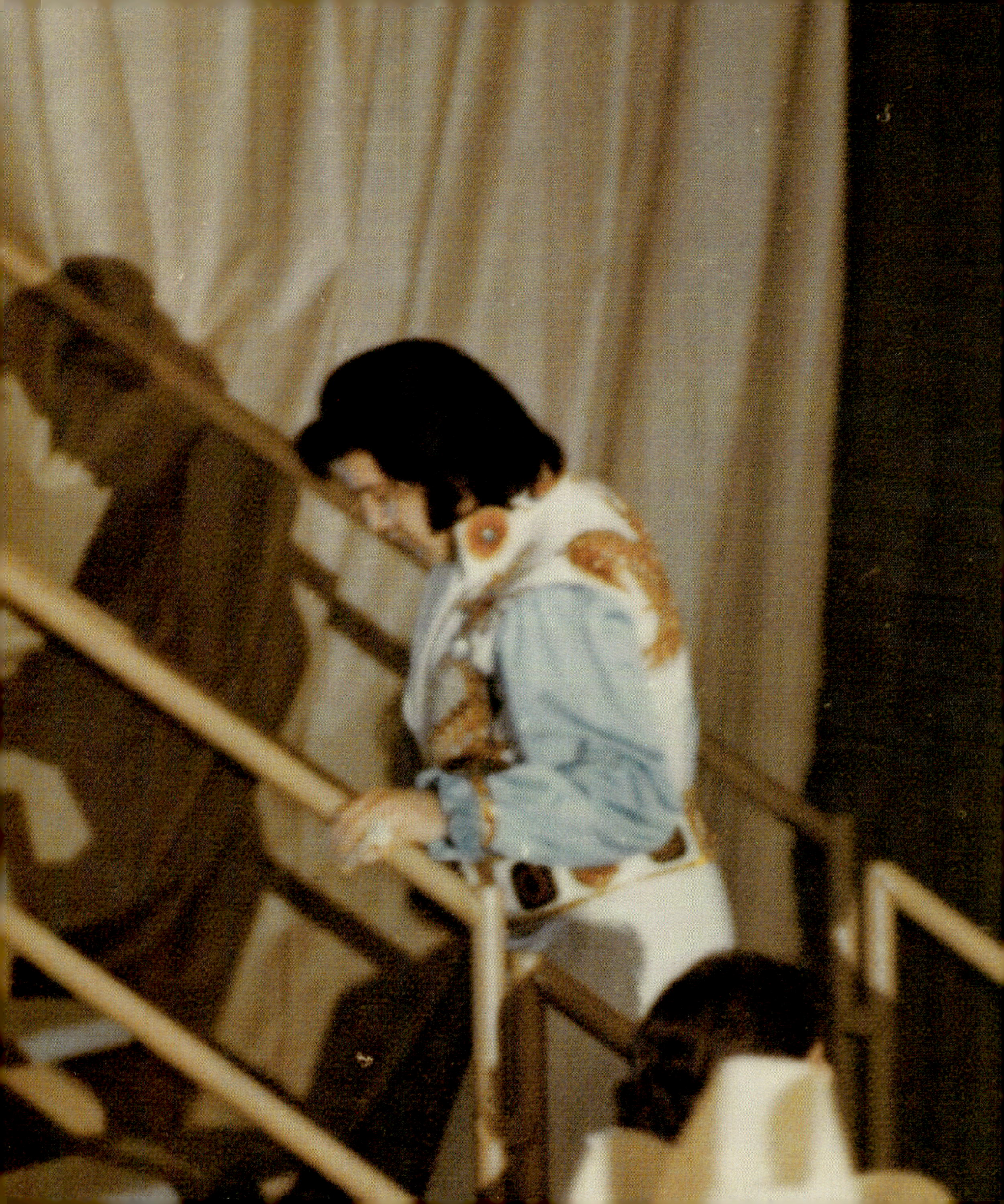

Journey through Asia

MASTERPIECES IN THE BROOKLYN MUSEUM OF ART

Journey through Asia

MASTERPIECES IN THE BROOKLYN MUSEUM OF ART

Amy G. Poster

with contributions by
Frances Z. Yuan, Layla S. Diba, Maryam Ekhtiar,
Aimée Froom, and Hyunsoo Woo

BROOKLYN MUSEUM OF ART
IN ASSOCIATION WITH PHILIP WILSON PUBLISHERS

This publication has been made possible, in part, by the Brooklyn Museum of Art's Asian Art Council. The section devoted to the arts of the Islamic world is supported, in part, by the Hagop Kevorkian Fund.

Publication of this volume was organized at
the Brooklyn Museum of Art by
James Leggio, Head of Publications & Editorial Services
Project editors: Kathleen M. Friello, Reiko Tomii, James Leggio
Editorial coordinator: Joanna Ekman

For Philip Wilson Publishers
Anne Jackson, Commissioning Editor

Designer: Langley Iddins
Cartographer: Trevor Bounford
Printed in Italy by Tonti & X-Press, Naples

ISBN 0-87273-148-0 (paperback edition)
ISBN 0-85667-564-4 (hardback edition)

Library of Congress Cataloging-in-Publication Data

Poster, Amy G.
Journey through Asia : masterpieces in the Brooklyn Museum of Art / Amy G. Poster ; with contributions by Layla S. Diba . . . [et al.].
p. cm.
Includes bibliographical references.
ISBN 0-87273-148-0 (pbk.) -- ISBN 0-85667-564-4
1. Art, Asian--Catalogs. 2. Brooklyn Museum of Art--Catalogs. 3. Art--New York (State)--New York--Catalogs. 4. Brooklyn (N. Y.)--Catalogs. I. Diba, Layla S. II. Brooklyn Museum of Art. III. Title.
N7260 .P66 2003
709'.5'07474723--dc21

2002012418

PHOTOGRAPH CREDITS

Photographs of objects in the collection of the Brooklyn Museum of Art reproduced in this volume are by: Patricia Layman Bazelon, no. 34; Dean Brown, Chief Photographer, nos. 12, 15, 18, 22, 23, 26, 35, 36, 45, 48, 51–53, 55–57, 67, 68, 76; Shin Hada, nos. 28, 101, 102; Justin Kerr, nos. 17, 33, 64; Phillip Popock, nos. 40, 69, 72; Gregg Stanger, no. 66; Bruce White, nos. 1, 5, 6. The following photographs are from the Brooklyn Museum of Art Archives: figs. 1, 2 (Culin Archival Collection), 3, 5–10, 12–14.

Contents

Foreword

As we begin the twenty-first century, already sometimes referred to as the "Asian Century," the economic, cultural, and political impact of Asia on the world is manifest. The importance of Asia is also evident in Brooklyn, where Asian communities are among the fastest-growing populations in the New York metropolitan area.

The Brooklyn Museum of Art's engagement with Asia and its artistic and cultural traditions is not a recent development, however. Over the course of a century of collecting, research, and exhibitions, the Museum has brought Asian art to an audience often unfamiliar with Eastern cultures. As globalization and technology make the world smaller and increasingly cosmopolitan, we hope that our collection will provide a rich foundation for understanding the diversity and complexity of Asian art and culture.

In honor of the centennial of our Department of Asian Art, I am pleased to introduce *Journey through Asia: Masterpieces in the Brooklyn Museum of Art*. As the first general survey of the Museum's Asian holdings, this book offers an overview of one of our nation's foremost collections of Asian art. Encompassing works from across Asia as well as the Islamic world, the catalogue highlights more than a hundred particularly splendid works of art, drawing upon and celebrating decades of pioneering research by the many curators and specialists who have worked closely with the Museum's collection. The earliest ethnological material acquired around the turn of the twentieth century has now expanded into a collection of more than twenty thousand objects that reflects the dynamic arts of the region and Brooklyn's connections to Asia.

The Brooklyn Museum of Art is one of the leading American museums to offer the public encyclopedic collections in an open, accessible environment. The BMA strives to foster understanding across cultures, within our diverse community and beyond. The collection of Asian art is an important component in the Museum's mission to achieve this goal.

This publication relied on the expertise of many individuals, foremost among them, Amy G. Poster, Curator and Chair of the Department of Asian Art, whose commitment to the project was vital to its successful completion. I would also like to thank the BMA's Asian Art Council and the Hagop Kevorkian Fund for their financial support for this publication.

For the ongoing support of the Museum's Trustees, we extend special gratitude to Robert S. Rubin, Chairman, and to every member of our Board. Without the confidence and active engagement of our Trustees, it would not be possible to initiate and maintain the high level of publication programming exemplified by *Journey through Asia: Masterpieces in the Brooklyn Museum of Art*.

Arnold L. Lehman
Director
Brooklyn Museum of Art

Acknowledgments

Journey through Asia: Masterpieces in the Brooklyn Museum of Art has been in my thoughts for a long time. Although the Museum has published many specialized catalogues devoted to specific areas of strength within its Asian holdings, it has never previously attempted to give a sense of the full range of the Asian collection. The present book, the fruit of a sustained effort by the Department of Asian Art over the last several years, is in fact the first general survey of the Asian collection published since the founding of the Department in 1903.

As with all books of this kind, its realization depended on the talents and dedication of many individuals. Frances Z. Yuan, formerly Assistant Curator of Asian Art, helped to organize the publication project during its formative stages and coordinated its initial editing. She worked tirelessly with all the curatorial contributors and the other Museum departments involved in the book. Thanks also go to the many current and former members of the curatorial staff who brought their knowledge and critical intelligence to the writing of this catalogue. The bulk of the entries are the work of Dr. Layla S. Diba, Dr. Maryam Ekhtiar, Dr. Aimée Froom, Hyunsoo Woo, Frances Yuan, and myself.

Although most of the research incorporated into the entries came from the curators and scholars, past and present, who have been instrumental in building or caring for the Brooklyn collection, we would also like to extend our thanks to the many specialists outside the Museum who contributed knowledge and expertise to individual entries. Melissa McCormick, Assistant Professor of Japanese Art at Columbia University, John Seyller, Professor of Art History at the University of Vermont, Savita Monie at the Asia Society, and Trevel Balser at the Indian Center of Art and Culture each authored entries in their respective areas of specialization. Yukio Lippit at Princeton University and Wheeler Thackston at Harvard University offered their advice and helped in the translation of certain texts.

Special thanks are also owed to the many departmental interns and volunteers who helped with this project since its inception in 1999. We would like to thank especially Tara Adrian,

Elizabeth Beller, Meghan Conaton, I-Hsuan Chen, Fanny Hsu, Anjali Kothari, Sarah Laursen, Ilaria Migliardi, Kent Ng, and Mari Takamatsu.

Deborah Wythe, Archivist, provided access to the Museum's archives as well as her own wealth of information on the institution's history, the central concern of my introductory essay to this book. Ruth Janson, Coordinator of Rights and Reproductions, expertly organized the illustrative materials drawn from the Museum's photography files. Dean Brown, Chief Photographer, and Gregg Stanger of the Photography Department tirelessly shot and re-shot many of the masterpieces in the collection.

At Philip Wilson Publishers, London, our thanks to Philip Wilson, Cangy Venables, Norman Turpin, and Anne Jackson for their enlightened interest in this project. At the Museum, Joanna Ekman helped to coordinate the interaction between the staff and our colleagues in London.

We are grateful for the partial financial support for this publication by the Asian Art Council of the Brooklyn Museum of Art and the Hagop Kevorkian Fund.

Finally, special thanks to Dr. James Leggio, Head of Publications and Editorial Services at the Museum, and to Reiko Tomii and Kathleen M. Friello, the project's editors. Their insight, guidance, and persistence – and their inexhaustible patience, not only with the text but also with the contributors – proved essential to the book's success.

AGP

The First Century of the Department of Asian Art

Amy G. Poster

The Brooklyn Museum of Art's Asian art collection, now beginning its eleventh decade, bears the indelible stamp of those who have shaped it, reflecting the personal interests of its curators, the collecting taste of its donors, and changing public fashions. Since its inception in 1903, the collection has evolved beyond the ethnologic focus of its first Curator to become a truly cross-cultural collection of East Asian, Southeast Asian, Indian, and Islamic arts. The Museum has always been committed to representing the diversity of Asia and the rich cultural and artistic heritage of the peoples of this region. However, as will be evident in this brief history, the Department of Asian Art, like most museum collections, was not formed systematically but grew as much by chance in areas that were of interest to curators and collectors at the time or as the result of the taste of the Museum's benefactors. The collecting strategies of the Museum's curators can only be deduced from the acquisitions made, as the intentions of the curators were not often delineated in the written record.

During the history of the Department of Asian Art, there have been many thematic exhibitions presenting the diversity of the Asian art collections. The range of these projects is illustrated by the selection of exhibitions and symposia cited here.

1900s

The Department of Asian Art was officially established in 1903 as part of the Museum's Department of Ethnology. Prior to 1903, however, Chinese and Japanese ceramics, many since deaccessioned, were donated by Carll H. de Silver (1846–1913), a merchant who worked in the China trade and later had a successful Wall Street career. De Silver was an early supporter of the Museum and Benefactor of the Brooklyn Institute of Arts and Sciences (the Museum's parent organization), and a Trustee of the Museum Governing Committee. He worked closely with Colonel Robert B. Woodward (1840–1915), not only a Trustee of the Brooklyn Institute of Arts and Sciences but also Chairman of its Governing

Committee. De Silver and Woodward may be considered the earliest patrons of the Asian art collections.

In 1903, the Institute appointed the Museum's first Curator of Ethnology, Stewart Culin (1858–1929). As Director of the University of Pennsylvania Museum of Archaeology and Paleontology, he had pursued, among other topics, researches on the life and culture of the contemporary Chinese American community.[1] Culin developed a strong interest in Asian cultures, yet his early collecting activities for the Brooklyn Museum focused on Native American material culture.[2] It was only toward the end of the decade that the Museum began to acquire significant Asian holdings. In 1909, Culin led his first field expedition to China and Japan, a buying trip that yielded approximately 1,800 objects for the Museum [FIG. 2].[3]

1910s

During Culin's long and productive tenure (1903–29), he spearheaded the Museum's collecting expeditions to Asia: to Ukiya, Tokyo, Yokohama, Sendai, Nikkō, and Kyoto in Japan and Shanghai, Hong Kong, and Canton in China from June 1909 to March 1910; to Japan, including the Kurile Islands and Hokkaidō, from May 1912 to January 1913; and to Japan, China, Korea, and India from October 1913 to May 1914.[4] In India, Culin visited Lucknow, Agra, Delhi, Jaipur, Ahmedabad, Bombay, Madras, and Candy (Sri Lanka), before proceeding on to Europe. Culin's objective in building the collection was to understand the "language of things," especially in the world of fashion and design. His collecting practice, continued from his Native American expeditions, consisted of traveling with knowledgeable Western and local contacts, commissioning or purchasing artifacts, and recording direct observations.[5] In his diaries, correspondence, and publications, he documented both the meaning and origins of the objects he collected. He also obtained objects of curiosity used for divination or ritual purposes.

One of Culin's many important correspondents who influenced the collection was Lockwood de Forest (1850–1932), an artist and designer who opened a factory in Ahmedabad, India, in 1882 for the manufacture of wood and brass objects for American interiors, based on designs inspired by the local Gujarati architecture. Culin traveled with de Forest on his collecting trip to India in 1913. The two of them not only visited Ahmedabad but also stopped in Delhi, where they obtained significant works, primarily textiles and carpets, from the Maharaja of Jaipur's collection; these were sold to

FIGURE 1
The Brooklyn Museum of Art traces its origins to 1823, with the founding of the Brooklyn Apprentices' Library. The Beaux-Arts building, located at 200 Eastern Parkway, Brooklyn, N.Y., and designed by McKim, Mead & White, architects, opened in 1897.

1. "Records of the Office of the Director: W. H. Fox, 1913–1933, Ethnography," Brooklyn Museum of Art Archives, File no. 27/2, 1922–33.

2. *Masterpieces in The Brooklyn Museum* (New York: The Brooklyn Museum in association with Abrams, 1988): 14–15.

3. *Museums of the Brooklyn Institute of Arts and Sciences Report for the Year 1910* (Brooklyn: [Museums], 1911): 60.

4. "Records of the Office of the Director: W. H. Fox, 1913–1933, Ethnography."

5. John Getz, *The Woodward Collection of Jades and Other Hard Stones* (New York: Privately printed, 1913); Deirdre E. Lawrence, "Culin: Collector and Documentor of the World," *Orientations* 20, no. 7 (July 1989): 20–27; Deirdre E. Lawrence and Deborah Wythe, comps., *The Brooklyn Museum: Guide to the Culin Archival Collection* (Brooklyn: The Brooklyn Museum, 1996).

Culin at the time by the art dealer Imre Schwaiger (1864–1940).[6] De Forest was a frequent collaborator with Louis Comfort Tiffany and the brother of Robert de Forest, then Director of the Metropolitan Museum of Art, whose agents also made acquisitions during this trip.

FIGURE 2
Stewart Culin with art dealer Togo Takayanagi in Hokkaidō, Japan, 1909

Culin was also responsible for forming the Museum's exceptional collection of more than a thousand objects from the native people of northern Japan, the Ainu. He was familiar with Ainu culture from his University of Pennsylvania days, when he installed the collection assembled in the field by Hiram M. Hiller. When he moved to Brooklyn, he used contacts acquired during his Philadelphia tenure to establish an important collection for the BMA. Funded by Herman Stutzer (1857–1933), Culin's expedition to Hokkaidō took place in 1912, where he met the Reverend John Batchelor (1854–1944), an English missionary in Hokkaidō from 1877 to 1940 who wrote the first Ainu-English dictionary (1889). In 1912, the BMA acquired Batchelor's collection. The Museum also gained for the collection a large portion of the Ainu objects assembled by Frederick Starr (1858–1933), Curator of the Field Museum, Chicago, for the Ainu exhibit at the 1904 Louisiana Purchase Universal Exposition in Saint Louis, in addition to purchases made by Culin throughout Japan.[7]

Culin assembled important works through gift and purchase in the United States, as well. In 1911, for example, he acquired at auction in New York a pair of thirteenth-century Buddhist cosmic diagrams (see no. 26) dating to the Kamakura period (1185–1333). The paintings were among the many works acquired in Japan in 1886 by the American artist John La Farge (1835–1910).

Whereas the objects Culin acquired on his trips were intended to educate the Museum's public about non-European cultures, gifts to the Museum quite logically tended to reflect collecting tastes of the gentry who were its benefactors. In this vein, the Museum received an important bequest in 1915 of 218 later Chinese jade and hard stone carvings from the Estate of Colonel Robert B. Woodward.[8] Additional gifts were provided by Samuel P. Avery, Jr. (1857–1920), son of the noted art dealer and collector of American art Samuel P. Avery (1822–1904). In 1909, he donated a sizable collection of Ming- and Qing-dynasty Chinese cloisonné enamels. His donations would grow to exceed some 360 Chinese objects,[9] catalogued by John Getz and displayed at the BMA in 1912.

6. Ellen S. Smart and Daniel S. Walker, *Pride of the Princes: Indian Art of the Mughal Era in the Cincinnati Art Museum*, exh. cat. (Cincinnati: Cincinnati Art Museum, 1985).

7. *Museums of The Brooklyn Institute of Arts and Sciences Report for the Year 1912* (Brooklyn: [Museums], 1913): 41.

8. Lawrence, "Culin: Collector and Documentor," 24.

9. Ibid.

The Department devoted the latter part of the decade to cataloguing and installing the collection from Culin's expeditions.[10] Contextual displays were a part of Culin's vision for presenting Asian culture at the Museum. In 1910, the Japanese Hall was installed; in 1917, a Jain Rest House, acquired in Ahmedabad, Gujarat, was put on exhibition; and two exhibitions were mounted of Japanese woodblock prints from the collection.

1920s

In the 1920s cataloguing and installation activities continued. In 1920, the Museum created the "Oriental Collections," separating the collections from the ethnography collection and moving the displays to their own galleries. In 1927, the Chinese Hall of State and the new Japanese Hall were installed on the first floor of the Museum, displaying the Chinese, Japanese, Tibetan, and Korean collections [FIG. 3].[11] Throughout the decade Culin supplemented his field acquisitions with purchases, such as objects from the Waddell Collection of Tibetan Art acquired in London in 1920.[12]

Culin's outstanding acquisitions in this period included nine pages of the *Qissa-i Amir Hamza* purchased at auction in 1923–24 (see no. 69). This manuscript, one of the glories of Indian Mughal painting, illustrates tales of the life of the Prophet Muhammad's uncle, Amir Hamza, produced for Emperor Akbar (r. 1556–1605).[13] Culin carried out careful research on the manuscript, seeking expertise from the German scholar Hermann Goetz.[14] Unfortunately, five of the nine *Hamzanama* folios were later deaccessioned, but the four that remain in the collection are the jewels of the Museum's Indian painting collection.[15] Other significant donations during this period include a late Chola-dynasty (c. 750–1310) bronze image of Shiva Nataraja (acc. no. 27.959), purchased in Madras, India, by Frank L. Babbott (1854–1933) and donated to the BMA in 1927 [FIG. 4].

Culin's death in 1929 brought this most significant chapter in the Museum's history to a close. His collections, which form the core of the Department of Asian Art, his archives, and his extensive library that was purchased by the Museum serve as Culin's legacy to the present day.[16]

Following Culin's death, the Museum hired Herbert J. Spinden (1879–1967), formerly Curator of Mexican Art at the Peabody Museum, Harvard, to serve as Curator (1929–50). Tassilo Adam (active 1899–1948), who had been working as an ethnologist for the Dutch Colonial Government in the Dutch East Indies for twenty-five years, was appointed to look after the Oriental collections, becoming Assistant Curator for Eastern Art in 1929 and Curator of Eastern and Near Eastern Art in 1934.

1930s

The decade following Culin's death was a period of dramatic change for the Museum and Asian art and culture. The Department of Ethnology was separated into several autonomous divisions, including the Department of Eastern and Near Eastern Art, established in 1931 and renamed the Department of Oriental Art in 1934.[17] Furthermore, the Museum's displays were reorganized to reflect contemporary ideas about world history. The galleries of Asian art

10. *Museums of the Brooklyn Institute of Arts and Science Report for the Year 1920* (Brooklyn: [Museums], 1921): 12.

11. Lawrence, "Culin: Collector and Documentor," 25.

12. Brooklyn 1920, 12. Registrar's records show that no Waddell Collection material remains in the BMA today.

13. R. Stewart Culin, "Illustrations of the Romance of Amir Hamzah," *Brooklyn Museum Quarterly* 11, no. 4 (1924): 139–43.

14. Amy G. Poster, *Realms of Heroism: Indian Paintings from The Brooklyn Museum*, exh. cat. (Brooklyn: Brooklyn Museum, 1994): 30–31, 61.

15. Ibid., 31.

16. *Museums of the Brooklyn Institute of Arts and Science: Report for the Year 1930* (Brooklyn: [Museums], 1931): 12.

17. *Masterpieces in The Brooklyn Museum*, 19, 21.

18. *Museums of the Brooklyn Institute of Arts and Science: Report for the Year 1934* (Brooklyn: [Museums], 1935): 10.

19. Amy G. Poster, *From Indian Earth: 4,000 Years of Terracotta Art*, exh. cat. (Brooklyn: The Brooklyn Museum, 1986): 7.

FIGURE 3
Installation view of Chinese Hall of State, Brooklyn Museum, 1927

were newly arranged by culture, in chronological order, resulting in the dismantling and relocation of Asian art in 1934 to the second floor, where it remains at present.[18] Tassilo Adam's tenure as Curator of Eastern and Near Eastern Art was devoted to the reinstallation of the permanent collection. By 1932, the Museum had completed several contextual exhibits, including a Damascus house, a Hindu street, and four re-created Chinese rooms from different periods [FIGS. 5, 6].

Subsequently, Laurance P. Roberts (1907–2002) headed the Department of Oriental Art from 1934 to 1946, presiding over these changes and the installation of the new galleries [FIG. 7]. Roberts was responsible for changing the name to the Department of Oriental Art in 1934 when he was hired from the University of Pennsylvania museum. During his tenure, the Museum often sought the advice of the preeminent scholar of Indian art Ananda K. Coomaraswamy (1877–1947), whose influence is shown most vividly in the collections he helped to form. For example, through his intervention, the BMA acquired sixty-nine objects from the Indus Valley site of Chanhu-Daro (Pakistan), excavated between 1935 and 1937 jointly by the Museum of Fine Arts, Boston, and the University of Pennsylvania. During this decade, the Museum purchased its first paintings from Rajasthan and the Punjab Hills in India directly from Coomaraswamy.[19]

Roberts served as Director of the Museum from 1939 until 1946. This was a felicitous association, when donors such as Frederic B. Pratt (1865–1945) helped to expand the holdings of East Asian and Islamic art. In 1939, Pratt made a major gift to the Japanese collection of a Kan'ei era (1624–44) genre painting, *A Cherry Blossom Viewing Picnic* (see no. 33), considered today to be one of the Museum's masterpieces of Japanese art. Pratt, one of six sons of the industrialist Charles Pratt, an original director of the Standard Oil Company, resided in Brooklyn and was President of the Pratt

FIGURE 4
Shiva Nataraja. South India, late Chola dynasty, 13th century. Bronze, H: 30 in. (76.2 cm.). 27.959, Brooklyn Museum of Art, Gift of Frank L. Babbott

FIGURE 5
Interior of the Damascus House, Brooklyn Museum, 1932

FIGURE 6
Installation view of Chinese Bedroom, Brooklyn Museum, 1932

Institute in Brooklyn. During his tenure as president, in 1894, Pratt traveled to Japan. His observations of the tour were reflected in his extensive writings and lectures at the Pratt Institute during the following year. He also invited the Japanologist and aesthete Ernest Fenollosa (1853–1908) to lecture there about Japanese art, religions, and culture.[20]

The profile of the Museum's Islamic collection was also enhanced early in the decade with the exhibition of nearly a thousand items entitled *Brooklyn Museum Exhibition of Persian Art and Its Reaction in the Modern World* (1931). In 1936, the Islamic section was the recipient of a valuable carpet fragment from sixteenth-century Safavid Iran (acc. no. 36.213 a–h). The fragment, which has been known as the "Angel Rug," was a gift of Herbert L. Pratt (1871–1945), son of Frederic and Caroline Pratt.

1940s

Asian art activities were curtailed considerably during the Second World War, particularly post-1942, when the Curator, Laurance P. Roberts, took leave to join the United States Army (1942–46).[21] During Roberts's leave, his wife, Isabel Spaulding Roberts (b. 1911), served in his place [FIG. 8]. Despite the war, the generous donations to the Brooklyn Museum by the Pratt family continued during these years. In 1943, significant donations were made to the Islamic collection, including the Egyptian fifteenth- to sixteenth-century *Mamluk Carpet* (see no. 95) and a sixteenth-century Iznik *Spherical Hanging Ornament* from Turkey (see no. 97), both given by Mr. and Mrs. Frederic B. Pratt. These objects remain the most important Islamic works in the collection.

The Japanese print collection had been established early in the century but was enhanced significantly in this decade through the donations of Louis V. Ledoux (1880–1948). Ledoux, a renowned connoisseur-collector of Japanese prints, served as President of the Japan Society of New York and as a Trustee of the Brooklyn Museum (1939–48).[22] Ledoux's library on the subject including his annotations is now part of the Art Reference Library of the BMA.

Following the Second World War, the attention of the Curator shifted to the Chinese collection when George N. Kates (1895–1990) served as Curator of Oriental Art (1947–49). Kates is best known for his work *The Years That Were Fat* (1952), which recounts his recollections of life in Beijing. In 1946, Kates organized the BMA exhibition *Chinese Furniture*, formed from his personal collection of hardwood furniture gathered during his years spent in China [FIG. 9].[23] Following this, he published *Chinese Household Furniture* (1948).

FIGURE 7
Laurance P. Roberts, Curator, 1934–46; Director, 1939–46

FIGURE 8
Isabel Spaulding Roberts, Acting Curator/Director, 1942–46

20. Professor M. Morton, Pratt Institute, conversation with author, July 1996.

21. *The Brooklyn Museum: Annual Report 1946* (Brooklyn: Brooklyn Museum Press, 1947): 9.

22. "Ledoux, Louis Vernon," *Who Was Who in America, Vol. 2, 1943–1950* (Chicago: Marquis, 1950).

23. Asian Art Department, "Vertical Files to 1979," Brooklyn Museum of Art Library.

FIGURE 9
Installation view of *Chinese Furniture*, Brooklyn Museum, 1946

Kates's collection was subsequently dispersed. In 1948–49, he also curated an exhibition of Chinese metalwork. Notable Chinese ceramics donated by the Frank L. Babbott family and generous loans of Chinese bronzes and jades by Ernest Erickson (1893–1983) and Alastair B. Martin (b. 1915) considerably enriched the Chinese collection.[24]

1950s

When George J. Lee (1919–76), a specialist in Chinese art educated at Harvard University, served as Curator of Oriental Art (1949–59), the holdings in the Museum's storerooms were reassessed and the collections of Chinese painting and Tang, Song, and Yuan ceramics were strengthened.[25] One of the decade's most important acquisitions was the 1952 Augustus S. Hutchins (1856–1948) bequest of 360 Chinese ceramics. This included the masterly and world-renowned fourteenth-century Yuan-dynasty (1272–1368) blue-and-white wine jar (see no. 17), depicting fish amid water plants. Lee reported that he was sent to survey and collect the Hutchins ceramics at the family estate on Long Island, and that after all the works were thought to have been loaded onto the Museum truck, he went to the garage to wash his hands.[26] There he found, left below the sink to catch water drops, this remarkable icon of the BMA collection. He also reported that when he arrived as a new curator, the Community Committee held a luncheon in his honor, where he was surprised to find another of the BMA Chinese ceramics, the Song-dynasty Ding ware basin (see no. 11), used as a centerpiece. Collectors such as Ernest Erickson and Alastair B. Martin, formerly Chairman of the Board of Trustees and still a board member, continued to lend generously to enhance the Chinese collection.[27] This period saw the beginning of several such long relationships, whereby the consummate eye of the collector elevated certain sections of the Department's collection to a new level. In the Korean field, a Koryŏ-dynasty (918–1392) celadon ewer (see

24. *The Brooklyn Museum: Annual Report 1949–1950* (Brooklyn: Brooklyn Museum Press, 1951): 7; Asian Art Department, "Acquisition Strategy" (1991): 1.

25. Ibid.

26. George J. Lee, conversation with author, July 1974.

27. *The Brooklyn Museum: Annual Report 1950–1951* (Brooklyn: Brooklyn Museum Press, 1951): 10.

28. Poster, *Realms of Heroism*, 31.

FIGURE 10
Installation view of *The Kevorkian Foundation Collection of Rare and Magnificent Oriental Carpets: Special Loan Exhibition*, Brooklyn Museum, April 23–May 28, 1967

no. 49) from the first half of the twelfth century, now considered one of the world's most remarkable Koryŏ celadon ceramics, was presented by Mrs. Darwin R. James III in 1956; the Museum has recently learned that this celebrated piece was first acquired by the donor's relative, Horace K. Underwood (1859–1916), a Presbyterian missionary who founded Yonsei University in Seoul at the turn of the century. The 1950s were also a time when the Japanese collection was significantly enhanced by new acquisitions of ceramics, lacquer, sculpture, and paintings. In 1959, the Department of Oriental Art purchased *Drying Fishnets in the Four Seasons* (see no. 32), a pair of screens attributed to Kaihō Yūshō (Japanese, 1533–1615) from the Momoyama period (1573–1615). The Indian section benefited from the donation of two groups of Hyderabadi portraits from James S. Hays (acc. no. 59.205) and Philip P. Weisberg (acc. no. 59.206).[28]

1960s

Lois Katz (b. 1932), Assistant and Associate Curator in Charge of the Department (1962–65; 1965–70), set the pace for the ensuing period, not only rediscovering treasures hidden in storage for decades, but also establishing a new art-historical approach to the collection, a pattern for further studies, and areas of collecting for the future.

In the 1960s, two significant loan exhibitions represented the Department's first foray into the realm of major international shows. With the encouragement of Lois Katz, in 1967, the Japanese loan exhibition *Japanese Ink Painting and Calligraphy from the Collection of the Tokiwayama Bunko Foundation* examined Muromachi-period (1392–1573) ink painting. In 1967, the Kevorkian Foundation sponsored a traveling exhibition of forty-one carpets, entitled *The Kevorkian Foundation Collection of Rare and Magnificent Oriental Carpets: Special Loan Exhibition* [FIG. 10].

FIGURE 11
Dōtaku. Japan, Yayoi period, 2nd–3rd century. Bronze, 34½ × 11½ in. (87.6 × 29.2 cm.). 67.198, Brooklyn Museum of Art, Gift of Mr. and Mrs. Milton Lowenthal

Much activity was centered on Indian and Islamic art under the tenure of Acting Curator Andree L. Cooney (b. 1927) during 1959–61 and that of Lois Katz from 1962 to 1970. In 1963–64, Ernest Erickson's extensive collection of Indian and Islamic art was exhibited in newly renovated galleries with an accompanying catalogue, *Asian Art from the Collections of Ernest Erickson and the Erickson Foundation, Inc.*[29] A monumental stone relief, representing the Buddhist deity Green Tara (see no. 66), was one of the decade's most significant acquisitions. This piece had been on loan to the Museum since 1937 and was purchased from the original owner in 1960. Among the important Japanese art acquisitions of the 1960s was a bronze bell (*dōtaku*) (acc. no. 67.198), donated by Mr. and Mrs. Milton Lowenthal, which dates to the second to third century A.D. during the Japanese Bronze-Iron age or Yayoi period [FIG. 11].

At the end of the decade, an endowment provided by the Hagop Kevorkian Fund established the first new curatorial department at the Brooklyn Museum of Art in almost fifty years.[30] The Department of Middle Eastern Art and Archaeology was established as a separate entity from the Department of Oriental Art, with the former Curator of Islamic Art at the Metropolitan Museum of Art, Charles K. Wilkinson (1897–1974), serving as Curator from 1969 to 1974.[31]

1970s

The pace of the Museum's activities in Asian and Islamic art quickened considerably in the 1970s. Wilkinson oversaw the installation of a gallery devoted to the Islamic world in 1972.[32] Building on the foundations of the rich collection acquired by Stewart Culin, Wilkinson amassed an exceptional collection of later Persian art of the Qajar dynasty (1785–1925), including gifts from his own collection. It is because of Wilkinson's interest in acquiring a representative range of all the arts of the Qajar period, an area largely ignored by other collectors, that the Brooklyn Museum of Art now holds in its trust one of the preeminent collections of Qajar art outside of Iran. Wilkinson and his wife, Irma, also donated one of the important portraits now in the collection, an early nineteenth-century Qajar-dynasty portrait in oil on canvas, *Prince Yahya* (see no. 101).[33] In addition, extensive archival material, consisting of Wilkinson's correspondence from his tenure at the BMA, contains important references to now-lost paintings by major artists of the Qajar period.

During the 1970s, the Department of Asian Art was under the curatorial direction of Dr. Stanislaw Czuma (b. 1935; Associate Curator, 1970; Curator, 1971–72), who departed to become Curator of Indian and Southeast Asian Art at the Cleveland Museum of Art, and Robert Moes (b. 1935; Curator of Oriental Art, 1973–88). Between 1969 and 1974, the Asian

29. *The Brooklyn Museum Annual, Volume 5: Articles and Reports 1963–64* (Brooklyn: [Museum], 1965): 133.

30. *The Brooklyn Museum Annual, Volume 10: Reports and Articles 1968–69* (Brooklyn: [Museum], 1969): 15.

31. Maryam Ekhtiar, "The Art of Qajar Iran," checklist of The Brooklyn Museum's holdings, with an annotated bibliography (1989).

32. Department of Egyptian, Classical, and Ancient Middle Eastern Art, "Vertical File to 1985," Brooklyn Museum of Art Library.

33. Maryam Ekhtiar, "The Qajar Visual Aesthetic: Highlights from The Brooklyn Museum Collection," *Orientations* 20, no. 7 (July 1989): 46; Layla S. Diba and Maryam Ekhtiar, eds. *Royal Persian Paintings: The Qajar Epoch 1785–1925*, exh. cat. (New York: Brooklyn Museum of Art in association with Tauris, 1998): 194–95, cat. no. 47.

Galleries were reinstalled. An area was devoted to the Korean art collection, which was the first permanent exhibition space for Korean art in the New York City area.[34] Several special exhibitions were prepared, including *Figures in Clay: Terracottas from Ancient India* (1973), inspired by the important gift of Dr. Bertram H. Schaffner (b. 1912) of Indian terracotta sculptures.[35] Moes, a former Curator of Asian Art at the Denver Art Museum and a specialist in Japanese art, brought new attention to the Japanese permanent collections with special exhibitions and accompanying catalogues. *A Flower for Every Season: Japanese Paintings from the C. D. Carter Collection* (1975) led to the acquisition of several major screens, including Nagasawa Rosetsu's (Japanese, 1754–1799) *Puppies in Moonlight* (acc. no. 77.202), donated by Patrick J. Gilmartin (b. 1933) and Edward Greenberg (b. 1941). *Along the Tōkaidō; Twelve Views of Utagawa Kuniyoshi* (1977), curated by Amy Poster, featured a little-known series by the artist.

The first of a series of BMA collection catalogues of Asian Art, *The Brooklyn Museum: Japanese Ceramics* (1979), was authored by Moes. This brought to light several recent acquisitions, including gifts of Sidney B. Cardozo (1916–2002), an important collector of contemporary Japanese ceramics. These gifts reawakened the Museum's interest in contemporary Japanese ceramics, an area that continues to be a focus of the collection. In the area of Chinese art, one of the Museum's significant early ritual bronzes, a wine vessel (*guang*; see no. 1) that had been on loan since 1950, was donated by BMA Trustee Alastair B. Martin from his personal collection, known as the Guennol Collection. Indeed, Martin's commitment to the Brooklyn Museum of Art has been remarkable and of long standing: he served as Chairman of the Museum's Board of Trustees (1984–89) and has provided leadership as a donor to the Museum for more than fifty years.

In the 1970s, the Museum also brought two special exhibitions organized by the People's Republic of China to the United States, *Chinese Paper-Cutting Art of Hou-Tien* (1974) and *Peasant Paintings from Huhsien County of the People's Republic of China* (1977).

1980s

Several exhibitions of Japanese art were mounted in the 1980s, including *Japanese Painting and Prints of the Shijō School* (1981) and *Mingei: Japanese Folk Art* (1985), with accompanying catalogue [FIG. 12]. The latter exhibition surveyed the BMA's comprehensive collection of folk art from Japan, and featured the Museum's early holdings of everyday art, the Ainu collections formed by Culin, and recent acquisitions including the donations of Dr. John Lyden (b. 1940) and Stanley Love (1926–1994). Henry D. Smith II and Amy Poster collaborated on the monograph *Hiroshige: One*

FIGURE 12
Installation view of *Mingei: Japanese Folk Art*, Brooklyn Museum, 1985

34. Asian Art Council, "Brooklyn Museum of Art," brochure [1996].

35. Amy G. Poster, *Figures in Clay: Terracottas from Ancient India*, exh. cat. (Brooklyn: The Brooklyn Museum, 1973): 1.

Hundred Famous Views of Edo, presenting the artist's last series of prints, of which Brooklyn owns a complete set of 119 pages and all variant states.[36] Departmental acquisitions focused on Japanese folk art, contemporary ceramics, paintings, and screens. The *Head of a Guardian* (see no. 28), a monumental Kamakura-period sculpture, originally from Kōfuku-ji in Nara and on loan to the Museum since 1954, represented another highly significant gift from the Guennol Collection in 1986.[37]

Two significant exhibitions of Indian paintings, *A Selection of Late 18th and Early 19th Century Indian Botanical Prints* (1980), lent by the British Museum (Natural History) and the India Office Library, London, and *Visions of Courtly India* (1982), a loan exhibition comprising Pahari School paintings from the private collection of William and Mildred Archer, noted British scholars in the Indian art field, were mounted at the Museum. In fact, the 1980s was a decade of major Indian art acquisitions (almost entirely through donation) in the Indian painting and sculpture fields, mirroring what had become a lively area of collecting in New York.

FIGURE 13
Installation view of *From Indian Earth: 4,000 Years of Terracotta Art*, Brooklyn Museum, 1986

The Korean collection was given its first exhibition of highlights in Robert Moes's *Korean Art from The Brooklyn Museum Collection* (1987) with accompanying catalogue. The Chinese section concentrated efforts on reevaluating the painting collection. In 1988, *Lacquer: A Panorama of Asian Decorative Arts* presented sixty-five examples of Chinese, Japanese, Korean, and Persian lacquer in a comparative exhibition from the Museum's permanent collection.[38] A symposium brought attention to the remarkable scope of this field and cross-influences of technique, forms, and decorative motifs.

In 1988, the name of the Department was changed to the Department of Asian Art and Amy G. Poster was appointed Curator and Chair (1988–present). At this time the Islamic collection was reassigned to the Department of Asian Art.[39] The Department of Asian Art became the focus of considerable activity with a roster of exhibitions and significant acquisitions, following a strategic plan to fill lacunae with major works of art. In 1986, the Museum received one of its greatest bequests with the donation of the long-term loan collection of Ernest Erickson, comprising 474 objects.[40] In the following year, an exhibition entitled *The Collector's Eye: The Ernest Erickson Collections at The Brooklyn Museum* displayed this newly acquired collection, including thirty-five Indian and seventy-five Islamic items.[41]

One of the first Asian art collector-support groups to be formed in the United States, the Oriental Art Council, subsequently renamed the Asian Art Council, was established at Poster's urging in 1986 to give Asian art collectors the opportunity to study the Museum's

36. *The Brooklyn Museum Report 1987–1989* (Brooklyn: [Museum], 1990): 20.

37. "Acquisition Strategy" (1991): 2; Poster, "Religious Arts of Medieval Japan in the Brooklyn Museum." *Orientations* 20, no. 7 (July 1989): 28.

38. *Museum Report 1987–1989*, 19.

39. *The Brooklyn Museum: Annual Report 1979–80–81–82* (Brooklyn: Brooklyn Museum Press, 1983): 22; *Museum Report 1987–89*, 19.

40. *Masterpieces in The Brooklyn Museum*, 22.

41. *Museum Report 1987–1989*, 20.

collection on a firsthand basis and to participate in the acquisition of new works.[42] In its sixteen years of existence, the Council has acquired major objects in all fields covered by the Department, in fact serving as the Department's principal purchasing resource. Partnership with collectors who acquired and donated objects to complement the Asian collections has enabled the Department to build its rich holdings of painting and sculpture despite the Museum's extremely limited purchasing resources.

The importance of cross-cultural interaction in understanding the nature of Asian art has increasingly become a focus of the Department of Asian Art's activities. The Department has participated in several major international special exhibitions: In 1984–85, the Museum was a venue for *Light of Asia: Buddha Sakyamuni in Asian Art,* a Los Angeles County Museum of Art exhibition that explored the image of Buddha in various cultures and historical periods. A catalogue essay, "The Buddha Image in Japan" and the Japanese catalogue entries were authored by Amy G. Poster. In 1986, in conjunction with the Festival of India in the United States, Amy Poster curated the first international exhibition of Indian terracottas, entitled *From Indian Earth: 4,000 Years of Terracotta Art,* drawn from collections in India and public and private collections worldwide [FIG. 13]. This exhibition established the BMA as a center of terracotta art collecting and research in the ensuing years.

The Islamic collection received a donation of nineteen carpets from the Beaupre Charitable Trust in memory of Joseph V. McMullan in 1984.[43] In that same year, Sheila Canby, Associate Curator of Islamic Art, presented the accompanying exhibition *Oriental Carpets from the Collection of Mrs. Joseph V. McMullan* in the refurbished Islamic Galleries. In 1985, Islamic arts were the focus of *Curator's Choice: Islamic Art in Africa,* and in the following year, the Islamic Galleries were reinstalled with a selection of highlights of the Islamic collection.[44] The Department continued to show its support for Qajar art by organizing the first international symposium on the subject, *The Art and Culture of Qajar Iran,* sponsored by the Hagop Kevorkian Fund in 1987. An accompanying checklist, *The Art of Qajar Iran,* was prepared by Maryam Ekhtiar, Assistant Curator of Islamic Art,[45] and a number of the symposium papers were subsequently published in the scholarly journal *Muqarnas* (vol. 6, 1989). In 1987, the Estate of Charles K. Wilkinson donated an important collection of nineteenth-century books to the Brooklyn Museum's Art Reference Library.[46] The personal library of Charles K. Wilkinson includes rare travel books, Persian lithographed versions of poetic texts from the late nineteenth century, and publications of Georgian museum collections of Qajar art.

1990s

Beginning in the late 1990s, the curators and the Museum in general began to reconsider the BMA's contribution to museum practice in the field of Asian art and culture. Realizing that the BMA was approaching its centennial date, the Department reexamined its collecting mission and recognized that this was a time to reflect on the past. In keeping with this vision, the Department initiated new research on the way objects came into the Museum in the early decades of the century.

In 1994, the Museum's collection of 250 Indian paintings and drawings was showcased

42. Asian Art Council Brochure.

43. *The Brooklyn Museum Report 1982–1986* (Brooklyn: [Museum], 1987): 28.

44. *Museum Report 1987–1989*, 19.

45. See n. 31.

46. *Museum Report 1987–1989*, 31.

FIGURE 14
Installation view of *Royal Persian Paintings: The Qajar Epoch 1785–1925*, Brooklyn Museum of Art, 1998

in the special exhibition *Realms of Heroism: Indian Paintings at The Brooklyn Museum* to celebrate the publication of the Museum's catalogue raisonné prepared by Amy Poster with contributions from Sheila Canby, Pramod Chandra, and Joan Cummins. In 1991, the Islamic Galleries were refurbished under the direction of the new Associate Curator for Islamic Art (1991–98), Layla S. Diba. The Department returned to some of its first acquisitions with a cloisonné enamel exhibition, *The Blue of Jingtai* (1990), derived from the extensive collection donated by Samuel P. Avery, Jr., in 1909.

The Cambodian art collection received a strong new impetus from the 1991 gift of Dr. Bertram H. Schaffner (in honor of his eightieth birthday) of a life-size Cambodian *Torso of a Male Divinity (deva-raja)* (see no. 85), whose geometric proportions and polished surface suggest Khmer patronage of the tenth century, and from the extraordinary continuing gifts of Georgia (b. 1946) and Michael (b. 1940) de Havenon in the Khmer and Indian fields. These gifts reflect the way a single gift or series of gifts can become catalysts for other great objects to come into a collection and change its nature. Once the Schaffner Khmer torso and the de Havenon works entered the Department, other collectors recognized the importance of having more than an isolated piece in one field; they saw the opportunity to build the Asian collection and contributed outstanding works of equal importance, rarity, and beauty.

The art of the ancient Khmer empire had always been acknowledged as an outstanding example of the efflorescence of Indian culture in the regions adjacent to the Indian subcontinent. The Museum collection now includes important objects from Thailand and Cambodia ranging in date from the great pre-Angkor periods (6th–8th century) to the well-known Khmer and Bayon periods of the twelfth through thirteenth centuries. Sculpture in the round has been favored over relief, and although many works are fragmentary, our goal has been to show more complete examples of quality.

More recently, the Department has recognized the importance of objects that transcend categorization according to national borders and has sought to emphasize the cross-cultural significance of Asian art and culture in its major acquisitions. Exhibitions have begun to reflect both the distinct qualities of the individual cultures represented and the connections between them. The new Asian Art Galleries planned for the near future will address these connections in a thematic presentation.

The 1996 reinstallation of the Chinese Galleries under the direction of John R. Finlay (Assistant Curator of Asian Art, 1994–98) and Frances Z. Yuan (Research Assistant, 1996, and Assistant Curator, 1998–2001) re-presented our own history of exhibitions and scholarship, reflecting the Chinese cultural pattern of returning to the past as a source for renewal for the present.

In 1998, the Museum also held the first major international exhibition of Qajar arts, *Royal Persian Paintings: The Qajar Epoch 1785–1925*, curated by Dr. Layla S. Diba (Hagop Kevorkian Curator of Islamic Art, 1998–2000). This interdisciplinary exhibition and catalogue explored representation, identity, revivalism, and modernity in the Qajar era [FIG. 14]. In 2001 Dr. Aimée Froom joined the Department as Hagop Kevorkian Associate Curator of Islamic Art.

Exhibition and research projects also provided an incentive to reassess other areas of the collection. With the cooperation and support of the Japan Foundation and the National Research Institute for Cultural Properties (Bunkazai Kenkyūjo), several of the Museum's pivotal works of Japanese painting have been restored and remounted by Japanese experts. These include the La Farge *Ryōkai Mandara* (see no. 26) and the *Drying Fishnets* screens (see no. 32) acquired earlier in the century. The Department continued to raise its profile abroad both by inviting foreign scholars to view its holdings and by initiating contact with institutions, particularly in Japan, that would exhibit works from the BMA at a time when the Museum was unable to do so.

In this manner, the Ainu collection was recognized internationally for the first time when it was surveyed by a team of Japanese scholars under the direction of Yoshinobu Kotani of Nagoya University.[47] Similarly, the Museum was invited to collaborate on three inventory-publication projects in conjunction with the collections of Japanese painting and sculpture, Japanese *ukiyo-e* prints, and Korean art and culture. These surveys have been sponsored respectively by the Cultural Ministries of the government of Japan, Ōta Memorial Museum, Tokyo, and the Korea National Research Institute for Cultural Property.

47. As a result of the Ainu inventory survey, an exhibition was mounted by the Arctic Studies Center of the Smithsonian Institution's National Museum of Natural History in 1999. See William J. Fitzhugh and Chisato O. Dubreuil, eds., *Ainu: The Spirit of a Northern People*, exh. cat. (Washington, D.C.: Arctic Studies Center, National Museum of Natural History, Smithsonian Institution in association with University of Washington Press, 1999).

The Department of Asian Art has continued to expand on the great legacy of its past curators and donors. In the past, the programs of the Department constantly built on the strengths of its collection, emphasizing its encyclopedic nature. Now the focus has shifted to reflect the multicultural face of Brooklyn, with its diverse Asian populations.

Entering the new millennium, the Brooklyn Museum of Art continues to attract audiences worldwide. The ongoing activities of the Department of Asian Art reflect the new conception of the BMA as a place of community engagement, and the Department reaffirms a clear balance between scholarship on an international plane and the desire to appeal to, and reach, our Brooklyn constituencies.

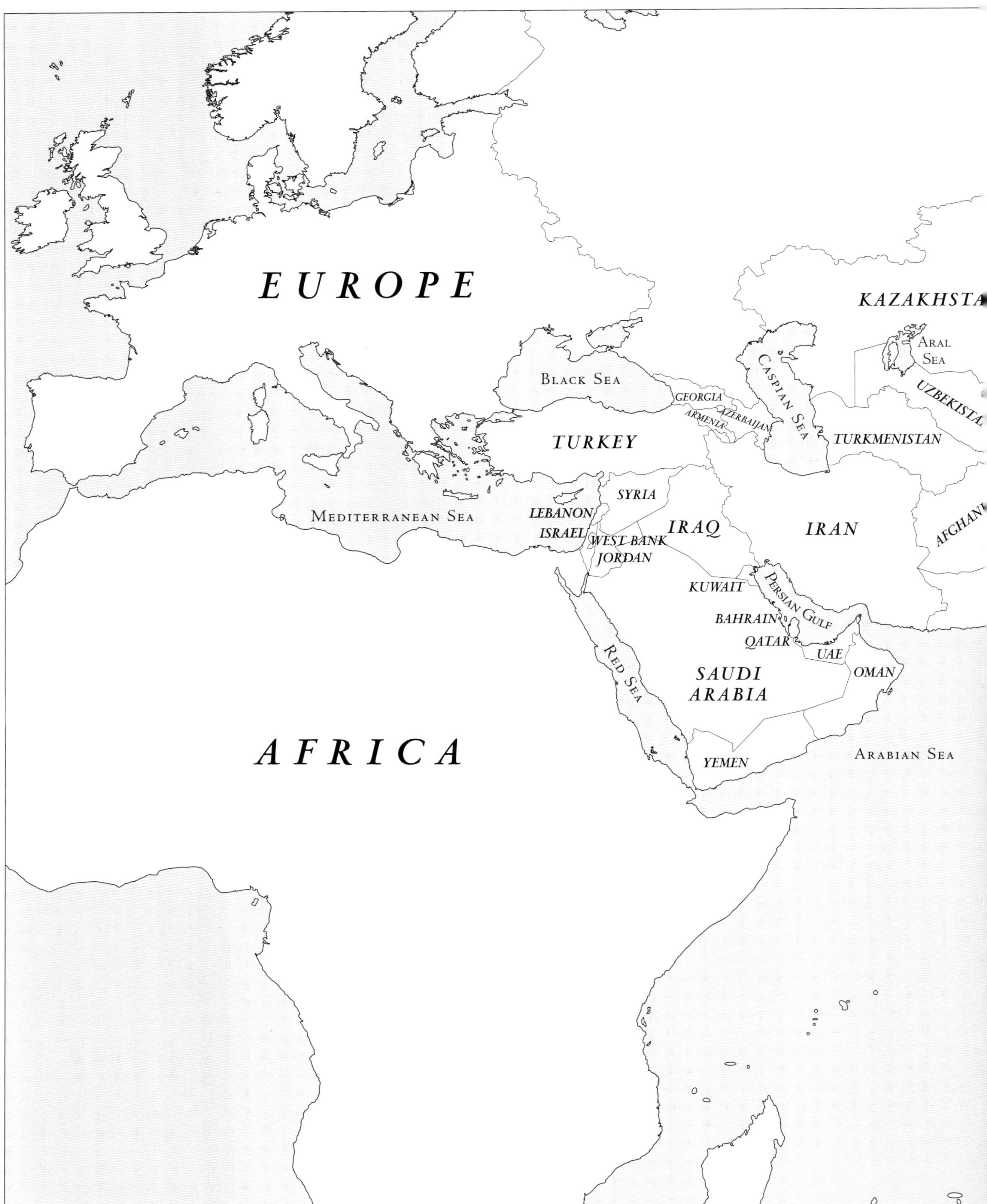

EUROPE
KAZAKHSTA
ARAL SEA
BLACK SEA
CASPIAN SEA
UZBEKISTA
GEORGIA
ARMENIA
AZERBAIJAN
TURKEY
TURKMENISTAN
SYRIA
MEDITERRANEAN SEA
LEBANON
ISRAEL
IRAQ
IRAN
AFGHAN
WEST BANK
JORDAN
KUWAIT
PERSIAN GULF
BAHRAIN
QATAR
UAE
OMAN
RED SEA
SAUDI ARABIA
AFRICA
YEMEN
ARABIAN SEA

RUSSIA
MONGOLIA
KYRGYSTAN
ASIA
CHINA
NEPAL
BHUTAN
BANGLADESH
INDIA
MYANMAR
(BURMA)
LAOS
Bay of Bengal
THAILAND
VIETNAM
CAMBODIA
SRI LANKA
Sea of
Japan
KOREA
JAPAN
South
China
Sea
Pacific Ocean
PHILIPPINES
BRUNEI
MALAYSIA
Sumatra
Borneo
Indian Ocean
INDONESIA
Irian
Jaya
PAPUA
NEW
GUINEA
Java
AUSTRALIA

Changing Definitions of "Asia" and "Asian Art"

Frances Z. Yuan

The works of art reproduced in this volume encompass most of the major regions and historical cultures identified with the continent of Asia. In the plate section of this book, the works are gathered under the five headings of China, Japan, Korea, South and Southeast Asia, and the Islamic world. Yet the immensity of the subject of Asian art must give pause to anyone trying to define workable, reasonably convenient categories like these for the purposes of discussion or presentation. The sheer physical scale of Asia, the extent of its cultural and national histories, and the enormous size and diversity of its populations ensure that any general definition of Asia, or of the categories within Asian art, will face immediate challenge. Indeed, there are those who might question our five plate-section headings, too, since some of these categories are nation-states, some are geographical regions, and one names a religious faith.

Rendering the question of definitions perhaps even more problematic is the obvious fact that this volume was written at an American museum by English-speaking authors. This circumstance gives further impetus to our wish to identify, and question, received definitions of Asia and Asian art, rather than perpetuate unacknowledged assumptions that may reflect a Western bias. Asia is a complex and often contradictory subject, and so is others' perception of it. The purpose of this brief introduction is to review some of the operative definitions of "Asia" and related terms, with an eye toward clarifying how those definitions influence the way we see Asian art.

WHAT ARE THE BOUNDARIES OF ASIA?

As a beginning, let us ask ourselves: Just what do we mean when we use the terms "Asia" and "Asian art"? The concept of "Asia" would appear to be almost too vast to grasp: nearly sixty percent of the world's population resides in Asia, and in terms of sheer land area, it is by far the largest of the traditional seven continents. Even in strictly geographical terms, as a glance at the map on pp. 26–27 might suggest, it is not an easy matter to identify Asia with any real precision.

Most typically, "Asia" refers to the large constituent regions usually called East Asia (principally China, Japan, and Korea) and Southeast Asia (notably Cambodia, Laos, Myanmar, Vietnam, and Thailand). To these can be added the Indian subcontinent of South Asia (i.e., Bangladesh, India, and Pakistan).

Complicating the situation, in various different formulations, certain other major regions may also sometimes be included, and sometimes not. Readily accommodated among these is Central Asia, including Mongolia and the Himalayan regions of Nepal and Tibet. But Central Asia also encompasses parts of China and Russia, and their presence pulls and twists our sense of the area in different directions – toward East Asia in the case of China, and toward Europe in the case of Russia. In fact, parts of the Russian Asiatic region of Siberia extend westward into the Ural Mountains, historically regarded as the frontier of Europe. These considerations render the place of Central Asia in a clear set of geographical definitions less self-evident than it might at first seem.

More problematic to locate within an overall definition of Asia is the Middle East, including, among other areas, the Arabian Peninsula, Egypt, Iran, Iraq, Jordan, Lebanon, and Syria. Works of art from the Middle East appear in this volume under the heading "The Islamic World." Nonetheless, it is open to debate whether Asia should be defined in a way that spans the Middle East or Islamic world; Egypt, for example, geographically speaking, is clearly part of Africa, as are other North African nations with large Islamic populations, while Iran might be thought of as part of West Asia.

The groups of islands within the expanse of the South Pacific, which are known collectively as Oceania, also raise issues when viewed as belonging to mainland Asia. In this book, artworks from Java, for instance, are grouped with those from Southeast Asia. Yet there are inevitable ramifications to the fact that the numerous states of so-called Island Southeast Asia, such as Indonesia, simply do not form part of the continental landmass. For one thing, some of the islands' cultures could be said to have affinities at least as close with aboriginal populations of Australia. For another, a case might be made that the island groups constitute their own maritime entity, largely independent of continental ties.

These questions concern the outer limits of what can be defined as Asia. Likewise, there are questions about which specific part of Asia a certain region properly belongs to. Where does a country like Afghanistan, for example, fit within the overlapping, conflicting definitions of the different segments of Asia? Are its ties stronger to South Asia, Central Asia, or the Middle East?

Moreover, underlying the vexed notion of "Asia" is a further ambiguity about whether it can even be identified as a separate continent in the first place. This is true because Asia does not constitute a "natural" geographical entity – unlike, say, the relatively clear-cut continent of Africa. In fact, Asia is physically attached to Europe along thousands of miles of shared territorial frontiers. Consequently, the very idea of Asia's classification as a discrete continent has often been challenged; alternatively, Europe and Asia together could be considered to form the single continent of Eurasia. Acknowledging the possibly more "natural" mega-continent of Eurasia tends to unsettle the whole matter of defining the precise boundaries of "Asia."

As these various issues suggest, the complex aggregate of geographical and cultural units making up the larger entity called Asia changes boundaries over time and from culture to culture; the consensus shifts. Taking these many factors into account, Asia begins to appear not as a timeless, mythic monolith, but rather as something much more provisional and loosely defined: a flexible, ever-changing collection of regions, states, and peoples forever redividing and regrouping.

THE OTHER NAMES OF ASIA

If Asia now appears to be many different places, we should also recognize that it has had a number of different names. Two in particular demand comment.

One of them, the Eurocentric term "Orient," has been used to set up a contrast with all that is Western, or "Occidental." Initially, however, the "Orient" referred to the Islamic world, namely Egypt, the Levant, and adjacent areas in southwestern Anatolia. Its use started at a time when India was perceived in Europe as the eastern extremity of the world. As application of the term evolved, the "Orient" expanded to cover all non-European areas of Eurasian civilization. In light of its original connection to the Islamic world, the "Orient" could disregard continental distinctions and stretch to include North Africa, and in certain definitions also parts of southeastern and southern Europe and Iberia, especially when Islamic populations have been dominant there. Only later was the working definition of the "Orient" largely limited to East Asia, Southeast Asia, and eastern Central Asia.

The second term, the "East," also operates within a binary pair, this time the opposite number being the "West." But in this case, the contrast or opposition was initially between the two halves into which the late Roman world was divided, with the "East" originally indicating the Eastern Roman Empire, especially its capital, Constantinople, established by the emperor Constantine as an alternative to the city of Rome and the Western Empire. Growing out of that initial distinction, "East" later came to indicate the Eastern Orthodox faith within Christianity. As Russia became more of a focal point, the concept of "East" gradually extended itself somewhat westward, to reflect the territorial disposition of a wide-ranging country straddling Europe and Asia. "East" also gained, in the mid-twentieth century, a specific Cold War geopolitical significance, designating the Communist countries of Eastern Europe, the so-called Eastern Bloc, which was sometimes also considered to include Communist China.

The reaction against these two Western-constructed words, "Orient" and "East," has been strong in academic discourse, as the terms' built-in European biases have become impossible to ignore. The word "Asia," however, unlike "Orient" and "East," was not formulated as part of a dichotomous pair. Relatively less imperialistic and Eurocentric, in the culturally sensitive present it has become the preferred term.

Still, "Asia" too has a history of fluctuating definitions. "Asia" as the name of a landmass originated historically with the ancient Greeks, who used it to designate the lands east of the

Aegean Sea. "Asia" joined the terms "Europe," denoting the lands to the north and west, and "Africa" (then called Libya), representing the lands to the south, as the components of a three-continent scheme of the ancient world, the forerunner of the seven-continent scheme commonly observed today. In its etymology, "Asia" has associations with the Phoenician word for "sunrise" and with the city of Assos, near Troy. As its historical development suggests, the word "Asia," though now more neutral-sounding than "Orient" or "East," seems to reflect a particular Mediterranean milieu. Yet it also has an "Asian" origin, deriving from "Ashuwa," an ancient kingdom in Anatolia located in present-day western or northwestern Turkey and documented in the records of the Hittite Empire.

CHANGING IDEAS OF ASIA AT THE MUSEUM

As preservers and interpreters of cultural artifacts, museums are well positioned to examine multiple ideas of Asia. Over the course of its history, the Brooklyn Museum of Art has interpreted and reinterpreted the definition of Asia, through its collections and exhibitions of Asian art.

The Department of Asian Art today oversees collections that include the arts of China, Korea, Japan, India, Southeast Asia, the Himalayas, and the Islamic world. It should be pointed out, however, that this curatorial department has been renamed four times during the Museum's history, reflecting changing views of Asia and Asian art, and changing geographical and cultural usage in the world at large.

In its early years, the Museum, observing what was then a common distinction, separately maintained a Department of Fine Arts and a Department of Ethnology. Originally, the latter had primary responsibility for Asian artworks (though it should be noted that Asian objects were in fact given to the Museum as early as 1898, even before the entity formally known as the Department of Ethnology was founded in 1903). The local patrons and the institutional curators who first collected art objects and antiquities from Asia in the nineteenth century did not categorically distinguish them from objects originating in the rest of the "non-Western" world (that is, beyond white Europe and America). Asian artifacts incorporated into the Department of Ethnology were valued as representatives of the cultures and customs from where they originated or were found.

Stewart Culin (1858–1929), the Museum's first Curator of Ethnology, may also be considered its first curator of Asian art. During his tenure, most Asian objects were deemed ethnological, yet at the same time, some works from Asia did find their way into the Department of Fine Arts. Many objects now considered Asian art – such as ceramics, lacquers, metalwork, paintings, prints, and sculptures – were actually divided between the two departments. Thus, William Henry Goodyear (1846–1923), Curator of Fine Arts, was the first custodian of Chinese and Japanese ceramics, Chinese cloisonné enamels, and jades, for instance, while Stewart Culin's Department of Ethnology focused on Buddhist sculpture, Japanese woodblock prints, and Chinese paintings, to name a few categories. In addition to this perhaps somewhat arbitrary division of responsibilities, there were other anomalies. For example, one of the earliest Asian objects in the Museum's collection, a Syrian glass perfume sprinkler given in 1901, spent most of its years in Brooklyn in the Department of Decorative Arts and was transferred to the Department of Asian Art only in 1992. As can be seen from these circumstances, during its early period, the Museum lacked a comprehensive definition of "Asian art."

In the 1930s, the Museum underwent a major restructuring. Its third principal curatorial division, the Department of Natural History, was disbanded and the collections of fossils, biological specimens, and related material were dispersed to colleague institutions. This change concentrated the institution's resources on the primary role of being an art museum. During the same period, the Department of Ethnology was divided into several culturally identified departments that through the subsequent years would continue collecting the arts of Africa, the Pacific Islands, and the Americas.

Out of this restructuring, what is now the Department of Asian Art began to emerge, adopting a number of interim names along the way. The Department of Eastern and Near Eastern Art was established in 1931 and was renamed the Department of Oriental Art in 1934. It included what is now called Islamic art. During that period, the art of the Middle East from pre-Islamic times was the province of a separate curatorial division, the Department of Ancient Art.

In 1969, these two distinct collections of art from the Middle East were consolidated into a new Department of Middle Eastern Art and Archaeology. That department existed independently for over a decade before Islamic art was reintegrated into the Department of Oriental Art in 1983, becoming once more identified with Asia. In 1988, a nominal change occurred again, when the Department of Oriental Art adopted its current designation as the Department of Asian Art.

Today, the terms "Asia" and "Asian Art" are the standard nomenclature used to denote the department and its collections at the Brooklyn Museum of Art, as well as at many other art museums worldwide. Yet there are still a number of venerable cultural institutions that choose to describe such collections as "Oriental" and "Eastern." At the same time, however, other institutions continue to seek alternative ways to reposit Asia's identity in the world and its role in global culture by pairing Asia with the Pacific, or by drawing it into an even larger array of geographical and cultural components and linking it with Africa as well as Oceania.

Such enterprises, in reshuffling the deck, so to speak, can be a tricky matter. The Museum's own presentations, even in the early years, did sometimes seek to rethink accepted categories and attempt to relate different cultural areas to each other in illuminating ways. But curators sometimes did this by emphasizing the cultural dominance of one particular entity. As the geographical purview of the Museum's Asian collecting activities grew, in the 1920s, the presentation centered largely on China. The installation of a major architectural piece, the Chinese Hall of State, in the large central exhibition area on the first floor of the Museum in 1927 included Korean, Tibetan, and Japanese objects as well. In a letter to the Museum's director, William Henry Fox, Stewart Culin explained that the exhibition would be so unexpectedly inclusive in scope because the Tibetan and Korean collections, like those of Japan, both represented the extent of China's influence and illustrated aspects of China's past through these different sources. Culin intended to emphasize the plurality of China by representing the civilization's entire history, the material culture of its various classes (including the Chinese diaspora in America), and its influence and links with other cultures. But such a presentation, however unintentionally, could under-represent, or misrepresent, the other distinct cultures of the region; it could promote a view of China as the one dominating influence across the face of Asia and against which all other cultures were to be measured.

Nonetheless, different voices were beginning to be heard, some of them trying instead to limit such notions of dominance and hegemony, and seeking a more nuanced view of the interaction among diverse, shifting cultural groups. While Culin, like his contemporaries in the field, had been prone to conflate different terms, sometimes using "Asia," "Orient," and "East" interchangeably, different viewpoints were emerging, reflected in an exhibition organized in 1940 by Laurance P. Roberts (1907–2002), who had been Curator of Oriental Art before being promoted to Director of the Brooklyn Museum in 1939. Entitled *As Others See Us; or, Occidentals Through Oriental Eyes*, the exhibition explored the perception of Europe and the United States in Asian art. Perhaps rather surprisingly, as we look back on it, the show's theme was openly post-colonial. It was prescient in granting an empowered voice to the "other," implicitly questioning what we now call the Eurocentric view of the world.

Today, the Museum's presentations try to do justice to the complex interplay among different cultures that is so evident in Asian art, rather than focus too exclusively on individual geographical regions. Among the reasons for pursuing this broader approach is the fact that, clearly, the arts of Asia are in great part religious in origin, and many artworks reflect the migration of religious influences throughout Asian history. The Museum's 1984 presentation of *Light of Asia: Buddha Sakyamuni in Asian Art* exemplified this approach, tracing the variations in different regional and cultural modes of depicting Shakyamuni, the historical personage of the Buddha, from the first representations of the Buddha in the second century A.D. to the present.

THE ISLAMIC WORLD

To further unravel the complicated nature of Asia, it may be helpful to narrow our focus, for the moment, to one or two particular regions. Areas whose relations to the larger landmass seem especially illuminating warrant examination as case studies in the difficulties of definition. And so this section and the next look at two regions that raise key questions about Asia's boundaries as well as about the Museum's practice. The first region is the Middle East, seen within the context of the larger Islamic world. The second, to be discussed a little later, is Southeast Asia.

The overlapping terms "Middle East," "Near East," and "Islamic world" cover much of the same cultural and geographical territory. At the same time, they also reveal the diverse contexts within which this region has been described. The term "Middle East," favored in modern political and economic writing, originated early in the twentieth century as a British military designation for an area that, by the end of World War II, was considered to be the territory from Libya to Afghanistan. Although the boundaries remain fluid, the Middle East generally comprises Egypt, Iran, Iraq, Israel, Jordan, Lebanon, Syria, Turkey, and the countries of the Arabian Peninsula. At times, it includes or has included North African countries, such as Libya and Morocco; countries of the subcontinent, such as Pakistan; the Sudan; the Ottoman presence in Europe; Afghanistan; and the Muslim presence in Spain and India. As this list might suggest, there is no absolute Middle East. The borders, countries, and cultures constituting it remain in flux.

The "Near East," a term often used synonymously with the Middle East, refers to the area of the ancient world from Turkey in the west to Iran in the east. It also consists of the western regions of the Ottoman Turkish Empire, including the Balkans, Greece, Turkey, and the eastern Mediterranean Sea. Since its chronological range extends from the campaigns of Alexander the Great (who died in 323 B.C.) to the Islamic conquest in the mid-seventh century A.D., the word "ancient" is almost always attached to "Near East," whereas the term "Ancient Middle East" very rarely occurs (although the Brooklyn Museum of Art does favor "Ancient Middle East" over the more commonly used term in describing its curatorial department of ancient art). Moreover, "Ancient Near East" and "Ancient Near Eastern" have strong associations with philology and antiquarianism that endure today.

While "Middle East" may be the most widely accepted term currently used, it is nonetheless inherently problematic because, like "Near East" or for that matter "Far East," it defines parts of Asia in terms of their relative distance, how near or far they are, from Europe.

The term "Islamic" has its own share of complications as a tool for classifying art. The Islamic faith is not confined to the Middle East, by any means, but is strongly represented in South and Southeast Asia in countries such as India, Pakistan, Bangladesh, and Indonesia. Indeed, Indonesia has the largest Muslim population of any nation on earth. Furthermore, the term "Islamic art" itself is something of a misnomer. In practice, it refers to works of art created by both Muslims and non-Muslims, and indeed sometimes these works have been made for individuals who do not practice the Islamic faith. It should be borne in mind that "Islamic art" can be either religious or secular in nature.

Identifying the cultural and geographical area of the Middle East as a part of Asia continues to be challenging. It has been called an "interstitial zone" or "intermediate civilization" between the larger cultural constructs of the "West" and the "East." When the concept of the "Orient" – originally referring to the peoples and cultures of the Middle East – began to be more closely identified with East Asia instead, the Middle East became more aligned with Europe, in some ways of thinking. This "Western" association defines the area either as a subset of Asia, with North Africa its annex, or as a semi-autonomous transitional zone on the European-Asian frontier. Although the Middle East is often caught in this continental tug-of-war, it continues to display a distinct, independent identity.

☙

At the Brooklyn Museum of Art, the question of whether or not Asia should be considered to include the Middle East extends beyond theoretical discussions: the debate has been part of the Museum's history and has altered the institution's curatorial structure more than once.

In the first decades of the twentieth century, when Asian art belonged primarily to the Department of Ethnology, the Middle East was unquestionably a part of Asia in the eyes of the institution. And early on, a commitment to Islamic art was demonstrated by the acquisition of the celebrated Mughal *Hamzanama* in 1924 (see no. 69) and the organization of the major traveling show *Brooklyn Museum Exhibition of Persian Art and Its Reaction in the Modern World* in 1931. Under its subsequent names as an independent curatorial entity – the Department of Eastern and Near Eastern Art (1931–34) and the Department of Oriental Art (1934–88) – the Museum department responsible for Asian art continued to include in its broad mandate the geographical region between Persia and Egypt.

Within the Department of Oriental Art, the term "Middle East" was understood to indicate the art and culture of the Islamic world, beginning historically about A.D. 700, with the rise of Islam. A separate curatorial division, the Department of Ancient Art, represented the art and cultures of the Middle East from pre-Islamic times.

In 1969, these two distinct collections of art from the Middle East were consolidated into a new Department of Middle Eastern Art and Archaeology. Charles K. Wilkinson (1897–1974), formerly Curator of Islamic art at the Metropolitan Museum of Art, was the inaugural curator from 1969 to 1974. The department remained an independent entity until 1983, when the Department of Oriental Art reclaimed the Islamic collection and Sheila Canby joined the staff as Associate Curator of Islamic Art. Pre-Islamic art of the Middle East returned to the Department of Ancient Art, which is now called the Department of Egyptian, Classical, and Ancient Middle Eastern Art.

Today, the Department of Asian Art continues its stewardship of Islamic art. The geographical boundaries represented by its activities in this collection area extend from Islamic Spain and North Africa in the west to Indonesia and Malaysia in the east.

Particular objects often raise questions about the validity or usefulness of too rigid an adherence to such categories and may underscore the extent of possible confusions among the divisions of Middle Eastern, Islamic, and Ancient Near Eastern art and culture. A prime example in the collection is a Marwan textile (no. 87), which originally came into the Department of Ancient Art in 1941 as a Coptic textile. However, when research on the inscription gradually revealed that this textile fragment was indeed from the earliest dated Islamic textile known, the Asian department recategorized it as Islamic art.

In recent years, the Museum has presented Islamic art within a more truly pan-Asian, even global, perspective. For example, the border-crossing exhibition *Lacquer: A Panorama of Asian Decorative Arts* (1988) showed for the first time the range of lacquers produced throughout Asia and the Islamic world. And now that Islamic culture in Africa has become a popular exhibition topic, it is useful to remember that the Brooklyn Museum was the first to introduce the rich visual traditions of the Islamic populations of Morocco, Tunisia, and Islamic West Africa, in the noted exhibition *Africa in Islam* (1985).

SOUTHEAST ASIA

Our second case study is Southeast Asia. Like the Middle East, it too is a distinct region of Asia that calls into question the seemingly intransigent borders of the larger continent. In many ways, the relationship of Southeast Asia to the rest of Asia encapsulates the complexities of defining a region geographically and culturally while also classifying it for the practical purposes of an art museum.

Consider the genesis of the term "Southeast Asia." Like the names of many countries in this region, "Southeast Asia" is a modern term that was not indigenously developed; the term was coined around 1900, initially to describe a trading and shipping zone. By World War II, it was an acknowledged designation for a world region, and in the ensuing Cold War era became a significant term employed in United States' foreign policy statements.

Traditionally, there has been a tendency to describe Southeast Asia as simply the area between China and India. Prior to the recognition of Southeast Asia as an entity in its own right, the region's representation as an annex of the two established civilizations could be seen in the English use of "East Indies" and "Further India," and in the names "Indochine" and "Insulinde" for the French colonies in the area. Lying between South and East Asia, Southeast Asia has been historically considered a "Janus-faced" region.

Another major complication arises from the fact that Southeast Asia overlaps or can be linked with Oceania (the island groups sometimes subdivided into Melanesia, Micronesia, and Polynesia) or even other Pacific Islands. Southeast Asia at present comprises ten independent countries, but just as important, physically the region is divided into a land-bound area and an island area. Mainland Southeast Asia, simply the southeastern section of the Asian continent, consists of Cambodia, Laos, Myanmar (formerly Burma), Thailand, and Vietnam. Island Southeast Asia encompasses the myriad islands in the Indian Ocean and South China Sea that surround continental Southeast Asia to the south and east. Island Southeast Asia, also called Insular or Maritime Southeast Asia, contains Brunei, Indonesia, Malaysia, the Philippines, and Singapore.

The problem of circumscribing a definitive Southeast Asia arises precisely out of the region's mainland-versus-island dichotomy. The strong maritime influence of the surrounding seas can hardly be overestimated. Southeast Asia reaches toward the South Pacific on one side and the Indian Ocean on the other, its complex coastline infiltrated with inlets, bays, and other bodies of water, as well as cut by rivers seeking the sea, at the same time that much of its land area is dispersed among groups and strings of islands large and small. This geological fragmentation amid waterways is why the region is often called the "Mediterranean" of the tropical world; the oceans and smaller seas make possible commercial, cultural, and religious exchanges as well as the distinctions and enduring regional frictions among the various peoples in the region.

The maritime landscape that partially describes Southeast Asia challenges the idea of a monolithic Asia that is land-bound. At the same time, it raises the question of whether parts of Island Southeast Asia are indeed best considered Asian.

Expanding on the maritime implications of Southeast Asia, the popular term "Asia-Pacific" has added a further complication to the lexicon, and so has the term "Pacific Rim." Both are widely employed in journalism and the social sciences. From an economic perspective, "Asia-Pacific" focuses on East and Southeast Asia, sometimes extending through the island groups to include Australia and New Zealand, and occasionally reaching as far into the Eurasian interior as India and, farther north, into eastern Russia. "Pacific Rim" might seem even more diffuse, seeming to span the extended ridge of continental shorelines surrounding the Pacific Ocean. But in practice, it is more closely identified with the trading relationship between Japan and the United States and, to a lesser extent, the rapidly developing Asian countries along the Pacific.

ଓ

When art from this complex of Southeast Asian regions is placed in a museum, what curatorial departments should be given responsibility for it? At the Brooklyn Museum of Art, the issue has revolved around how, or whether, Southeast Asian art might be divided between the Department of Asian Art and a separate department that is responsible for art of the Pacific Islands. From the perspective of the Museum, tribal Southeast Asian art belongs to Oceania while non-tribal Southeast Asian art belongs to Asia.

As with all areas in Asia, Southeast Asian art was collected early in the Museum's history. One of the institution's first presentations of Southeast Asian art was the *Exhibition of Ancient and Modern Art of the Dutch East Indies,* held in 1929. Organized by the curator Tassilo Adams (active 1899–1948), who had worked for the Dutch colonial government in the Dutch East Indies, the exhibition displayed material from Bali and Java. From our current standpoint, the objects shown would now reside in two curatorial departments: at present, Mainland Southeast Asia is the domain of the Department of Asian Art, while the Department of the Arts of Africa and the Pacific Islands oversees the collection of Island Southeast Asia. However, back in 1929 these distinctions were neither addressed nor of great concern: the Southeast Asian material for the exhibition was part of the Department of Ethnology, although organized by a curator of Oriental art. At that time, there was no felt need to classify and reclassify the area of the Dutch East Indies.

The division of the collection remains caught in a classificatory dilemma in which vestiges of many different definitions created at different times continue to coexist. The forces pulling Island Southeast Asia toward the mainland, on one hand, and toward the Pacific Islands as an independent entity on the other are clearly the main issue. But there are other conflicting forces at work in the process of definition, producing some surprising realignments. The Museum's holdings of tribal art of the Pacific furnish an interesting instance. Indigenous material from the Pacific Islands is generally the curatorial responsibility of the Department of the Arts of Africa and the Pacific, retaining a connection with the Museum's older ethnological framework, which classified such objects as "primitive" art. The Museum's important collection of utensils, ritual objects, and costumes of the Ainu, a separate indigenous people of northern Japan, was once classified with primitive art. However, this material has recently been transferred to the Department of Asian Art, becoming part of its Japanese collection (see no. 43). This step was taken in light of the interest in Japan in preserving the culture of indigenous peoples from its northern region, and also acknowledges the growth of related research projects and preservation efforts.

Here we see a body of material shifting out of the curatorial entity responsible for the Pacific Islands, but on this occasion to join a collection devoted to East – not Southeast – Asia.

CULTURAL IDENTIFICATION OF EXPORT ART

The "biographies" of art objects – not only where and when they were made, but also who subsequently acquired them – can complicate the matter of cultural identity. The life that a work leads after its creation, when it leaves home and is purchased and collected elsewhere, can become as much a factor as its place of origin.

Especially thorny issues can grow out of the later lives of artworks made specifically for export. Take, for instance, a brilliantly embroidered textile with roundel motifs from Chinese Turkestan (no. 92). Although it was produced in an area currently considered to be technically within China and historically associated with Central Asia, the Museum classifies it as an Islamic object, since the textile was produced for the Islamic export market. (It should be noted that similar textiles are kept in the Chinese collections at some other museums.)

For somewhat parallel reasons, Chinese export art made for the Western market is generally held at the Museum by the European and American Decorative Arts collections, being classified according to the market for which the object was made. Nonetheless, Japanese export lacquer for the Portuguese market, such as an elaborate portable writing desk (no. 31), is in the Museum's Japanese collection, not the European Decorative Arts collection. Though its form is European, the piece employs motifs that are both Indian and Japanese, yet all reinterpreted within a new Asian art form.

In other instances, too, objects made for export continue to be classified and presented in terms of their country or culture of production. A thirteenth-century lacquer coffer (no. 16) exhibits strong connections with Tibet in its surface designs and metal hardware but was in fact made in the traditional Chinese center of lacquer manufacture, the city of Wenzhou, along the coast of China. While the work may have been produced for export and was believed to have been discovered in Tibet, the object is nonetheless classified as Chinese and was acquired with the Chinese collection in mind.

CULTURAL IDENTIFICATION OF CONTEMPORARY ART

Different questions about cultural classification arise when we turn to contemporary Asian art. Since the Department of Asian Art continues to collect recent art, its acquisitions sometimes overlap with other curatorial divisions, principally the Department of Contemporary Art and the Department of Prints, Drawings, and Photographs. Contemporary Japanese ceramics are a particular strength of the Department of Asian Art, with a segment of the permanent galleries focused on this flourishing tradition. Yet the mid-career retrospective devoted in 1999 to the Japanese artist Mariko Mori, who makes photomurals, videos, and installation pieces, was coordinated by the Museum's Department of Contemporary Art.

The situation can be even more fluid when other curatorial divisions handling other kinds of materials are involved, as with *Japonism in Fashion: Japan Dresses the West*, coordinated by the Costumes and Textiles Division of the Department of Decorative Arts. This 1998 exhibition traced the impact of traditional Japanese costume design on Western fashion in the nineteenth and twentieth centuries as well as exploring the influential work of contemporary Japanese designers. Like the issues raised by objects made for the export market, here, too, the perceived identity of the works has much to do with the market they are intended for. Indeed, the mixing of different cultures' characteristics within these hybridized fashion designs becomes an integral part of their appeal to the purchaser. Crossover is part of their point.

Perhaps the mixed media on view in the exhibition *My Reality: Contemporary Art and the Culture of Japanese Animation* at the Museum in 2001 posed the most suggestive challenge to cultural classification. As with so much contemporary art, the work in the exhibition derived much of its interest from the dynamic interplay between different popular cultures (in this case, those of Japan and the United States); its special charge derived as well from the free interplay between artistic materials and media often thought of as distinct, but now mixing ideas, motifs, and techniques from film, painting, sculpture, installations, and so on. These two aspects would seem to be related: this was an art in which the mixing of media helped convey the idea of mixing national identities. In an age of multiculturalism, a great deal of the art being created today takes as its very subject the questioning and redrawing of traditional cultural boundaries, addressed by questioning the limits of established artistic media.

CONCLUSION

Asia may be thought of as a palimpsest in which the present is overlaid on the complex inscriptions of the past. Individual histories are constantly written and rewritten, spanning the ages, from before the ancient Greek invention of the word "Asia" for the lands east of the Aegean Sea, to the empowered sense of "Asia" accepted by Asian peoples in the twenty-first century. The term encompasses dozens of separate nation-states and the dynamics among all the many cultures, peoples, and regions lying between the Ural Mountains on the west, the Pacific Ocean on the east, and the Indian Ocean on the south.

The present survey of working definitions of "Asia" and "Asian art" suggests not a definitive answer but rather a multitude of additional questions and further contradictions and qualifications. Myriad competing factors push and pull different states into different regional and cultural groupings, giving us much to consider beyond the underlying fact of a shared landmass. How are we to evaluate shifting commonalities of geography, culture, religion, politics, economics, and social values when we try to define Asia? Since no single definition of Asia can do full justice to its extraordinary wealth of varied heritages, we may in the end acknowledge that there is not one Asia but rather many different Asias. The mandate of an encyclopedic collecting institution such as the Brooklyn Museum of Art is, in part, to celebrate the rich, diverse plurality inherent in this complex geographical and cultural entity.

NOTE TO THE READER

Japanese, Chinese, and Korean names are given in the traditional order, surname first, except in the case of individuals who have chosen to adopt the Western system.

In transliterating the Chinese language, the pinyin romanization system has been employed, except in quotations and bibliographical citations from sources using alternate methods. Macrons have been used to indicate long vowels in Japanese names and words (Hōryū-ji). Commonly known city names and words adapted into English have been given without macrons (Kyoto, Shinto). Korean long vowels have been indicated by breves (Chosŏn, Mirŏk). In Sanskrit, accented s's are transcribed as "sh" (Shakyamuni, Kshitigarbha).

Dimensions of works are given, unless otherwise noted, in order of height by width, for two-dimensional objects; and height by width by depth, for three-dimensional objects. Diameter is given at widest point.

Literature citations and parenthetical notes in entry texts are keyed to the Bibliography.

Entry authors:
Tara Adrian (*TA*)
Trevel Balser (*TB*)
Layla S. Diba (*LSD*)
Maryam Ekhtiar (*ME*)
Aimée Froom (*AF*)
Yukio Lippit (*YL*)
Melissa McCormick (*MM*)
Savita Monie (*SM*)
Amy G. Poster (*AGP*)
John Seyller (*JS*)
Hyunsoo Woo (*HW*)
Frances Z. Yuan (*FZY*)

Plates and Commentaries

RUSSIA
MONGOLIA
INNER MONGOLIA
Liaoning
Beijing
HEBEI
Ding
Cizhou
Anyang
Yellow River
CHINESE TURKESTAN
CHINA
KOREA
JAPAN
Luoyang
HENAN
JIANGSU
HUBEI
Indus River
Yangtze
Mount Lu
NEPAL
Jingdezhen
ZHEJIANG
HUNAN
Longquan
Wenzhou
JIANGXI
FUJIAN
Ganges River
YUNNAN
GUANGDONG
TAIWAN
INDIA
Hong Kong
Bay of Bengal
South China Sea
Pacific Ocean

China

Chinese art at the Brooklyn Museum of Art consists of more than eighteen hundred objects that cover more than five thousand years of Chinese culture and civilization from Neolithic times to the present. Although the collection contains a variety of media including sculptures, paintings, textiles, metalwork, and lacquers, ceramics and decorative arts are particular strengths. The Museum's holdings of cloisonné enamels, many from the Chinese imperial collection, are unequaled outside of Asia. One of the earliest groups of Chinese art acquired by the BMA, the enamels were a gift of the American dealer and collector Samuel P. Avery, Jr. (1857–1920), in 1909. Funerary arts related to early Chinese tombs and burials, ritual arts linked with ancestor worship, Buddhism, and Daoism, and arts of the imperial court and scholar-elites are among the key subjects that define the Chinese collection at the Brooklyn Museum of Art.

Chinese art and cultural artifacts have long been collected at the Museum. During the early twentieth century, attention to China at the BMA corresponded to the ethnographic preoccupation of comprehending a unified civilization through objects. Current interest focuses on China's diversity and multiculturalism and its cultural and artistic connections with its neighbors. Also significant is China's cultural past, particularly the ways in which the development of China's civilization is frequently predicated on its enduring respect for its past.

FZY

1

Ritual Wine Vessel (*Guang*)

China, late Shang dynasty, 13th–11th century B.C.
Bronze
6½ × 3¼ × 8½ in. (16.4 × 8.3 × 21.6 cm.)

72.163a, b, Gift of the Guennol Collection

Unlike the forms of other bronze wine-pouring vessels, the ovoid *guang* was rather short-lived, enduring only from the late Shang into the Western Zhou dynasties (c. 11th–9th century B.C.). A latecomer in the repertoire of wine vessel shapes, the *guang* has no ceramic prototype and belonged to a new group of vessels and variations of established forms produced in the central Shang capital of Anyang in Henan province.

The *guang*'s brief existence is an example in the evolution of bronze forms and ornament that occurred during the transition between the two dynasties. While certain visual components from the Shang dynasty survived in Western Zhou bronzes, other characteristics were consciously eliminated. In general, the quantity and variety of ritual wine vessels decreased under the Zhou rule as the forms for food and water vessels proliferated. The *Shu jing* (Book of Documents), considered the foundation of Chinese political philosophy, supports this development through the Zhou dynasty's claim, in their assertion of the right to rule, that the fall of the previous Shang kings derived from their heavy indulgence in alcohol. Although the *guang* form eventually disappeared by the middle of the Western Zhou period, it did attain a certain degree of importance during the early Western Zhou along with several other wine vessel types. Sets of *fangyi, zun,* and *guang* were highly valued, as surviving elaborately decorated examples attest (Rawson 1990, 34).

This late Shang *guang* is an exceptional example of the vessel type, with its lid in the form of a toothy bottle-horned dragon, and a *taotie* (monster mask) frieze on the body of the vessel. Whereas it may not be as flamboyant as certain contemporary examples, the *guang* is superbly cast and elegantly designed. The contours and decorative reliefs are sensitively integrated into an organic whole. Although not as heavily adorned with bold animal motifs as some later *guang* tend to be, it nevertheless exudes a dynamic power in its sculptural form and crisply articulated surface.

FZY

LITERATURE

Brooklyn 1988, 84, cat. no. 51.
Finlay 1996, 71, no. 19.
Brooklyn 1997, 36.
Fane and Poster 2000, 20, no. 11.
Yuan 2000, 84, no. 1.
Yuan 2001, 106, fig. 5.

2

Ritual Tripod Vessel (*Ding*)

China, late Shang to early Western Zhou dynasty, 12th–11th century B.C.
Bronze with black inlay
8 7/16 × 6 7/16 × 6 3/8 in. (21.4 × 16.4 × 16.2 cm.)

1997.178, Anonymous gift

This ritual vessel reflects the variety and rich complexity of shapes in ritual bronzes during the late Shang and early Western Zhou dynasties, from around the eleventh to the ninth century B.C. While the semi-spherical tripod with two handles bears the basic attributes of the *ding* bronze vessel form, its three-lobed body closely resembles the body of the *li*, another Shang vessel type. The *ding* and the *li* were ritual food containers with shapes that took precedence in pre-existing Neolithic pottery forms. During the Shang dynasty (c. 1600–c. 1045 B.C.), the *li* shape was often integrated with other vessel types. The *Erya*, the earliest Chinese dictionary (3rd century B.C.) describes a close resemblance between the two types, remarking that the *li* is a *ding* with hollow legs (Jiang 1987, 235).

Consistent with other lobed *ding* vessels from the late Shang and early Western Zhou, this fine example bears a single cast inscription, most likely a clan sign, on the interior wall above a leg. The *taotie* (monster mask) motifs in low relief against a *leiwen* spiral background and centered over a cylindrical foot also conform to the surface design on similar "transitional"-period *ding*. The animal masks embellishing the swell of each lobe are complete articulations of the motifs, in contrast to the fragmented depictions on the contemporaneous *guang* (see no. 1).

The vessel features remains of earth from burial and a patina extending from a smooth, gray-green surface of the original casting to azurite and malachite encrustations with light tan patches. The encrustation reveals a faint textile impression. The *ding* also exhibits a matte black material inlay in the intaglio areas of the *leiwen*-patterned ground and in the lines defining the eyes of the various animal masks. This substance also covers a portion of the joins between the body and the legs.
FZY

LITERATURE

Yuan 2001, 107, fig. 6.

3

Garment Hook

China, Warring States period, c. 5th–4th century B.C.
Olive green nephrite
4⅞ × 2 × ½ in. (12 × 5 × 1.4 cm.)

2002.36.4, Gift of Mr. and Mrs. Raymond Hargreaves

Jade, or nephrite, has been a metaphoric medium throughout Chinese history. Its qualities of translucent beauty, durability, and hardness have been associated with Confucian values of moral integrity, justice, and perseverance, respectively. This garment hook, used to fasten a belt or robe (see cat. no. 4), exemplifies the jade culture of the Warring States period.

The powerful silhouette of the hook's plaque in the form of a dragon is emphasized by a complex surface pattern polished to a high sheen. As one of the most important early jades in the BMA collection, the piece epitomizes the low-relief "rush mat" or incised spiral design of interlocking and semi-geometric patterns that is present only in jade plaques of this era.

The piece is designed with the head of a dragon at one end and a tiger-headed hook at the other; the tiger dramatically bites the dragon's tail. The dragon's mouth is open with a pronounced jaw, raised scrolled ears, and an S-curve body profile. As is common in jades of the Warring States period, the reverse of the plaque repeats the same decoration. The form and surface decoration of the garment hook, especially the shallow incised stylized floral motif on the neck of the dragon, are related to jades found at Zincun.

Nephrite, a mineral of extreme hardness, was never carved, but worked with bamboo tools and an abrasive. Blocky shapes of nephrite pebbles were fashioned into elaborately decorated ornaments and arc-shaped belt hooks like this one. Such jades not only were used as personal ornaments, but were placed in burial mounds to serve a protective function, guarding the deceased and conferring immortality.

AGP

4

Garment Hook in the Form of a Fish

China, late Eastern Zhou–Western Han dynasty, 3rd–2nd century B.C.
Bronze inlaid with gold, silver, and blue mineral or glass
2⅜ × 6 5/16 × 1¾ in. (6 × 16 × 4.4 cm.)

51.137, Gift of Mr. and Mrs. Alastair B. Martin, the Guennol Collection

This elaborate bronze garment hook inlaid with precious metals and minerals is remarkable for its large size and uncommon depiction of a fish. Similarly large and intricately decorated inlaid garment hooks served more as evocations of status, ceremony, and conspicuous consumption than merely as functional fastenings for a belt or robe. The naturalistic fish motif and the use of a blue mineral or glass for the eyes date the work to the late Eastern Zhou to early Western Han dynasty, from around the third to second century B.C. The garment hook maintains the Zhou regard for colorful effects with its rich inlay of precious metals and the Han penchant for realism in its fish form.

In China the garment hook, also known as the belt hook, initially was a functional accessory used to secure garments. Worn by both men and women, it was usually made from bronze with a button on the back of one end and an upturned hook on the other. Belt hooks, ranging from ten to twenty centimeters in length, like the example shown here, would be horizontally attached to a cloth or leather belt. Knowledge about the use of the Chinese garment hook comes from a kneeling bronze figure from a Warring States period (403–221 B.C.) site at Sanmenxia in Henan province. The figure is dressed in a robe tied with a belt and secured by a garment hook.

While animal-inspired designs often appear on garment hooks, they typically represent such motifs as birds or felines in combat scenes, associated with the region outside of China known as the northern steppes. The image of the fish is uncommon in the repertoire of early bronze inlay designs. Although the motif itself existed in the Chinese visual vocabulary as early as the Neolithic period (c. 10,000–2100 B.C.), examples comparable to this fish-shaped belt hook have yet to surface.

FZY

LITERATURE

Brooklyn 1967, 144–45.
Fane and Poster 2000, 86, fig. 60.
Yuan 2000, 85, fig. 2.

3

4

5

Hill Jar and Cover

China, Han dynasty (206 B.C.–A.D. 220)
Earthenware with green lead glaze
H: 11½ in. (29.2 cm.); DIAM: 8¾ in. (22.2 cm.)

1995.49 a, b, Purchase gift of Dr. Bertram H. Schaffner, Mr. and Mrs. Milton F. Rosenthal, Mr. and Mrs. Greg Fitz-Gerald, and Mr. and Mrs. Robert L. Poster; Helen Babbott Sanders Fund, Charles Stewart Smith Memorial Fund, Caroline A. L. Pratt Fund, and Caroline H. Polhemus Fund

The use of *mingqi*, or "spirit goods," during the Han dynasty marked a change in funerary practices and customs. Rather than actual possessions, replicas of prized objects and personal goods were produced in less expensive materials for interment with the dead. Ceramic reproductions of amenities and aspects of daily life, such as servants and buildings (see no. 7), were provided for life in death. This hill jar is a *mingqi*; although it emulates the basic form of a metal wine-warming vessel with its cylindrical body, tripod legs, and faux ring-handles, the earthenware copy infuses its appearance with elements of Han cosmological symbolism. Not seen on the metal prototype is the hill jar's cover, which is in the shape of Mount Bo, a sacred mountain inhabited by Daoist immortals; also added is a continuous mountain landscape encircling the vessel's exterior in low relief. Amid the undulating peaks of this landscape frieze is an assortment of real and imaginary creatures. Most notable are animals symbolizing the four cardinal directions of the universe – the dragon (East), the phoenix, (South), the tiger (West), and the tortoise (North) – which became part of Han cosmology by the first century A.D. Animal imagery also extends to the legs supporting the vessel. The image of a mother bear clutching her young suggests a northern Chinese influence. The dynamic pictorial imagery decorating the vessel may allude to the concept of the sacred mountain as an intermediary space between the visible world and the spirit world.

This vessel is unique among the many examples that exist to this day. Although the landscape and animal motifs follow a standard pattern, the hill jar's dimensions are larger and more monumental than usual. A short inscription of two characters, which reads as "*juma*," between a handle and one of the animals makes the hill jar even more unusual. The exact meaning of the characters remains elusive.

FZY

LITERATURE

Finlay 1996, 70, fig. 17.

6

Wine Vessel (*Zun*) in the Form of a Goose

China, Han dynasty (206 B.C.–A.D. 220) or later
Bronze
11½ × 6 3/16 × 17½ in. (29.2 × 15.7 × 44.5 cm.)

54.145a, b, Gift of Mr. and Mrs. Alastair B. Martin, the Guennol Collection

Used for heating and holding wine, this bronze vessel, called a *zun*, takes the form of a standing goose with an extended neck that serves as a spout. It is also a striking sculpture, which represents the goose in an animated stance with a remarkable degree of naturalism. Two small lions support a handle connected to an opening on the goose's back. Incised hatched lines delineate the eyes, webbed feet, and feathers on the tail, as well as the design on the handle. Although this work is a celebrated early Chinese bronze in the Museum's collection and an exceptional example of its type, a conclusive date for it remains elusive.

The vessel bears numerous characteristics that suggest a range of dates. While X-ray radiography has determined the possibility of a Han-dynasty (206 B.C.–A.D. 220) date, the handle with the two lions suggests a later Tang-dynasty (618–907) attribution and a strong influence from Central Asia and Sassanian Iran. The engraved zigzag patterns on the tail feathers indicate an addition after the casting of the vessel, again suggesting a Tang date. From the tenth century on, when a strong penchant for studying and excavating early bronzes as well as a taste for archaistic forms began, goose-shaped vessels similar to the Brooklyn vessel proliferated. These later archaistic versions were often bejeweled and inlaid with precious metals and enamels. Early documentation of a similar goose-shaped vessel is found in the collection of the Northern Song (960–1127) emperor Huizong (r. 1101–25) and illustrated in the catalogue of his imperial collection of ancient bronzes first printed around 1125. The stance, expression, and details of the Museum's bronze vessel are almost analogous. This illustration was also the inspiration for a Northern Song Ru ware example of this vessel, according to the album of the Ming (1368–1644) collector Xiang Yuangbian (1525–1590), which documents this imperial ceramic version.

FZY

LITERATURE

Archives of the Chinese Art Society of America 1953, 84, fig. 3.
Lee, G. 1955, 2–4.
Brooklyn 1967, 142–43.
Finlay 1996, 71, fig. 21.

7

Tomb Tower

China, Eastern Han dynasty (25 B.C.–A.D. 220)
Earthenware with green lead glaze
H: 42 in. (106.7 cm.)

1997.142a–e, Purchased from the Schloss Collection with funds given by Dr. Richard and Ruth Dickes, Lucille and Martin E. Kantor, Dr. Robert and Bernice Dickes, Florence and Irving Kingdon, Dr. Bertram H. Schaffner, Dora Wong and Diane H. Schafer; Frank L. Babbott Fund

Among *mingqi*, or "spirit goods," made exclusively for Eastern Han (25 B.C.–A.D. 220) tombs in northern China are tall earthenware buildings, such as this tomb tower. Perhaps imitating contemporary Chinese architecture from around Henan province, where numerous similar multi-storied edifices have been discovered, this tower provides clues about life and culture during the Eastern Han and possibly about attitudes toward afterlife and funerary customs.

The three floors of this tower teem with activity. On the second- and third floor-balconies are pairs of seated figures, perhaps officials or soldiers, with their hands clasped. They peer outward, as do the figures in doorways on these floors. A dog guards the courtyard entrance and a bird nests on the roof. The figures and creatures all face in one direction. Although the actual significance of such towers remains unresolved, this building and the many figural elements offer symbolic meanings of wealth, power, and protection. The bird suggests the heavenly realms and is a feature that occurs only in northern architectural models.

With the lack of extant Han-dynasty architecture, much of our current knowledge is derived from multiple sources – tomb architecture, earthenware models, the pictorial tradition, and contemporary textual references. Whether or not tomb towers represent actual Han edifices is a continuing debate. Actual architectural elements are represented in these models, such as the tiled roofs and brackets (*dougong*) with and without dragon heads. There is a marked distinction between tomb architectural models excavated from northern and southern China. While models found in the south are usually compounds consisting of a courtyard with several buildings, models in the north are typically multi-storied buildings. Henan province, where the Eastern Han capital (present-day Luoyang) was situated, has the highest number of such elaborate towers.

FZY

8

Plaque of a Ram

China, Tang dynasty (618–907)
Silver
5 × 6 in. (12.8 × 15.5 cm.)

L2001.6, Promised gift of Mr. and Mrs. Leopold Swergold

In contrast to jade, bronze, or gold, silver was not readily accessible in early China since only small amounts of alluvial silver existed. Subsequently, the precious white metal was not as greatly sought after and valued as these other precious materials. Although the Chinese worked with silver as early as the Shang dynasty (c. 1600–c. 1045 B.C.), it did not become a popular artistic medium until the first millennium A.D., when China was exposed to foreign influences, particularly from the ancient Near East and Central Asia. Interest in working with silver grew during the late Six Dynasties period (220–589) and Tang dynasty (618–907) after China was introduced to artifacts from Sassanian Iran and the tribes and kingdoms from the northern borders.

This plaque has been identified in the past as an ibex, but it may represent a long-haired ram or goat. Molded in silver, the long-haired ram is shown with a shaped muscular torso, long horns, and slender hoofed legs. The body is engraved with repeated lines that depict the animal's long and heavy coat. The open mouth and staring eye combined with the dynamic presentation of movement suggest that the animal is fleeing from a pursuer.

This work was formerly in the collection of Mr. and Mrs. Myron S. Falk, Jr. A nearly identical silver plaque in the Santa Barbara Museum of Art appeared in the exhibition *Early Chinese Gold and Silver* (no. 58).
AGP

LITERATURE

Smith College Museum of Art 1957, cat. no. 20.
Trubner 1957, cat. no. 351.
China Institute in America 1971, cat. no. 58.
Dayton Art Institute 1984, 90, cat. no. 57.
Christie's 2001, 239, lot no. 190.

9

Qingbai Ware Ewer with Phoenix Head

China, Tang or early Song dynasty, c. 10th century
Stoneware with translucent glaze
H: 14 9/16 in. (37.1 cm.); DIAM: 6 7/8 in. (17.5 cm.)

54.7, Ella C. Woodward Memorial Fund and Frank L. Babbott Fund

From around the tenth to the fourteenth century, the southern region of China produced a popular white stoneware called *qingbai* (literally "bluish-white") ware, named so after the bluish-white color of its glaze. Descriptions of this stoneware often likened the glassy, transparent quality of the glaze and its color to unblemished, icy jade. Modifying the ceramic technology from China's north, numerous southern Chinese kilns generated *qingbai* wares, with the Jingdezhen kilns in Jiangxi province as the premier production center. Owing to the tremendous demand for this ceramic ware in the domestic and export markets, kilns in Fujian, Guangdong, and neighboring southern Chinese provinces began producing this refined stoneware with a white porcelaneous body and luminous glaze.

This ewer with a phoenix head is an extraordinary example of early *qingbai* ware. One of only a handful of vessels of this type, the ewer stands out for its overall pristine condition and sensitive depiction of the bird's features. The crisp, well-defined contours of the vessel form indicate close ties with an Islamic metal or glass prototype.

The ewer reportedly was discovered in Indonesia and is related to a similar phoenix-head ewer in Jakarta, which was originally made in Chao-an in Guangdong province. While many *qingbai* wares were exported to Southeast Asia, archaeological excavations in present-day northeastern China demonstrate the popularity of this type of southern white ware among the semi-nomadic Qidans of the Liao dynasty (907–1125). Liao ceramics also have incorporated and adapted the form of the ewer with phoenix-head spouts, showing the impact of this form and decoration (Krahl 1998, 20–21.).

FZY

LITERATURE

Brooklyn 1967, 146–47.
Finlay 1996, 74, fig. 27.
Brooklyn 1997, 36.

10

Saddle Ornaments

China, Liao dynasty (907–1125)
Silver
Section A: 11½ × 13½ × 1½ in. (29.2 × 34.3 × 3.8 cm.)
Section B: 17 × 17¾ × 3 in. (43.2 × 45.1 × 7.6 cm.)
Section C: 7¾ × 2¾ × ½ in. (19.7 × 7 × 1.3 cm.)

1990.72a–c, Purchased with funds given by Mr. and Mrs. Herbert Irving

Horses and horsemanship were synonymous with the identity of the Qidans, a powerful semi-nomadic people who established a separate border dynasty, the Liao (907–1125), in northern China during the tenth century. Texts and paintings by Chinese contemporaries concerning their non-Chinese neighbors and excavated material from Liao tombs in Liaoning and Inner Mongolia reveal the vibrant equestrian tradition maintained by the Qidans. Horses were not only important culturally, but also central to the Qidans' hunting and military prowess and as political and economic commodities. After years of warfare, in 1005 the Qidans and Chinese began diplomatic relations and exchanged gifts through their respective envoys. Historical sources recounting these transactions describe that while the Qidans presented horses and other gifts reflecting their semi-nomadic lifestyle, the Chinese bestowed items that catered to Qidan taste. Saddle ornaments with dragons and phoenixes, similar to the example seen here, were described in these literary documents (Fontein and Wu 1973, 186, cat. no. 97).

These three components are from a larger set of ornaments that once framed a wooden saddle. Pairs of confronting phoenixes surrounding a flaming pearl are the dominant design elements. Research conducted by former Assistant Curator Xiaoping Lin suggests that the saddle was intended for a woman of royal standing; images of phoenixes in frescoes and funerary objects, including saddles, were pervasive in the tomb of the Liao princess Chenguo, dated to 1018. The intricate design and refined quality of the metalwork indicate the great skill and effort involved in its creation. The Liao and Chinese influences in these saddle ornaments bring up issues of intercultural interactions and the lengths to which the Qidans adopted Chinese art and culture. In the manufacture of silver and gold objects, the Qidans maintained metalwork traditions from the Tang dynasty (618–907). The shape of the ornaments follows a Tang prototype. However, some experts propose that certain metalwork associated with the Liao style may actually be export ware produced by the Chinese for the Qidans (Fontein and Wu 1973, 186).

FZY

LITERATURE

Archives of Asian Art 1991, 106, fig. 10.

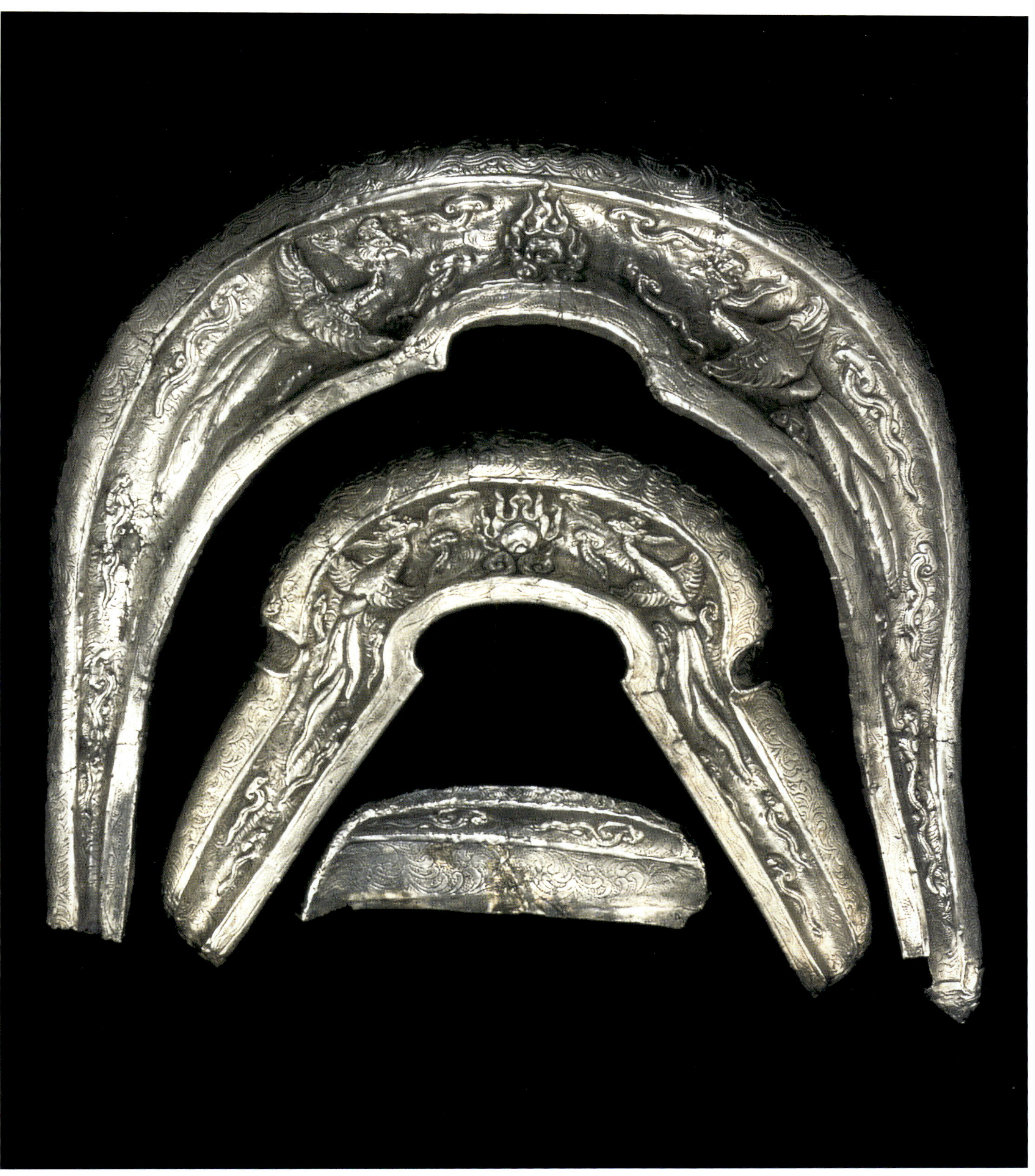

11

Ding Ware Basin with Incised Floral Decoration

China, Northern Song dynasty (960–1127)
White porcelain with ivory-colored glaze and silver band
H: 5 in. (12.7 cm.); DIAM: 9⅝ in. (24.5 cm.)

47.219.20, Anonymous gift

Among the prized ceramics produced during the Song dynasty (960–1279) were the fine white porcelains from the imperially sponsored Ding ware kilns in Hebei province. Historically, northern white ware introduced two technological innovations to the long-standing tradition of Chinese ceramics – the process of firing wares upside down to economize space in the kiln; and mold-impressed decoration. Although Ding kilns produced a variety of ceramic wares, they were most noted for the white porcelains they supplied to Chinese officials and the imperial court during the Northern Song (960–1127).

This large basin with incised decoration is a superb and distinctive example of Northern Song Ding ware owing to its unusually large size and the perfection of the porcelain body. There is a refined quality in the whiteness of the body, the exceptional ivory-colored glaze, and crisp incised surface decoration. The fluency of line of the graceful billowing waves and scrolling lotus blossoms on the interior and peony flowers on the exterior never overwhelms the vessel's sleek contours or interferes with the pristine color and quality of the transparent glaze. As revealed in many imperial ceramics of the time, this basin embodies the Song aesthetic – an elegant integration of form, color, and design.

According to textual references during the ensuing Southern Song (1127–1279), Ding ware's fall from imperial favor during the late Northern Song was owing to the so-called unsightly unglazed rims (literally named "rough mouth") that resulted from firing the wares upside down. This was a reason why many Ding ware vessels bear gold, silver, and copper bands around their rims. However, metal bands served a decorative purpose as well. The practice of decorating edges with precious metals stems from the Han dynasty (206 B.C.–A.D. 220) and was considered a means of embellishing an object. Metal bands were not exclusively used to disguise unglazed rims, but often covered glazed rims as well.
FZY

LITERATURE

Japan Ceramic Society 1956, 50, no. 6.
Asia Society 1960, 85, cat. no. 33.
Spelman 1977, 69, no. 105.

12

Seated Buddha Shakyamuni

China, Liao dynasty, 965 or 1025
Gilt bronze
H: 8¾ in. (21.5 cm.)

1999.42, Gift of the Asian Art Council in memory of Mahmood T. Diba; Mary Smith Dorward Fund

Detail of inscription

Gilt bronze icons of Buddhist divinities were ritually and aesthetically significant early in China's reception of Buddhism. These deeply venerated, portable images were initially introduced into China by missionaries, travelers, and pilgrims. By the end of the Eastern Han period (25 B.C.–A.D. 220), around the second century, the Chinese began to cast their own bronze Buddhist icons, establishing a vibrant sculptural tradition that reflects China's own heritage as well as its engagement with non-Chinese cultures. This exquisite figure represents a Buddhist gilt bronze from the Liao dynasty (907–1125), a period under the rule of the Qidans, a semi-nomadic group originating in eastern Inner Mongolia who occupied northeastern China.

Seated and dressed in a long, flowing, Chinese-style robe, this Buddha Shakyamuni (C: Shijiamouni Fo), or historical Buddha, is presented in a softly stylized hieratic pose. He manifests the traditional physical attributes of the Buddha – elongated earlobes, snail-curl hair, cranial bump (S: *ushnisha*), and distinctive tuft of hair (S: *urna*) between his eyes. He also displays the gesture of preaching with his right hand and the vow-fulfilling gesture with his left. It is said that the gleaming surfaces of gilded bronze icons were intended to reproduce the sunlike radiance of the Buddha's body. The gilding, in superb condition, manifests a divine brilliance while the figure's supremely calm and introspective gaze imparts a benevolent spirituality. This is further captured by the gently calligraphic folds of the robe.

Most noteworthy about this work is the four-character inscription (see detail). Reading "*yi chou sui zao*," or "made in the *yi chou* year," it enables us to ascribe this Buddha to either 965 or 1025. Within the limited number of Liao Buddhist bronzes, examples with inscriptions are rare.

FZY

13

Bodhisattva Guanyin

China, Yunnan province, Dali Kingdom, 11th–12th century
Bronze with traces of gilding
18⅞ × 4½ in. (47.9 × 11.4 cm.)

1995.48, Gift of the Asian Art Council

The area of present-day Yunnan province in southwestern China was under the rule of the independent and indigenous Nanzhao and Dali kingdoms from the mid-seventh to the thirteenth century. Serving as a crossroads for Tibet, China, and Southeast Asia, the region often had unsteady relations with neighboring powers but was an important site for trade and cultural exchange. This bronze figure of the bodhisattva Guanyin exemplifies the cultural cross-pollenization that occurred in this area and provides insight into the genesis of the "Yunnanese style."

The cult of the Buddhist bodhisattva Guanyin, the God of Mercy (S: Avalokiteshvara) was supposedly introduced to Yunnan by a seventh-century Indian monk who was perceived to be an incarnation of the bodhisattva. The monk also visualized Guanyin, who eventually replaced the Buddha as the principal Buddhist deity in the region. Guanyin as the supreme compassionate savior became significant in the religious life of ruling families and to the cultural identity of the Nanzhao and Dali kingdoms.

Belonging to a small number of extant Yunnanese cast bronze images of Guanyin, this figure bears characteristics consistent with other examples in the group – the same upright posture, slender and linear physique, and general iconography. Standing barefoot, bejeweled, and garbed in a simple skirt, he raises his right hand in the gesture of exposition (S: *vitarka mudra*) while his left hand is extended in the gesture of wish-granting (S: *varada mudra*). Within his elaborate hairstyle is the image of a seated Buddha Amitabha, who is intrinsic to the identity of the bodhisattva. Traces of gilt on the surface suggest that the statue was at one time heavily gilded.

Although conflicting views on the stylistic and iconographic origins of gilt bronze Yunnanese Guanyins exist, associations with Indian and Southeast Asian sculptural traditions are particularly compelling. The bronze images take influence from eighth- to eleventh-century Bengali sculpture under the Pala dynasty (8th–12th century), which then spread through Southeast Asia, particularly the maritime and commercial kingdom of Srivijaya in the Malay Archipelago. These bronzes reveal a complex process of exchange that resulted in a distinct national style.

FZY

LITERATURE

Brooklyn 1967, 37.
Finlay 1996, 75, fig. 25.

14

Cizhou Ware Pillow in the Form of a Tiger

China, Jin dynasty, dated 1182
Earthenware with black, orange, and white slip
4⅜ × 14½ × 6¾ in. (11.1 × 36.8 × 17.1 cm.)

1993.56, Gift of the Asian Art Council

Initially developed during the Sui dynasty (581–618), ceramic pillows became popular items produced throughout northern and southern China from the seventh to the fourteenth century. Functioning mainly as headrests, they also warded off evil spirits and were used for traveling. Moreover, ceramic pillows served as armrests for sutra-writing and pulse-taking.

The Cizhou kilns in northern China were famous for producing often lively and elaborately designed ceramic pillows and other non-imperial wares. Animal-shaped pillows, namely tiger-shaped forms, were particularly fashionable items produced at Cizhou kilns during the Jin dynasty (1115–1234).

Mold-made and painted to simulate a crouching tiger, this earthenware pillow captures the spontaneity typical of folk ceramics from Cizhou kilns. Unrestrained calligraphic strokes of black slip not only delineate the tiger's stripes and charmingly fierce facial expression, but also delicately depict a bird perched on a bamboo branch in an oval panel on the tiger's back. The apotropaic element of this pillow is dictated by the tiger imagery, which according to Chinese lore would frighten away malevolent spirits.

While many tiger pillows still survive, examples with inscriptions, such as this one, are rare. On the unpainted base of this pillow (see view of base) is a lengthy inscription, which reads "*ren ying zheng yue shisan ri zhidao zhenzi jia sanshiyi wen zu.*" Recording the date of the original purchase of the pillow and the price paid, it has been translated by the ceramic specialist Fan Dongqing as "purchased for 31 wen on the thirteenth day of the first month of the *renying* year." The second character of the cyclical date "*ren ying*" is slightly effaced but appears to correspond to 1182.

FZY

LITERATURE

Finlay 1996, 76, fig. 30.

View of base

15

Pillow with Incised Decoration

China, Song dynasty (960–1279)
Stoneware with white slip and green lead glaze
5½ × 14¾ × 8⅝ in. (13.9 × 37.8 × 22 cm.)

2001.6.2, Bequest of Mr. and Mrs. Myron S. Falk, Jr.

In contrast to the often delicately designed and subtly glazed ceramics produced for the Song imperial court (960–1279), potters at the Cizhou non-official or folk kilns in Hebei province developed a great number of inventive decorative styles and techniques with their dramatic and colorful stonewares. Initially influenced by the designs of Yaozhou and Ding wares and the use of slip popularized by Tang-dynasty (618–907) ceramics, Cizhou ceramics were first characterized by slip-carved works and green and three-color glazed wares, and subsequently by spontaneous calligraphic painted decoration. Among the diverse types of Cizhou ceramics, wares with green glaze over painted black decoration were one of the last decorative styles to be produced. The popularity of Cizhou wares began in the late Five Dynasties period (906–960) and extended into the Song (960–1279) and Jin (1115–1234) dynasties. The kilns experienced a decline in favor by the Yuan dynasty (1279–1368) in the face of the growing dominance of porcelains at the central imperial-sponsored Jingdezhen kilns.

This bean-shaped pillow with its surface decoration and emerald-hued lead glaze exemplifies the spirit of Cizhou ware. In the center of the pillow, an infant boy is depicted with his arms raised above his head and clutching a flowering peony vine. Set against a background of faintly incised striations, the figure is flanked by two flowering peonies. A meandering leaf pattern, also against a striated background, decorates the sides.

The image of an infant boy grasping peony flowers was a design motif used on ceramics and textiles during the Northern Song dynasty (960–1127). It is believed that the motif of young boys afloat with flowers was initially Indian in origin and reached China with the inception of Buddhism but held a completely secular meaning to the Chinese. Motifs of male children associated with flowers symbolized good fortune and the wish for many successive generations of male progeny. The peony flower is less commonly shown than the lotus, however; the Chinese character for lotus, *lian*, is a homonym of the Chinese character for succession.

FZY

LITERATURE

Lee, S. 1953, 264.
Cahill 1962, no. C10.
Smith College Museum of Art 1975.
Christie's 2001, 20, fig. 3.

16

Lacquered Leather Traveling Coffer

China, Southern Song or Yuan dynasty, c. 1250
Lacquer over leather, bamboo, wood, metal mounts
17¼ × 28⅜ × 15 in. (43.8 × 72.1 × 38.1 cm.)

1996.68, Gift of the Asian Art Council

Produced in China for the Central Asian market, this magnificent and well-preserved lacquer traveling coffer exemplifies the intercultural connections between China and other Asian cultures.

Medallions containing mythical and real animals and floral motifs set against elaborately decorated backgrounds adorn the coffer's surface, represented through the lacquer techniques of *qiangjin* and *qiangcai*, in which gold leaf or gold powder and pigmented lacquer, respectively, are added to lines engraved into the lacquer ground. The central medallion on the front depicts a landscape with a mythological lion chasing a brocaded ball; a goose flying with a stalk of grass in its beak is portrayed in a similar medallion on the back. Within a panel on the lid a pair of phoenixes (*fenghuang*) confront one another.

An inscription under the front of the lid (see detail) reveals that the Ou family from the city of Wenzhou was the manufacturer. Wenzhou in Zhejiang province was celebrated as a center of lacquerware since the Northern Song dynasty (960–1127). Radiocarbon dating has established the coffer's date to around 1250, or between the early and late thirteenth century, during the period when the Mongols invaded China in 1279.

Former Curator of Islamic Art Layla S. Diba noted the increasing significance of lacquer as a trade item between China and Persia and as a new source for artistic exchange during the thirteenth and fourteenth centuries. Her research has documented that Chinese lacquers were exported to Egypt, eastern Iran, and Central Asia since the mid-fourteenth century. George Kuwayama has also discussed textual documentation of Yuan-dynasty lacquers to Southeast Asia in the thirteenth century. Lacquer sutra boxes employing the same *qiangjin* technique as the coffer, with Yuan-dynasty dates, are preserved in Japanese temple collections. The artistic relationship among lacquer, painted ceramics and blue-and-white porcelains, and textiles from the thirteenth and fourteenth centuries has long been recognized and examined. A comparison between the coffer and the fourteenth-century silk textile from Chinese Turkestan (see no. 92) illustrates such a possible dialogue. Tony Anninos has noted the similarity in design elements and decorative technique of the coffer with other lacquered leatherware recovered from Tibet.

FZY

INSCRIPTION

Inscribed, under the front of cover: "*Wenzhou xinhejie anningfang xia Ou jia shenghuo*" (Made by the Ou family of Wenzhou, Xinhe Street, Anning ward)

LITERATURE

Anninos 2000, 101–17.

Detail of inscription

17

Blue-and-White Wine Jar with Fish and Aquatic Plants

China, Yuan dynasty, 14th century
Porcelain with underglaze cobalt blue decoration
H: 11 15/16 in. (30.3 cm.); DIAM: 13 3/4 in. (34.9 cm.)

52.87.1, The William E. Hutchins Collection, Bequest of Augustus S. Hutchins

From the fourteenth century, the use of cobalt blue as a decorative pigment initiated a decisive conceptual shift in the history of Chinese ceramics. Whereas taste in ceramics formerly stressed the purity of form and glaze and the subordination of surface decoration, blue-and-white porcelain wares of the Yuan dynasty (1272–1368) projected a different preference – the emphasis of surface decoration over form. Many early examples of underglaze cobalt-blue porcelains were stimulated by Islamic and Persian patronage, and the mineral cobalt was imported in the fourteenth century from West Asian sources.

This magnificent wine jar, one of a small number of similarly decorated jars of the period, is an important example of early blue-and-white ware from the imperially sponsored kilns of Jingdezhen in Jiangxi province. Dominating the vessel's surface is the dramatic image of fish amid a lush environment of aquatic plants. As the Chinese ceramic specialist Wang Qingzheng remarks, water is never depicted within this pictorial frame, but its presence is suggested by the movement of the water reeds. Interestingly, this is contrasted with the band of crashing waves encircling the vessel's neck.

While eelgrass, pondweed, water crowfeet, duckweed, and blossoming lotuses are clearly depicted as the underwater flora, only two fish, the carp and perch, have been firmly identified; the remaining two could represent a type of mackerel and tuna. Fan Dongqing has noted that the specific species portrayed corresponds to the suggestion of an auspicious visual pun in the image. The Chinese names of the four fish form a homonym for the phrase "*qingbai lianjie*," or "pure and honest." The message from this visual wordplay suggests that the wine jar may have been for a specific clientele, perhaps a Chinese government official. Moreover, vessels with closed forms were made for domestic markets. Large plates and objects based on metalwork forms were often reproduced in blue-and-white ware for the Middle Eastern export market since they conformed to Islamic feasting customs.

FZY

LITERATURE

Japanese Ceramics Society 1956, 51.
Savelle 1957, vol. 2, 275.
Koyama 1959, 119, 399, fig. 527, pl. 142.
Brooklyn 1967, 154–55.
Lee and Ho 1968, cat. no. 155.
Medley 1986, 185, fig. 135.
Brooklyn 1988, 87, cat. no. 54.
Grabar 1992, 196, fig. 172.
Finlay 1996, 75, fig. 28.
Brooklyn 1997, 38.
Eskenazi 2002, 19, 22–24.

18

Longquan Wine Jar with the Eight Immortals

China, late Yuan to early Ming dynasty, 14th century
Porcelain with green glaze and unglazed relief
H: 9 5/16 in. (25.2); DIAM: 10 5/16 in. (27.7 cm.)

52.49.33, The William E. Hutchins Collection, Bequest of Augustus S. Hutchins

The Eight Immortals (*baxian*), the most popular deities in Daoist mythology, are emblematic of the eight conditions of life: youth, old age, poverty, wealth, the populace, nobility, the masculine, and the feminine. Although they often appear on paintings and a variety of decorative arts, the Eight Immortals are an uncommon decorative motif on complete celadon vessels from the Yuan (1272–1368) and Ming (1368–1644) dynasties.

The workshops at the Longquan kilns, the celebrated celadon-producing center in southeastern China, were the first to decorate ceramic vessels with the Eight Immortals. Yuan-dynasty Longquan sites at Linjiao and Dayao have yielded fragments with incised or sculptural figures of these deities; however, intact examples with the Daoist theme are very rare. This wine jar provides a striking illustration of the Longquan kilns' early contribution in the use of relief imagery on ceramic wares (He 1996, 203, no. 363).

Typically, these celadon wine vessels have the Daoist paragons framed within unglazed and mold-impressed panels. This wine jar is distinguished because the Immortals are unframed and in low sculptural relief. On the jar, the Immortals depicted are, reading from right to left: Li Tieguai (Iron Crutch Li) holding a crutch; Zhong Liquan, holding a fan; Lü Dongbin with flywhisk and sword; He Xiangu, carrying a lotus blossom; Cao Guojiu, wearing a Confucian official's cap (shown at center, opposite page); Lan Caihe, identified by clappers (*jieban*) and a basket of flowers; Zhang Guolao; and Han Xiangzi (Master Han Xiang) with a flute. He Xiangu is the only woman depicted.

The Eight Immortals are the best-known figures in Daoist mythology. First appearing in pre-Tang (618–907) literature, they were usually portrayed separately. By the Yuan dynasty, they gained popularity, first in dramas and then as subjects in a variety of visual media, ranging from wall paintings and textiles to ceramics and lacquerware. It was during this time that the Immortals were identified as a group.

FZY

LITERATURE

Finlay 1996, 72, fig. 23.

19

Lacquer Dish

China, Ming dynasty, Jiajing era (1522–66)
Carved cinnabar lacquer on wood
H: 1½ in. (3.5 cm.); DIAM: 8 in. (15 cm.)

L2002.5, Promised gift of Patricia Falk, from the Collection of Pauline B. and Myron S. Falk, Jr.

This exquisitely carved cinnabar lacquer dish with the decoration of a rampant dragon amid blossoming plants was intended for imperial use, as indicated by the reign mark of the Jiajing emperor (r. 1522–66) that is incised with gold on the underside of the base. The body of the shallow, circular dish has an upturned rim and a wide base. The red lacquer surface layers are carved down to a yellow ground on both the interior and exterior. The decoration on the interior consists of a large medallion with a central four-clawed dragon. A vaporous *shou* character issues from its jaws, which hold stems of *lingzhi* fungus rising from rocks and waves, all auspicious symbols. The background is carved with a flower-and-leaf design. On the exterior, a carved frieze of meandering *lingzhi* scrolls appears above a key fret band that encircles the foot ring. The imperial reign mark of the Jiajing emperor is carved in a vertical line in the middle of the red-lacquered base and infilled with gold. The dragon would have originally been five-clawed, since this is an imperial dish; at a later date, however, the fifth toe on each foot was removed.

AGP

LITERATURE

China Institute in America 1972, cat. no. 51.
Christie's 1990, lot no. 225.

20

Pair of Yokeback Armchairs

China, late Ming dynasty, first half of the 17th century
Huanghuali wood
43⅝ × 23 × 24 in. (111 × 58.5 × 61 cm.) each

78.246.1, .2, Gift of Alice Boney

This pair of armchairs, with well-proportioned and graceful linear contours and emphasis on the natural grain and color of their *huanghuali* hardwood, embodies the qualities of restrained elegance associated with Chinese furniture design from the Ming (1368–1644) and early Qing (1644–1911) dynasties. Yokeback armchairs that have top rails and arms with protruding ends, as depicted here, are known in China as the official's hat armchairs (*guanmaoyi*) or the official's hat armchairs with four protruding ends (*sichutou guanmaoyi*).

The yokeback chair design has survived over many centuries, manifesting a unique aspect of Chinese furniture – the persistence and unwavering popularity of certain furniture styles. The earliest known representation of this type of chair dates from the sixth century and shows Buddhist monks seated on low examples. Prior to this time in early China, from the fifteenth century B.C. to the third century A.D., the Chinese knelt or sat cross-legged on low platforms covered with mats. During the Song dynasty (960–1279), the use of elevated furniture and the social practice of sitting with pendent legs became widespread and not limited to the elite and powerful. At this time, the design of the armchair with protruding crest rails became higher and more ergonomic (Berliner and Handler 1995, xxvii, 59).

Besides presenting a pleasing aesthetic, the upward curve of the protruding top rail serves a practical function. Originally, these chairs would have had padded cushions on the seat and a cloth draped over the top to ward away the cold. The upward curving ends were a means of keeping the cloth in place.

The armchairs are highlights from a small collection of Ming and Qing hardwood furniture at the Brooklyn Museum of Art and are a gift of the late noted connoisseur and dealer Alice Boney.

FZY

LITERATURE

Archives of Asian Art 1980, 118, fig. 6.

21

Large *Famille Rose* Vase

China, Qing dynasty, Kangxi to Yongzheng era, early 18th century

Porcelain with overglaze enamel decoration
H: 17 15/16 in. (45.6 cm.); DIAM: 7 1/4 in. (18.5 cm.)

32.1126, Gift of the Executors of the Estate of Colonel Michael Friedsam

Famille rose overglaze enamels initiated significant changes in Chinese porcelain decoration during the eighteenth century. The semi-opaque and opaque polychrome enamels, namely a transparent colloidal gold-derived rose pink and opaque lead-arsenic white, expanded the color palette and offered the artisan an opportunity to treat the porcelain surface as if it were a painting. Graduated tones of color and the ability to shade and model surface decoration did not exist with earlier enamel pigments. This magnificently decorated mallet-shaped vase represents a very early example of *famille rose* enamel on porcelain, dating to around the 1720s. Introduced toward the end of the reign of the Kangxi emperor (1662–1722), this type of enamel pigment did not fully emerge until around 1730.

Adorning the exterior are two mythical birds, either a pair of phoenixes (*feng*) or a phoenix and her mate, the *huan*, in a rock-strewn landscape with peonies and peach blossoms. According to the ceramic specialist Fan Dongqing, this dramatic scene is a rebus expressing a wish for a rich and honorable household (*tang fugui*). The juxtaposition of the phoenix and peony usually symbolizes a happy life, while a phoenix and the *huan* connote a blissful marriage. Auspicious messages even extend to the decorative motifs on the vessel's shoulder and neck. Small groupings of antique bronzes, jades, paintings, and books within ovoid panels on the vessel's shoulder are known as the auspicious "Hundred Antiquities" (*bogu*). The figures in the narrative scenes encircling the neck convey wishes for a successful career and promotions in the near future.

FZY

LITERATURE

Finlay 1996, 78, fig. 33.

22

Bian Shoumin (Chinese, 1684–1752)

One Hundred Geese

China, Qing dynasty, late 17th to early 18th century
Hanging scroll, ink on paper
Overall: 124 × 49⅞ in. (315 × 126.7 cm.);
image: 77⅞ × 37⅞ in. (195.6 × 96.2 cm.)

1996.66, Purchased with funds given by Susan Beningson, Dr. and Mrs. Richard Dickes; gift of the Asian Art Council; Carll H. de Silver Fund

Wild geese and reeds (*luyan*) was a popular pictorial theme that emerged in tenth-century China. During the Song dynasty (960–1279) the image tended to be a poetic evocation of moods and sentiments associated with seasonal change; however, during the Yuan dynasty (1272–1368) the theme communicated didactic and social messages (Song 1996, 30). Wild geese in a natural landscape often reflected the scholar-gentleman's desire for reclusion, away from worldly affairs. Their freedom in the wild was a symbol of social transience.

The daily activities of geese – eating, calling, resting, and flying – as the "one hundred" geese in this Qing-dynasty (1644–1911) work show, carried a multitude of meanings. During the Song and Yuan dynasties, these four aspects of geese in Chan (Zen) Buddhism signified the four correct demeanors (*siyiwei*): correct dwelling, walking, sitting, and reclining. In Ming (1368–1644) court paintings, the four positions of the bird specified the natural order of things, as in the proper relationships among people. These might be the relationship between the emperor and his court or relationships between friends.

Painting geese was a specialty of Bian Shoumin, a painter, calligrapher, and poet. A native of Huai-an, Jiangsu province, Bian was best known for employing the splashed ink (*pomo*) technique in representing geese amid reeds. His association with this subject matter also extended to the name of his residence, "the library amid reeds." It was here that many celebrities sought the artist called "the nobleman of Huai-an."

This hanging scroll is unusual in its monumental scale. Typically, Bian's paintings are more intimate since his format of choice was the album leaf. Here numerous geese are sensitively represented in monochrome ink. Set in a soft, misty landscape of water and reeds, more than seventy-five geese are portrayed in the four basic positions. The large size of the work may provide a clue to its function, perhaps as a birthday painting, since the subject matter and the number of geese convey auspicious connotations.

FZY

23

Shrine with an Image of a Bodhisattva

China, Qing dynasty, Qianlong era (1736–1795)
Shrine: cloisonné enamel on copper alloy; image: bronze or copper with semi-precious stones
Overall: 25⁹⁄₁₆ × 9¹³⁄₁₆ × 19 in. (64.9 × 24.9 × 48.3 cm.)

09.520a, b, Gift of Samuel P. Avery, Jr.

An amalgam of Chinese and non-Chinese traditions is demonstrated in this lavishly designed Buddhist shrine with an image of a Tibetan bodhisattva. The canopy-like structure of the shrine is probably Indian in origin. As first recognized by former Assistant Curator Xiaoping Lin, the form of the shrine corresponds to a well-known baldachino in St. Peter's Basilica created by the Italian artist Gian Lorenzo Bernini (1598–1680). The imperial dragons curling around the four ornate columns, as well as the cloud forms and Buddhist elements decorating the cloisonné enameled surfaces, are Chinese motifs.

An artistic eclecticism was prevalent in the imperial arts during the reign of the Qianlong emperor (r. 1736–95). In the seventeenth and eighteenth centuries, Jesuit missionaries introduced European engravings to China, which inspired Chinese artists to incorporate Western designs into their work. Emperors also employed Jesuit artists and architects. Several imperial buildings synthesized European and Chinese architectural styles, such as the palace complexes of the Yuan Ming Yuan, or the Garden of Perfect Brightness outside of Beijing.

Even cloisonné technology was influenced by the Jesuits, as new techniques explored in palace workshops during the early eighteenth century were under the guidance of French and Italian Jesuit missionaries (Brinker and Lutz 1989, 142).

In many ways, the shrine and statue reflect Qianlong's reactions to foreign powers. The interest in things European and their incorporation into the Qing court arts and architecture had political repercussions on China's relations with European powers. The numerous Sino-Tibetan Buddhist sculptures and ritual paraphernalia produced for the Qianlong court may also reflect the political relationship between Tibetan lamas or relate to the Qing imperial patronage of Tibetan Buddhism.

When the statue and shrine entered the Museum's collection in 1909 as part of a large gift of Chinese imperial cloisonné from the New York art collector and dealer Samuel Putnam Avery, Jr., they were perceived as a pair. However, it has been since suggested that the bodhisattva may indeed predate its architectural surroundings and that the shrine was constructed intentionally for the statue.
FZY

LITERATURE

Getz 1912, 53, cat. no. 87.
Lin 1990, 30–37.

24

Qian Song (Chinese, 1807–1860)

Tianhuang Seal

China, Qing dynasty, first half of the 19th century
Soapstone
3¾ × 1¼ in. (9.5 × 3.2 cm.)

1996.122, Gift of Alastair B. Martin in memory of his beloved friend Ellen E. Schmidt

The meticulously carved miniature landscape on this seal is a well-known literary theme in China, referring to a poem known as the "Ode to the Red Cliff" (*Zhibi fu*). The scene of two gentlemen seated in a small boat before a towering cliff is taken from the famous prose-poem by Su Shi (1036–1101), a Northern Song (960–1127) scholar-gentleman, calligrapher, and poet. Written while the author was exiled in Huangzhou in Hubei province in 1082, the ode records a boat trip to the Red Cliff in Huanggang. The Red Cliff was also the site of a historically significant naval battle in 208; there the Han general Liu Bei (161–223) defeated Cao Cao (155–220), founder of the Kingdom of Wei, and prevented him from taking over the south of China. This battle was recounted in the historical dramatization *Romance of the Three Kingdoms* (*Sanguo zhi yanyi*).

Since the poem's genesis, the Red Cliff has been a literary theme popular in the visual realm. Decorating a variety of media, the theme is often the subject of paintings and represented on lacquers, ceramics, and cloisonnés, and in bamboo and soapstone carvings. Here the scholar's seal is carved from a *tianhuang*, or "field yellow" soapstone of the *shoushan* family, typically found in the rice fields of Fuzhou in the southern province of Fujian. With its characteristic warm, lustrous butterscotch color, the *tianhuang* stone has been a highly prized material for seals ever since the Ming dynasty (1368–1644).

The engraved inscriptions on the sides and base of the seal refer to the individuals who carved the landscape relief and the person to whom this seal was dedicated. The famous nineteenth-century seal-carver and calligrapher Qian Song carved the seal-script relief legend on the base for a Mr. Chunru. The legend, which reads "*xiangxue zhai*," may be translated as meaning "in the collection of Xiangxue zai." On one side of the seal there are two inscriptions. One is the name of the artist for the literary scene, Jingchuan, who may also be Yang I, a well-known seal carver. The other is a dedicatory inscription from Qian Song to a Mr. Chunru, which reads: "Dedicated to Chunru, the distinguished connoisseur, for eternity. Shugai." (Shugai is the sobriquet of Qian Song.)

FZY

LITERATURE

Brooklyn 1991, 110–11 [Poster].
Kuo 1992, 79, cat. no. 26.
Finlay 1996, 79, fig. 35.
Fane and Poster 2000, 60, fig. 37.
Yuan 2000, 86, fig. 3.

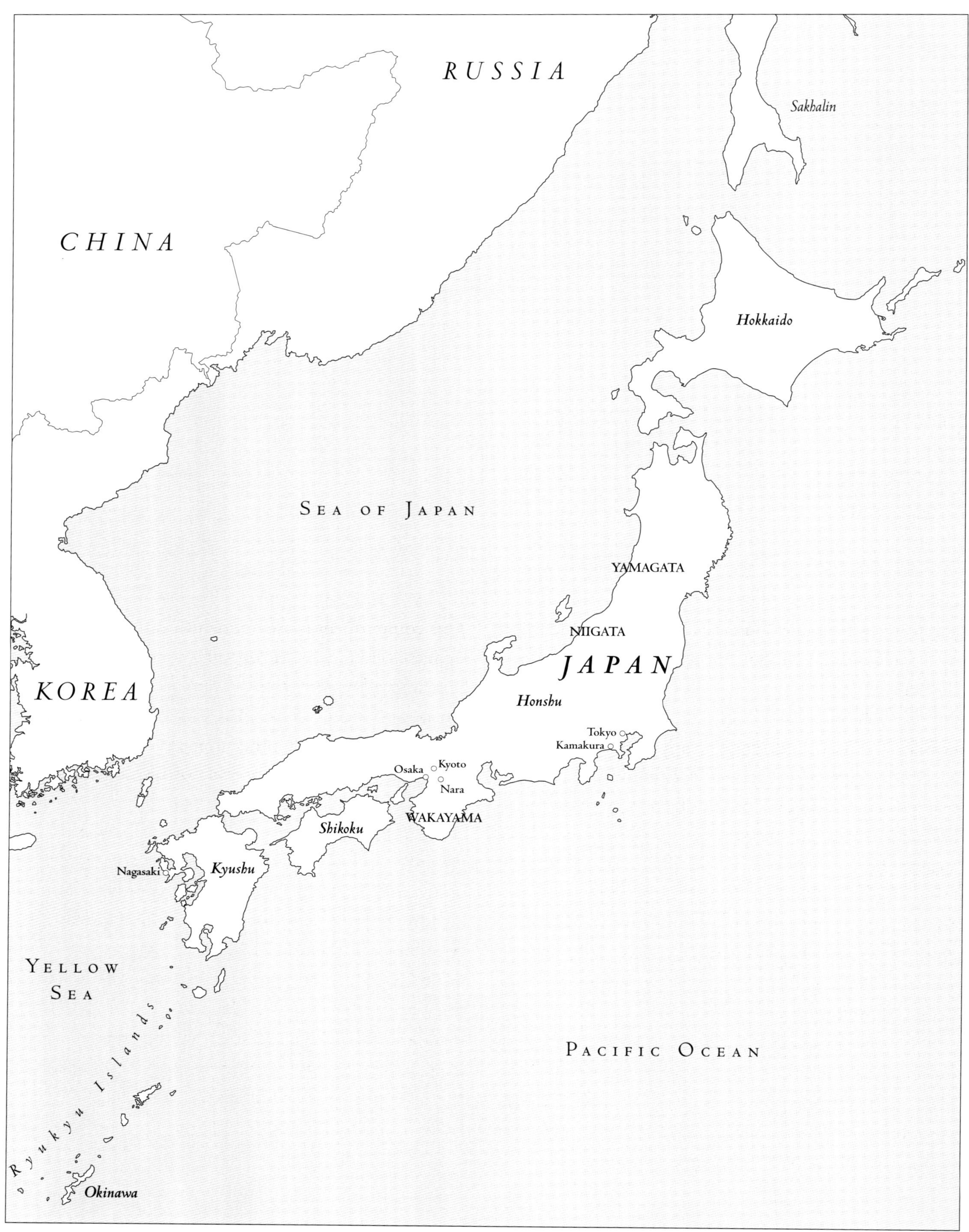
RUSSIA
Sakhalin
CHINA
Hokkaido
Sea of Japan
YAMAGATA
NIIGATA
JAPAN
KOREA
Honshu
Tokyo
Kamakura
Osaka
Kyoto
Nara
WAKAYAMA
Shikoku
Nagasaki
Kyushu
Yellow Sea
Ryukyu Islands
Pacific Ocean
Okinawa

Japan

Japanese art forms the largest area within the Asian art collection at the Brooklyn Museum of Art. Consisting of more than eight thousand objects, the Japanese art collection represents a wide range of media and styles and features the sacred, imperial, urban, and folk arts of Japan from the Jōmon period (10,500–400 B.C.) to the present day.

The Museum has an extensive history of cultural exchange with Japan beginning early in Stewart Culin's (1858–1929) tenure as Curator of Ethnology. Culin made three expeditions to Japan from 1909 to 1912 to build the collection. Donors during the same period, such as the Brooklyn industrialist Frederic B. Pratt (1865–1945), who traveled to Japan in 1894, began contributing some of the Museum's most important Japanese works. The early seventeenth-century genre screen of *A Cherry Blossom Viewing Picnic* (see no. 33) is a prime example of Pratt's gifts.

The Japanese art collection is also noted for its outstanding woodblock prints. These range from *ukiyo-e* works including the distinguished Torii School actor prints and a rare complete set of the *One Hundred Famous Views of Edo* by the nineteenth-century artist Utagawa Hiroshige (see no. 40) to twentieth-century works called *sōsaku hanga* ("creative prints").

Representing the contemporary artistic traditions in Japan has been a long-standing aim of the BMA. This commitment is exemplified within the area of Japanese ceramics by the ongoing collection of works by renowned masters and the younger generation of artists who are currently active in Japan. The folk art tradition in Japan is another strength of the collection. This group of works, consisting of textiles, basketry, and furniture, is unusually extensive and well preserved.

Exceptional within the Japanese collection is the collection of artifacts of the Ainu, a separate indigenous people of northern Japan. This collection reflects the broad range of interests of early curators at Brooklyn before the Museum became solely an arts institution in the 1930s. The largest and considered the finest of its type in North America, the Ainu collection includes utensils, ritual objects, and costumes that date primarily to the Museum expedition to Japan, Hokkaidō, and the Kurile Islands in 1912.

AGP

25

Haniwa Figure of a Shamaness

Japan, Kofun period, 5th–6th century
Earthenware with traces of red pigment
18 × 8¾ × 7½ in. (45.7 × 22.2 × 19 cm.)

79.278.1, Gift of Mr. and Mrs. Stanley Marcus

In the beginning of the fourth century, a group of people calling themselves the Yamato people migrated into Japan and Korea. The Yamato built mound tombs for their important dead, constructing the largest tombs for the emperors. The tomb chambers were filled with luxury goods meant to serve the deceased in the spirit world, artifacts nearly identical to those from Kaya Federation (42 B.C.–A.D. 562) and Silla Kingdom (57 B.C.–A.D. 668) tombs in southern Korea. *Haniwa*, however, are unique to Japan. They are large, hollow earthenware cylinders, either plain or shaped like weapons, buildings, animals, or human figures. This *haniwa* represents a Shintō priestess who would have presided over the funeral ceremony of a Yamato (Japan) chieftain.

The figure is hand-built of clay and low-fired. She wears a coatlike flared robe, closed diagonally across the chest, which passes over her right shoulder and leaves her left shoulder and breast uncovered. She wears a string of oval, circular, and rectangular beads around her neck and a flat, crescent-shaped headdress. Her stance and facial features contribute to the power of this object: her eyes are hollow and open, her mouth is a horizontal cut, and her eyebrow ridge is raised and demarcated by red pigment. Her ears are flat appendages.

Red pigment striations mark her lower robe, neck, cheeks, eyebrows, and forehead. The figure is fragmentary: the arms are missing, and like almost all extant *haniwa*, the figure has been reassembled from shards.
AGP

LITERATURE

Archives of Asian Art 1981, 97, fig. 4.
Brooklyn 1988, 94, cover and cat. no. 61.
Brooklyn 1997, 42.

21.240.1

26

Kongō-kai Mandara and Taizō-kai Mandara

Japan, Kamakura period, 13th century
Pair of hanging scrolls, ink and color and cut gold-leaf on silk
Overall: 84½ × 50⅛ in. (214.6 × 127.3 cm.) each; image: 46¹¹⁄₁₆ × 38⅞ in. (119 × 98.7 cm.) each

21.240.1, .2, Museum Collection Fund

This pair of *mandara,* or mandalas, depicts the principal cosmic diagrams venerated in Esoteric Buddhism in Japan, particularly of the Shingon (True Word) sect. Esoteric Buddhism, introduced from China by Kūkai (774–835), founder of the Shingon sect in Japan, promises that Enlightenment is possible in one's lifetime without long years of waiting for rebirth in a distant paradise. Part of the means of attaining enlightenment requires a study of revealed mysteries and the cosmology represented by the mandalas. Following these teachings, *mandara* demonstrate a pervasive symmetry of composition, conceptually representing the theme of Heaven.

The central deity of Shingon is Dainichi (S: Mahavairochana), the Cosmic Buddha of Infinite Light, whose manifestations occupy key places in this pair of *mandara* based on Buddhist texts (sutras). In the *mandara* of the *Kongō-Kai* (Diamond World) (21.240.1; left), as in other versions, Dainichi occupies the top center position of nine squares. The squares contain

21.240.2

arrangements of deities and are framed by borders containing deities and ritual symbols, most commonly *kongō-sho* (S: *vajra*) or thunderbolt-scepters.

This hieratic framework is also present in the accompanying *Taizō-kai* (Womb World) *mandara* (21.240.2; right), in which Dainichi is seated in an open lotus flower at the center of the diagram, surrounded by the Buddhas of the directions. The *mandara* as a pair form the *Ryōkai Mandara* (Mandala of the Two Worlds).

The works are monumental in scale and meticulously detailed in a bright palette of green, red, blue, and yellow, highlighted with minuscule strips of cut gold-leaf (*kirikane*). The BMA *mandara* are considered to be among the finest early painted *mandara* of this period. They were purchased from the estate of the American artist John La Farge (1835–1910), who acquired them in Japan during a three-month journey there in 1886 with the historian Henry Adams (1838–1918).
AGP

LITERATURE

Matsuoka 1930, 130–32.
Brooklyn 1967, 170–73.
Varley 1977, fig. 20.
Poster 1989, 32, figs. 4–5.
Guth 1995, 29–30, figs. 2–3.
Brooklyn 1997, 41.
Leidy and Thurman 1998, cat. nos. 41–42, 116–17.
Lorber 2001, fig. 14.

27

Tale of the Wisteria Robe

Japan, Kamakura period, 15th century
Handscroll, ink on mica-flecked paper
$6\frac{5}{8} \times 405\frac{1}{4}$ in. (16.8 × 1029.3 cm.)

81.198, Anonymous gift

The *Tale of the Wisteria Robe* (*Fuji no koromo monogatari*) is a narrative scroll by an unknown author that traces the trials and tribulations of its protagonist, Yamabushi, from the internecine rivalry with his siblings over his father's succession, to his life as a peripatetic mountain ascetic (the literal meaning of Yamabushi), to his reunion with his three children after a lengthy separation. The wisteria robe of the title refers to a fragrant garment associated with Yamabushi that signals his presence in key episodes throughout the narrative and symbolically invokes his true identity as a nobleman despite his humble appearance as a wanderer. In this penultimate scene in the scroll, Yamabushi's children mourn on receiving news of his death. Subtle details convey the melancholy atmosphere of the household. At right, a son identified as Chūnagon (a high-ranking courtier) faces a Buddhist priest who has borne the sad tidings and wipes away tears with his sleeve while holding a letter that demonstrates the strong bond between father and son. In the next room, his half sister (with her back to the viewer) similarly grieves the loss of her father.

Tale of the Wisteria Robe exemplifies the genre of monochromatic narrative painting known as *hakubyō*, or white drawing. While *hakubyō* adopted compositional techniques common to polychrome narrative painting, the elimination of color opened up new expressive possibilities and allowed it to develop a visual language all its own. Important features of this genre include an emphatic representation of the long, flowing hair of the female figures, depicted with glossy black ink, and an attention to the details of interior decor. An abstract interplay of forms results from the contrast between the

Detail

ruler-drawn architectural lines that structure the compositions and the ghostly, curvilinear forms of the figures contained within them.

The unpainted areas of *hakubyō* images invited the addition of inscriptions, which supplement the text that precedes each painting and imbue the narrative with lively dialogue. The Brooklyn scroll is especially notable for its abundant use of such dialogic inscriptions, whose cascading vertical columns not only enhance the scroll's visual appeal, but also document the spoken Japanese of the early Muromachi period (1333–1573). Originally one lengthy scroll, *Tale of the Wisteria Robe* was subsequently dispersed. The Brooklyn scroll contains the second half of the tale, while most of the first half remains in a Japanese private collection. Fragments from the scroll can be found in both the Freer Gallery of Art in Washington, D.C., and the Cleveland Museum of Art. At almost seventeen centimeters in height, it is a rare example in an American collection of a "miniature handscroll," one of a number of highly personal and sophisticated handscrolls measuring half the height of regular handscrolls that were produced and appreciated by elite members of Japanese society during the medieval era.

MM

LITERATURE

Narazaki 1960, 305–11, pls. 2–3.
Shinto 1970.
Addiss 1980, cat. no. 36.
Itō Y. 1990, 151–85.

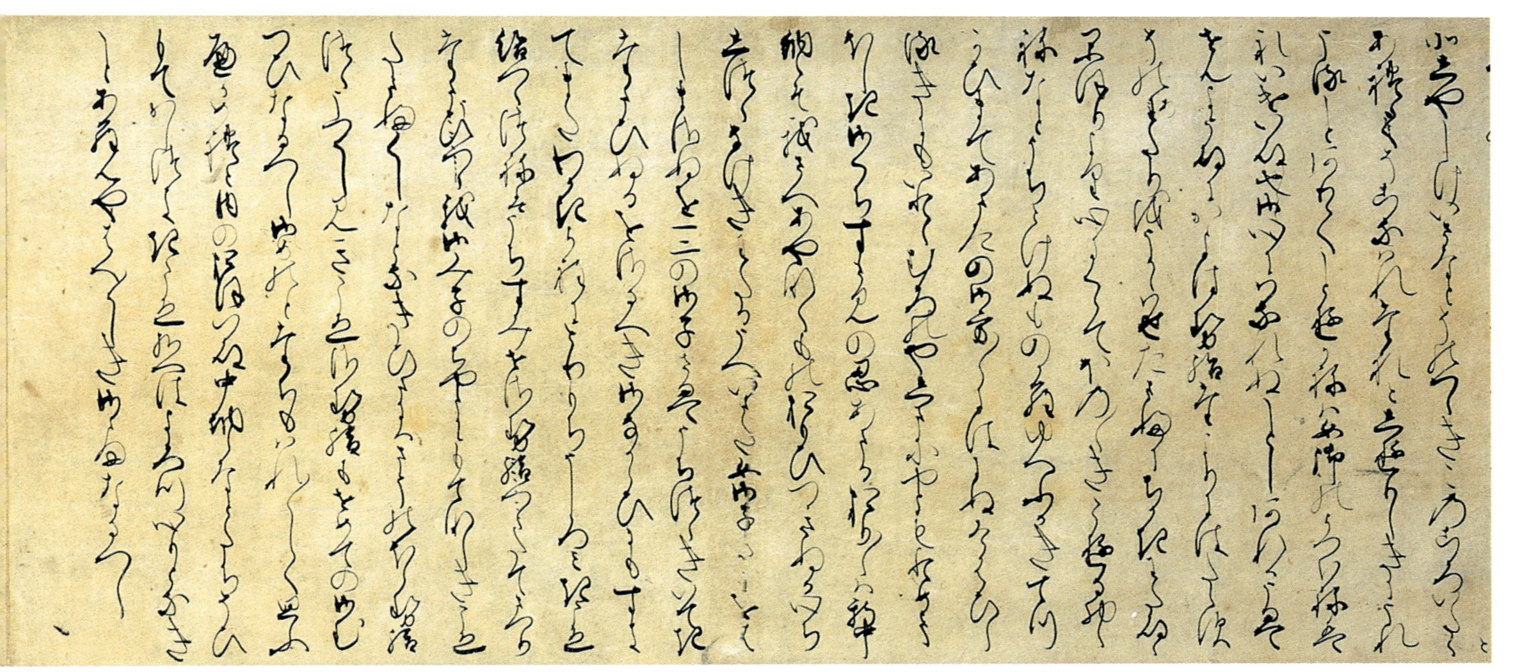

28

Head of a Guardian

Japan, Kamakura period, 13th century
Hinoki wood with color, inlaid rock-crystal eyes, and filigree metal crown
22 1/16 × 10 1/4 × 13 15/16 in. (56.1 × 26.1 × 35.4 cm.)

86.21, Gift of Mr. and Mrs. Alastair B. Martin, the Guennol Collection

This over-life-size head is from a figure of one of the Shitennō, the four guardian kings of the cardinal directions. Acquired by the Guennol Collection in 1954, the head was at one time owned by the Nara temple Kōfuku-ji. The fiery eyes, furrowed brow, prominent nose, and open mouth present a ferocious mien typical of these Heavenly Guardians, whose role was to protect the temple's sacred precincts.

The vitality of its expression is emblematic of the role of Kōfuku-ji in the brief but pivotal time during the early part of the Kamakura period (1185–1333) when the Nara temples were rebuilt and refurbished following a period of political instability. At this time, a renaissance of naturalism in sculptural style also occurred as sculptors such as the early thirteenth-century masters Unkei (1148?–1223) and Kaikei (d. 1223) and their followers created portraits and divine images with a new realism that was an amalgam of previous Nara styles. This piece compares in expression and detail to the Shitennō carved for the Nan'en-dō (Southern Octagonal Hall) at Kōfuku-ji in 1189 by Kōkei (1151–1200), an earlier Kamakura artist from the late twelfth century. The work itself can be dated to the thirteenth century by the decorative techniques applied and the realism of the countenance.

The head is carved from two blocks of wood, into which the topknot is inserted. The inset rock-crystal eyes are painted on the reverse and each detail of the physiognomy and headdress is deftly carved and finished with polychrome, presenting an expressive realism. Examination of the interior has revealed graffiti of the painter. The filigree crown is a later replacement.
AGP

LITERATURE

Tokyo Bijutsu Gakkō 1933, 7, 16, pl. 78.
Mayuyama 1966, 334, pl. 63.
Rubin 1975, 283–86.
Poster 1989, 28–29, fig. 1.
Poster 1996, 67, fig. 12.
Brooklyn 1997, 42.
Fane and Poster 2000, 47, cat. no. 25.

29

Gyokuen Bonpō (Japanese, c. 1348–c. 1420)

Orchids, Bamboo, and Thorns

Japan, Muromachi period, early 15th century
Pair of hanging scrolls, ink on Korean paper
Overall: 72½ × 58 in. (147.3 × 44.5 cm.) each;
image: 25 × 12¼ in. (63.5 × 31.1 cm.) each

73.123.1, Gift of the Roebling Society; 73.123.2, Asian Art Acquisition Fund

Ink-wash paintings of orchids have been fashionable in China since at least the thirteenth century. Scholar-artists trained in the Confucian classics associated the plant with Confucian ideals of refinement and virtue. Chan (Zen) priests, for whom orchids carried no symbolism, also liked to paint them. According to the fourteenth-century Japanese compendium of poems, *Kūgeshū* (1343), the orchid in poetry symbolized virtue in the face of suffering, as well as uncompromising moral character and loyalty (Shimizu and Wheelwright 1976, 227).

During the first half of the fourteenth century, large numbers of Japanese Zen student-monks went to China, where many of them mastered Chinese literature and calligraphy as well as Zen philosophy. Gyokuen Bonpō came from the next generation of monks, fewer of whom studied in China, and he never made the trip to the continent. Nevertheless, he became quite famous in Japan for his skill in Chinese poetry, Chinese calligraphy, and ink paintings of orchids. His paintings of wild orchids followed the style of the Chinese master Xuechuang (or Puming; active 14th century) and the Japanese Tesshū Tokusai (active 1342, d. 1366).

Bonpō was one of the great *bunjin-sō* or literati monks of the early fifteenth century. After serving the priest Shun'oku Myōha (1311–1388) first at the Tōshō-ji monastery in Kamakura and then at Nanzen-ji in Kyoto, he became the abbot of Kennin-ji and later of Nanzen-ji. The shogun Ashikaga Yoshimochi (1386–1428) was his patron. His signature on the left hanging scroll (73.123.2) in grass-style calligraphy reads *"Gyokuen ransha hitsu,"* "painted by Gyokuen, the Lazy One" (ibid.).
AGP

LITERATURE

Archives of Asian Art 1974–75, 114, fig. 5.
Shimizu and Wheelwright 1976, 244–47, 277, cat. no. 34.
Brindle and White 1982, 12, 17, fig. iv.
Brooklyn 1988, 96, cat. no. 63.
Stanley-Baker 1992, 12, 33, pl. 4-d.

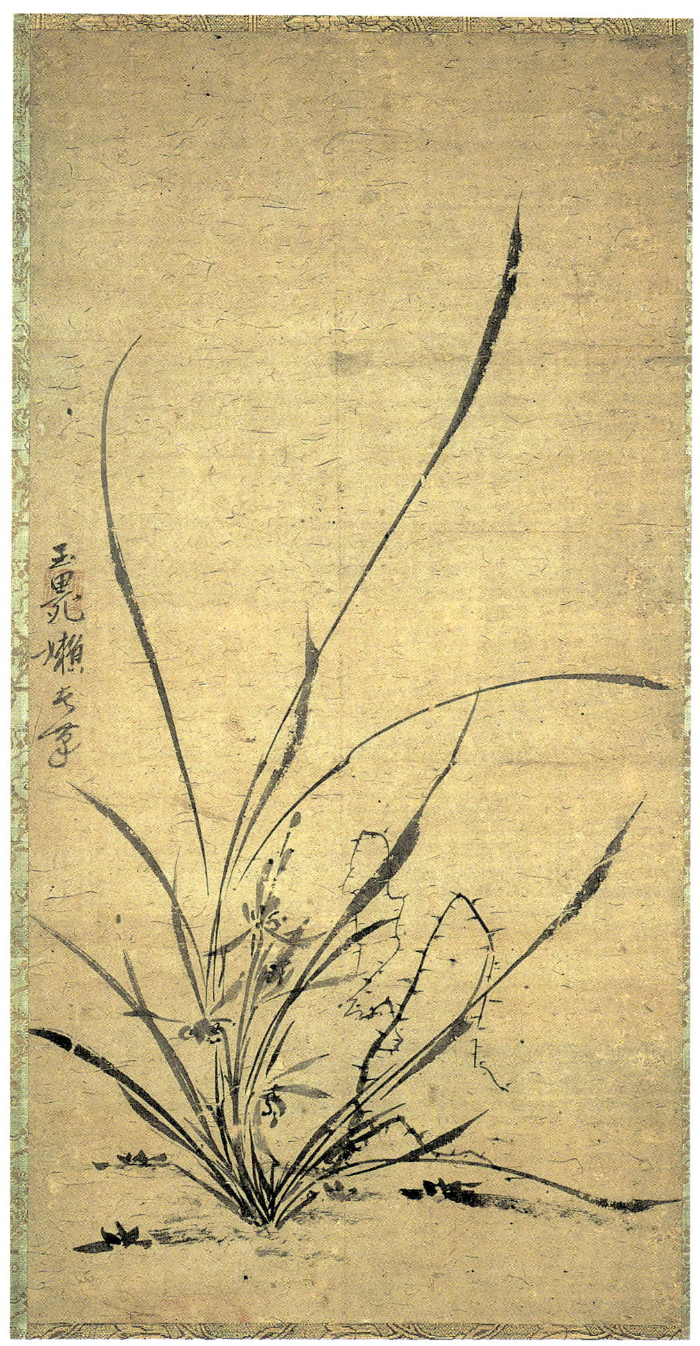

73.123.2

73.123.1

30

Negoro Wine Ewer

Japan, Muromachi period, 15th century
Lacquer on wood core
H: 12 in. (30.5 cm.); DIAM: 9 in. (22.9 cm.)

74.4, Gift of Robert B. Woodward, by exchange; Asian Art Acquisition Fund

Following the prototype of the Chinese *meiping* ceramic form from Song-dynasty (960–1279) China, this wine bottle has a softly rounded shape that expands from its high shoulders and tapers down to a flat, disc-shaped circular foot. It is covered with a monochromatic red-orange lacquer partially rubbed to expose a black lacquer undercoating.

Lacquer was used in Japan throughout its history to decorate household furnishings, musical instruments, and other utilitarian objects. It also became a popular and practical material for the serving utensils used in Buddhist temples. A wide variety of lacquering techniques evolved in Japan, including that of Negoro ware, in which red lacquer was applied over a black lacquer undercoating. As a consequence of regular use, the black lacquer shows through in some places, resulting in abstract patterning of black and red, with unique asymmetrical patterns and color combinations. This effect came to be prized in Japan over the centuries, making Negoro lacquer extremely sought after by collectors.

Negoro wares were originally produced in the late twelfth century for everyday and religious use by the monks of Negoro-ji in ancient Kii province (present-day Wakayama prefecture). Their forms are simple and restrained and their usage purely functional. They reflect the austerity of the Zen Buddhists and are modeled on Chinese prototypes. Negoro-ji was a temple known along with Enryaku-ji at Mt. Hiei in Kyoto and Kongōbu-ji at Mt. Kōya (also in Wakayama prefecture) for its soldier-monks and religious strength.

AGP

LITERATURE

Archives of Asian Art 1976–77, 107, fig. 8.
Ramamrutham 1989, 77, fig. 4.
Dunn 2001, 70, 75, pl. 28.

31

Export Lacquer Portable Desk (*Barqueño*)

Japan, Momoyama period, late 16th–early 17th century
Black lacquer with gold flecks, mother-of-pearl inlay, and metal fittings
17 15/16 × 13 3/8 × 24 1/2 in. (44 × 34 × 62.2 cm.)

84.69.1, Gift of Dr. and Mrs. John Lyden

A large body of lacquer wares produced in Japan for the Portuguese market during the brief four decades of the Momoyama period (1573–1615) survives. Catering to the demand for export lacquerware from Japan, artisans created objects that were manufactured to Western specifications in both function and design. Such works, including this *barqueño*, or portable desk, have been described in Japan as *nanban* (literally, "southern barbarian"), a term referring to things that are European or European-influenced.

This type of cabinet was used as a portable writing desk. When opened, it reveals drawers arranged around a central recessed niche. The Brooklyn desk displays a synthesis of indigenous Japanese techniques and decorative motifs obviously non-Japanese in inspiration, with forms adapted to the Western market. For example, the form of the central compartment recalls the *mihrab* arch, the prayer niche in a mosque's wall facing Mecca. A tree of life, a motif not found in the Japanese aesthetic vocabulary, is painted in gold, meandering over the back panel and door interiors of the cabinet. Inspiration for these motifs can be traced to Gujarat in western India, where they were most likely transmitted eastward via the Portuguese trade.

The lacquer technique is typically Japanese. Intricate details are rendered through the technical and artistic virtuosity of mother-of-pearl inlay and borders embellished with gold-flecked lacquer. An impressive decoration of interlocking folding fans and family crests appears on the front, top, and sides of the desk.

AGP

LITERATURE

Ramamrutham 1989, 76–77, fig. 6.

32

Attributed to Kaihō Yūshō (Japanese, 1533–1615)

Drying Fishnets in the Four Seasons

Japan, Momoyama period, early 17th century
Pair of six-panel screens, ink, color, and gold on paper
Overall: 66 1/16 × 148 1/2 in. (168.1 × 377.2 cm.) each;
image: 59 3/16 × 141 1/2 in. (150.4 × 359.4 cm.) each

59.7.1, .2, Carll H. de Silver Fund and Ella C. Woodward Memorial Fund

One of the most important works in the Brooklyn Museum of Art's Asian art collection is this pair of folding screens depicting fishnets hung up to dry along a seashore. Horizontal bands represent sandbars and clouds, which contrast with fishnets drying on wood posts placed in the immediate foreground, interspersed with green reeds. Subtle details of boats in the distance are painted in gold on the blue ground and enhanced with gold wash, which suggests water and mist. The passage of seasons from spring and summer (59.7.1) moves from the right to the snow-topped bamboo poles draped with nets at the far left (59.7.2). The concentration of pictorial elements at the outside ends of the painting with open space at the center is a typical convention in many of Yūshō's screen compositions.

The image in the screens symbolizes "Fishing Village in Evening Glow," one of the Eight Views of the Xiao and Xiang Rivers (J: *Shōshō hakkei*), a traditional theme developed in the Five Dynasties era in China (907–60). The eight scenes associate time, season, and mood with the area where the Xiao and Xiang Rivers meet in Hunan province. The theme was popular among Southern Song (1127–1279) artists, originally as an evocation of exile and political isolation. After Zen culture was introduced into Japan during the thirteenth century, the subject and its poetic meaning were welcomed by Japanese artists, forming a thematic basis for many idealized landscapes. In this composition, the absence of boatmen or other human figures suggests that the artist has adapted the established subject.

59.7.2

During the Momoyama period (1573–1615) in Japan, the great wealth assembled by the warriors and merchants was reflected in the growth of decorative screen painting, in which exquisite design and monumental scale received their fullest expression. The subject of the Xiao and Xiang Rivers realized its greatest decorative potential in the folding screen format, combining a celebrated Chinese poetic theme with the technique and style of Japanese screen painting.

Kaihō Yūshō was affiliated with the Zen temple Tōfuku-ji in Kyoto, where his exposure to Chinese paintings has been acknowledged. Altogether there are eleven known pairs of screens of this subject attributed to Yūshō or his studio. Since the screens are unsigned and have no seals of the artist, several scholars have questioned whether Yūshō or artists of his studio painted the work. The BMA screens compare to an important pair of *Drying Fishnet* screens in the Imperial Household Collection, Tokyo.

AGP

LITERATURE

Hisamatsu 1987.
Kokka 1942, 375, pls. 6–7.
Osaka City Museum 1942, pls. 17–18.
Paine and Soper 1955, 96.
Archives of the Chinese Art Society of America 1960, 65, fig. 2.
Brooklyn 1967, 174–75.
Murase 1971, 78–81, cat. no. 16.
Soper 1971, 43, 69.
Chiba City Museum of Art 1996, 46–47, 214, no. 13.

59.7.1

33

A Cherry Blossom Viewing Picnic

Japan, Edo period, Kan'ei era (1624–44)
Four-panel folding screen, ink, color and gold on paper
Overall: 39⅜ × 105⅞ in. (100 × 269 cm.);
image: 33⁹⁄₁₆ × 86½ in. (85.2 × 219.7 cm.)

39.87, Gift of Frederic B. Pratt

A Cherry Blossom Viewing Picnic, painted by an anonymous artist during the early seventeenth century, is an important document of Japan's early modern popular culture. The establishment of the new capital of Edo (modern-day Tokyo) in 1603 led to an era of political stability in Japan. The Edo period (1615–1868) witnessed tremendous economic development and social change, especially in the great cities of Edo, Kyoto, and Osaka. The retinues of the samurai elite, merchants, and artisans became powerful supporters of political activities, as well as patrons of a burgeoning urban artistic tradition. The new prosperity warranted new subjects in art, reflecting the fashionable entertainment activities of the townspeople and scenes of urban life.

The *Cherry Blossom Viewing* screen can be considered an archetype of *ukiyo-e* painting (literally, "pictures of the floating world"). The genre mainly consists of woodblock prints portraying popular actors, beautiful women, or famous sites in Japan, though many of these subjects and styles first appeared as large-scale paintings. Artists gradually focused on specific scenes of daily activities, especially entertainment in the pleasure quarters. Rich costumes, particularly of actors, courtesans, and even the lowest-echelon bathhouse girls, are portrayed in meticulous detail. Cherry blossom viewing was a popular diversion of the urban establishment, and the Brooklyn screen is one of the earliest known examples of this subject.

The Brooklyn screen portrays a procession of highly fashionable men and women shown against a plain background with gilded and embossed clouds. The women, dressed in beautiful variegated kimonos and playfully carrying a long pipe and decorative swords, are pleasure women (*yūjo*). The central figure wearing the red silk kimono, or *kosode*, is the most important individual in the group. While various levels of meaning concerning the scene exist, romance is implied by the action of a woman extending a branch of cherry blossoms with a poem strip (*tanzaku*) to the men following behind. Two of the men can be identified by their double swords as lower-class samurai. Representing the clientele that frequented the pleasure quarters, they are emblematic of the hedonism during the peaceful Edo period. The screen was originally part of a pair that we know was separated during the late nineteenth century. Its counterpart, which depicts the higher class of pleasure women from the Yoshiwara district seated beneath a cherry tree, is in a Japanese private collection.

AGP

LITERATURE

Brooklyn 1967, 180–83.
Takeda T. 1967.
Hashimoto 1968, 53–54.
Yawata 1975.
Takeda H. 1977, 50–51, pl. 30.
Kobayashi 1979, pl. 9.
Okudaira 1982, 23–28.
Kobayashi 1981, pl. 5.
Itō H. 1984, 77–95, no. 35.
Brooklyn 1988, 98–99, cat. no. 65.
Goodwin 1988, 40–49.
Kennedy 1990.
Murase 1990, 169, 174–75.
Kobayashi and Kano 1992, 142, fig. 92.
Satō 1993, 33, 46–47, fig. 31.
Poster 1996, 62–62, cat. no. 4.
Brooklyn 1997, 43.
Nagata 1997, 22–23, cat. no. 1.
Tokugawa Museum of Art 1997, 136–37.
Poster 1999, 15, fig. 1.
Shibundō 2000, fig. 5.

34

Views In and Around Kyoto

Japan, Edo period, c. 1645
Pair of six-panel screens, ink, color, and gold on paper
62 × 144 in. (157.5 × 365.8 cm.) each

54.144a, b, Gift of W. W. Hoffman

The Brooklyn screens are a well-known example of Japanese genre painting, a popular expression of the long-standing *meisho-e* (pictures of famous places) tradition. In the sixteenth and seventeenth centuries, such screens depicting the urban landscapes of Kyoto were produced to document the customs, popular destinations, and activities of Japan's ancient capital: hence, their names, *Views In and Around Kyoto* (*Rakuchū rakugai*).

The screens mark the time when Kyoto was being rebuilt and expanded following a period of war-ravaged destruction. Typically, Kyoto is presented as a panoramic overview, dominated by the area of Higashiyama (Eastern Hills). In the BMA screens, the central attraction is the lively procession and floats of the Gion Festival. This depiction of the annual summer event in the city's merchant district helps to date the screens by the procession's path before the outscaled Imperial Palace at the center-left of the left screen (54.144a). Another unusual event included here is the "women's Kabuki" depicted in the Imperial Palace enclosure in the fifth panel of the left screen.

The right screen (54.144b) shows the western part of Kyoto, including such places as Nijō Palace, the Kyoto residence of the ruling Tokugawa family, and the Katsura Palace, one of Kyoto's private imperial retreats, which was built in the first quarter of the seventeenth century.

In seventeenth-century versions of the *Views In and Around Kyoto*, the scenes emphasized tend to include

54.144a

those appreciated by Japanese commoners, as well as the nobility and samurai; thus, the commission of these screens is unknown. The rich colors and lavish use of gold with raised patterns in the scallop-edged clouds suggest the possibility of a special commission, but neither an official atelier nor a patron is known, and so the two screens are thought to be the work of anonymous town-painters, called *machi-eshi*.
AGP

LITERATURE
Murase 1971, 110–17, cat. no. 22.
Varley 1977, fig. 42.

54.144b

35

Soga Shōhaku (Japanese, 1730–1781)

River Landscape

Japan, Edo period, 18th century
Hanging scroll, ink on paper
Overall: 83⅝ × 26$^{15}/_{16}$ in. (212.4 × 68.3 cm.);
image: 54¾ × 21⅞ in. (139.1 × 55.5 cm.)

1998.39, Gift of the Asian Art Council in memory of Council Member Barbara Young

This painting depicts a distant retreat, possibly a Buddhist temple, within a remote river landscape. Boats on the river, wild geese descending in the distance, and figures (fishermen, monks, or perhaps even travelers around the precipitous mountain peaks) evoke a serene atmosphere. Although suggestive of summer, such landscapes in Japanese painting traditionally signify the passing seasons. The painting may also depict the celebrated Eight Views of the Xiao and Xiang Rivers (J: *Shōshō hakkei*), a popular landscape subject for Chinese-style painting in Japan, often compressed into one scene.

This scene is typical of ink painting in the Muromachi period (1333–1573); it is from earlier *suiboku-ga* (ink paintings) that Soga Shōhaku drew his inspiration for this work. The composition is characteristic of older landscapes with its strong asymmetry, expanses of voids, deep recession, and high vantage point. Yet Shōhaku conceived it in a more contemporary manner, as a series of dark, superimposed, contrasting ink tones, a composition with a remarkably powerful light and dark structure and sense of consistent spatial recession.

Soga Shōhaku, Itō Jakuchū (1716–1800), and Nagasawa Rosetsu (1754–1799) are known as the "three eccentrics" of the eighteenth century. Of them, Shōhaku took eccentricity to the extreme in both his lifestyle and his art. His surname "Soga" refers to an important monk painter of the Zen monastery of Daitoku-ji in Kyoto, Soga Jasoku (Dasoku; d. 1483), whose style served as the basis of an informal lineage of ink painters through the sixteenth and seventeenth centuries. Although Shōhaku first studied the painting methods of the Kano School, he soon found them ill-suited to his restless style and turned to the antique styles of the Soga School instead. He attempted to affiliate himself with that line, incorporating Dasoku's name in signatures and seals. The *River Landscape* signature reads "Dasokuken Shōhaku."

Shōhaku's assiduous study of past masters enabled him to revitalize earlier composition techniques ignored by contemporary painters of decorative screens. The restraint evidenced in this work is recognized in Soga Shōhaku's later works, which date from the 1770s.
AGP

36

Kitagawa Utamaro (Japanese, 1753–1806)

Courtesans Strolling Beneath Cherry Trees Before the Daikokuya Teahouse

Japan, Edo period, probably 1789

Color woodblock print

Ōban triptych, $15\frac{3}{8} \times 10\frac{3}{8}$ in. (39.1 × 26.4 cm.) each

1995.137a–c, Gift of the Estate of Charles A. Brandon, by exchange; purchased with funds given by Mr. and Mrs. Richard M. Danziger, Joan Easton, Mrs. Myron S. Falk, Jr., George S. Friedman, Mr. and Mrs. Mark Kingdon, Klaus F. Naumann, Robert Rosenkranz, and Mr. and Mrs. David Young; Asian Art Acquisition Fund

The image of the Green Houses of the Yoshiwara, the red-light district of Edo (present-day Tokyo) from the seventeenth through nineteenth centuries, was shaped largely by the work of the Japanese master Kitagawa Utamaro. This triptych exemplifies the combined talents of Utamaro and his publisher Tsutaya Jūzaburō (1748–1797), two of the most important figures in the world of *ukiyo-e* (pictures of the floating world) in the late eighteenth century. The print also provides a sumptuous evocation of the Yoshiwara spirit of extravagant excess, with courtesans and their attendants dressed in brilliant brocades and admiring cherry blossoms that were specially transported to the Yoshiwara each spring.

The Yoshiwara was a walled enclosure surrounding the so-called Five Streets in the city of Edo. It was a section of the city where gaudy display prevailed and the normal edicts limiting conspicuous consumption by townsmen did not. The Yoshiwara was also where men were judged by their wealth and stylish flair and not by their standing in the feudal hierarchy that governed Japanese society elsewhere. It was this Yoshiwara and the women who resided in it that became Utamaro's primary focus.

In this outstanding design, three high-ranking courtesans are shown in formal poses, reflecting the strict etiquette expected even for prostitutes. In a novel relaxation of censorship, this print presents the courtesans, child attendants known as *kamuro*, and apprentices, or *shinzō*, all

named in the inscriptions. The women are identified as Nabiki (Wakamatsuya), at the right; Yoshino (Wakamatsuya), at the center; and Kasugano (Ōgiya), at the left.

Part of the festivities for viewing cherry blossoms in spring is the practice of attaching written poems to cherry trees. Here in the right-hand sheet is a poem on the *tanzaku* hanging from the cherry tree by the noted poet Yadoya Meshimori (1753–1830). Later known as Rokujuen, founder of the Go-gawa poetry group, Yadoya was an important figure in the world of *kyōka* poetry. Just one year before the publication of this triptych, he had collaborated with Utamaro on the exquisite *Book of Insects* (*Ehon mushi erami*) also published by Tsutaya Jūzaburō.

The research of Asano Shūgo reveals that the scene in the print specifically represents the Daikokuya Teahouse, a popular restaurant of the Yoshiwara district in Edo. It was in such teahouses that courtesans would frequently await the arrival of their patrons. After the great 1787 fire consumed most of the area, Daikokuya moved from Nakanochō to Ageyachō street and apparently reopened in the spring of 1789. Perhaps commissioned as an advertisement for this event, the print is of special historical significance.

AGP

LITERATURE

Mirviss 1995, cat. no. 3.

37

Tōshūsai Sharaku (Japanese, active 1794–95)

Actor Segawa Kikunojō III as Oshizu

Japan, Edo period, 1794
Color woodblock print
14 7/8 × 9 1/4 in. (37.8 × 23.5 cm.)

42.83, Gift of Frederic B. Pratt

This print of the actor Segawa Kikunojō III (1715–1810) is one of the most celebrated portraits of the *onnagata* (male actor in a female role) by the late eighteenth-century artist Tōshūsai Sharaku. It portrays the sardonic expression of a character in the Genroku era (1688–1709) play, *Hanaayame Bunroku Soga* (The Iris saga of the Bunroku era), a drama that retells the true story of the vengeance of ten brothers for their father's assassination in 1701. Oshizu, the wife of Tanabe Bunzō, is shown. The play was performed in May 1794 at the Miyako-za, one of three theaters presenting Kabuki in Edo's entertainment district.

The psychological drama of this subject is suggested by the powerful image of a close-up bust portrait (*ōkubi-e*), one of the hallmarks of Sharaku's actor prints. Sharaku utilized this format to bring life and the personality of the performer to the image as well as to document the role performed. The mica ground is another distinctive feature of Sharaku's portraits; his signature and publisher's seal were stamped over the mica following the printing. As with all of Sharaku's prints, this bears the ivy-leaf emblem of the publisher, Tsutaya Jūzaburō (1748–1797).

The artist was active for only ten months, from May 1794 to January 1795 in the lunar year, during which he produced 140 actor prints. After that he disappeared, and no other works with that artist's signature are known. The mystery of his identity is still unsolved. It has been said that Sharaku was a Noh actor, Saitō Jūrōbei, who served the lord of Awa, a province of Shikoku Island near Osaka, but this has not been documented. Many theories have been proposed as well to show that Sharaku was a professional artist.

AGP

LITERATURE

Brooklyn 1988, 97, cat. no. 64.
Tōbu Museum of Art 1995, 33, cat. no. 6.
Brooklyn 1997, 43.
Ōta Memorial Museum of Art 1999, 48, 102, cat. no. 40.

東洲齋寫樂画

38

Ōhara Donshū (Japanese, d. 1857)

Blind Men Appraising an Elephant

Japan, Edo period, 19th century
Hanging scroll, ink and colors on paper
Overall: 92 × 46½ in. (233.6 × 118.1 cm.);
image: 67 × 37½ in. (170 × 95.2 cm.)

1993.57, Gift of the Asian Art Council, Mr. and Mrs. W. G. Clark, Georgia and Michael de Havenon, Mr. and Mrs. Greg Fitz-Gerald, Dr. and Mrs. George Liberman, and Khalil Rizk; Frank L. Babbott Fund

In the Edo period (1615–1867), Japanese artists began to introduce new narrative subjects to the field of Buddhist painting, ranging far beyond the iconic subject matter of earlier traditions. Expressive figures of blind men are frequently employed in later Japanese Buddhist painting to represent the vulnerable and precarious condition of those who are spiritually blind.

Although elephants are not native to Japan, this witty subject might have been familiar to Japanese artists from foreign sources. In 1728 the first white elephant was brought to Japan from Thailand. The scene of the elephant being examined by blind men is a metaphor for the human condition: each individual presumes to know the nature of the universe through his limited personal experience of it. The subject is found as early as the fifth century A.D. in the *Hitopadesha*, the Indian version of Aesop's fables, and continues to be represented throughout Asian literature and painting.

The composition of this work closely follows an earlier Chinese precedent called "Washing the White Elephant," which we know from several late Ming (1368–1644) examples, such as a painting by Ding Yunpeng (1547–1621) from 1604 that represents the annual event in China when the elephants of the imperial court were ritually cleansed. Donshū's contemporary, the woodblock print artist Katsushika Hokusai (1760–1849), also treated this subject in his *Manga* (Sketchbook), which dates to around 1814–19.

Donshū, whose work represents a variety of subjects and techniques, deliberately chose this large-scale format to be executed in the *haiga* style, the genre known for spontaneous brush technique often associated with *haiku* poems. The abbreviated and expressive depictions enhanced by a rapid yet precise brushwork provide an objective insight into human nature. The work is at once comical and charming without being pedantic.
AGP

LITERATURE

Archives of Asian Art 1994, 89, fig. 7.

39

Ninnami Dōhachi (Japanese, 1783–1855)

Bowl in the Shape of a Gourd

Japan, late Edo period, mid-19th century
Stoneware with underglaze iron oxide decoration
2½ × 8 13/16 × 7⅛ in. (6 × 22.4 × 18.1 cm.)

1994.93, Gift of the Executors of the Charles Brandon Estate, by exchange

A follower of Ogata Kenzan (1663–1743), the nineteenth-century potter Ninnami Dōhachi is best known for delicate hand-built clay forms as well as naturalistic treatment of the painted motifs applied to his ceramics. This shallow stoneware bowl epitomizes Dōhachi's ceramic style with its shape of a gourd or the fruit of the evening glory plant (*hisago*). The work dates from the potter's later period as indicated by his trumpet-shell seal engraved on its base. This is the time when the artist worked at his Momoyama kiln in Kyoto, from 1842 to 1855.

The style of this piece is undoubtedly reminiscent of the work of the famed Kyoto potter and aesthete Ogata Kenzan, whom Dōhachi often copied in specific works. Dōhachi is regarded as one of the greatest followers of Kenzan and Hon'ami Kōetsu (1558–1637), who were leaders of the Rinpa painting and decorative arts tradition. By 1811 at the age of twenty-nine, Dōhachi had acquired a variety of skills and knowledge of artistic pottery-making from his teacher, Okuda Eisen (1753–1811). He then became an independent potter. We do not know if he worked in any other media. He quickly received national patronage of the ruling classes, such as the *daimyō* nobility (the Suminokura family, the Takamatsu clan as in this work, and the Kishū branch of the Tokugawa family, for example) and several Buddhist temples. He is associated with the temple Ninna-ji in Kyoto, from which he was given one character in his name.

The extensive exhibition and publication history of the piece testifies to its extraordinary cultural importance. As a follower of Kenzan, Dōhachi found artistic expression within the tradition of Japanese ceramics. Dōhachi produced many excellent copy-works (*utsushi*) as well as ceramics in his own creative style, which is characterized by two distinctive techniques: a simple, low-fired Raku-type ware for tea bowls and a decorative type, employing naturalistic motifs painted in iron glazes and other pigments.

The Museum owns the original storage box that is traditionally signed and sealed by the potter and other packing materials, such as the original cord and wrapping cloths. The artist's signature occurs on the box lid and a colophon is given on the outer box.
AGP

LITERATURE

Akanuma 1977, 67, cat. no. 28.
Sadō Shiryōkan 1982, cat. no. 32.
Tokyo National Museum 1985, 208, cat. no. 289.

40

Utagawa Hiroshige (Japanese, 1797–1858)

Plum Estate, Kameido

From the series *One Hundred Famous Views of Edo*
Japan, Edo period, 11th month, 1857
Color woodblock print
13⅜ × 8⅞ in. (34 × 22.6 cm.)

30.1478.30, Brooklyn Museum of Art Collection

The Brooklyn Museum of Art's collection of the *One Hundred Famous Views of Edo* (*Meisho Edo Hyakkei*) is considered to be one of the finest specimens of Utagawa Hiroshige's *ukiyo-e* woodblock prints in the world. The series was produced by the publisher Uoya Eikichi, based on the designs of the artist in 1856–58. One of only eight known complete series, the BMA set has gained international attention and is considered the keystone of the Museum's collection of Japanese woodblock prints.

Plum Estate, Kameido is more than a mere landscape design. It is a literary allusion to a famous plum tree known as the "Sleeping Dragon Plum," which, according to Henry Smith, was the primary highlight of the Plum Estate (Umeyashiki). The tree attracted the attention of Shogun Yoshimune during the early eighteenth century with its fragrance and was thus elevated to celebratory status in Edo (present-day Tokyo). Through the artist's innovative foreground framing, the viewer attains an unusual perspective of this celebrated tree, renowned for its size, powerful fragrance, and exquisite double blossoms. The unique characteristic of this enormous tree was the fact that the low branches entered the soil and re-emerged at a distance, like an image of a "sleeping dragon." By Hiroshige's time, the tree had spread over an area of approximately fifty square feet. Unfortunately, nothing of the tree survives at the site today except a stone roadside marker in a sea of small factories and shops.

Hiroshige's landscape designs set a precedent in the medium of woodblock prints (and, through their influence, in Western painting) by introducing a fusion of many new technical and artistic approaches. Vincent van Gogh's (1853–1890) 1887 interpretations of Hiroshige's *Plum Estate, Kameido* and *Sudden Shower over Shin-Ōhashi Bridge and Atake*, along with Claude Monet's (1840–1926) version of *Inside Kameido Tenjin Shrine* (1899), are based on compositions from Hiroshige's masterpiece.
TA

LITERATURE

Smith and Poster 1986, cat. no. 30.
Varnedoe 1989, 56, 59, fig. 46.
Nagata 1997, 60, cat. no. 78.
Singer 1998, 288, cat. no. 146.

名所江戸百景
亀戸梅屋舗
廣重画

41

Leather Fireman's Coat

Japan, Meiji period, late 19th century
Stencil-dyed leather
49¼ × 53 9/16 in. (125.1 × 136 cm.)

12.83, Brooklyn Museum of Art Collection

One result in Japan of the Buddhist prohibition against taking life was the rarity of the use of leather until modern times. Nevertheless, the technique of dyeing animal skins by smoking, which resulted in a warm, orange-brown color, was introduced to Japan from India in about the fifth century. Its use was apparently reserved for the samurai class. The technique is still called *inden*, an old Japanese word for India. In this fireman's coat, the design was reserved by blocking part of the surface with a stencil.

During the Edo period (1615–1868), the use of leather by commoners was banned by the Tokugawa government as one of a series of sumptuary measures. Leather became popular again during the Meiji period (1868–1912), and such stenciled leather was commonly used for firemen's coats. Such a coat was too valuable to wear in actual fire fighting but was reserved for ceremonial use. The *mon* (crest) stenciled in pigment on the upper back is the emblem of a particular fire company; when paired with the stylized ideograms seen here, it creates a strikingly powerful composition.
AGP

LITERATURE
Moes 1985, 158, cat. no. 94.

42

Bingata Kimono

Japan, Meiji period, late 19th century
Stencil-dyed cotton
50 × 48 in. (127 × 121.9 cm.)

12.889, Brooklyn Museum of Art Collection

Bingata is a term used to describe the famous multiple-color stencil-dyeing of Okinawa. The term is derived from *bini* (red dye) and *kata* (stencil). The technique was introduced to the Ryūkyū Islands from South China in the fifteenth century. It soon grew popular with the Okinawan royal court, which became its principal patron. The court sought to regulate its production, reserving certain patterns and colors for the nobility and assigning them to wearers according to their rank at court. Patterns of smaller designs and a predominantly blue color scheme were permitted for commoners.

Cotton is not native to the Ryūkyū Islands, having been introduced to Okinawa in 1611. The spectacular colors of the Brooklyn robe are mainly red, yellow, and purple on a light blue ground. The crane and pine motif, produced in the typical stencil paste-resist dyeing and freehand paste-resist dyeing techniques, is a familiar symbol of longevity and an auspicious invitation of long life for the wearer of the robe.
AGP

LITERATURE

Moes 1985, 170, cat. no. 102.

43

Woman's *Attush* Robe

Japan, Meiji period, late 19th century
Elm-bark-fiber cloth with appliqué and embroidery
$49\frac{5}{8} \times 52\frac{3}{8}$ in. (126 × 133 cm.)

12.690, Museum Expedition 1912, Purchased with funds given by Herman Stutzer

After the introduction of the backstrap loom, Ainu ancestors began weaving *attush*, cloth made from the inner bark of the elm tree and from linden and nettle plants. Men were responsible for producing the bark, but women executed the weaving, sewing, and decorating of the clothing. Designs were embroidered on old clothing or fabric scraps obtained from the Japanese and sewn onto the *attush*.

This woman's robe is considered the best of its type in North America because of the quality of its chain-stitch embroidery in red and white. It is made of nettle plant (J: *irakusa*) fiber and is called *retarpe* or *tetarape*, meaning "white things" in the Ainu language. Most *retarpe* were produced in Sakhalin and have designs linking them to styles used by the Nivkhi and Manchurian Chinese groups. This stunning example displays the traditional design motifs. For the Ainu, the placement of the designs so as to enclose the area of the neck, the sleeves, and the base of the garment prevented evil spirits from entering the wearer's body. The Ainu maintain that these motifs do not have symbolic meaning. The form of the robe is consistent with Ainu formal garments and differs from the traditional Japanese robe in that the sleeves are tapered rather than square-cut.

This is one of more than three hundred pieces collected by John Batchelor (1854–1944), a British missionary in Hokkaidō, Japan, who authored the first Ainu-English dictionary in 1889. He sold it to Stewart Culin for the Museum in 1912, when Culin was in Japan on a trip sponsored by the Brooklyn Museum.
AGP

LITERATURE
Moes 1985, 186, cat. no. 113.
Lawrence 1989, 24, fig. 4
Fitzhugh and Dubreuil 1999, 160–61, figs. 20.8a–b.

44

Kuruma-Dansu

Japan, Meiji period, late 19th–early 20th century
Zelkova (*keyaki*) and cryptomeria (*sugi*) wood with iron fittings
37⅛ × 21⅜ × 44⅛ in. (94.4 × 54.3 × 111.8 cm.)

75.126, Designated Purchase Fund

In Japanese, *kuruma* means "wheel" or "vehicle," and the wooden wheels on this type of *tansu*, or chest of drawers, served an obvious purpose, enabling the chest and its contents to be moved, especially in case of fire. The interior of this *tansu* has a full-width shelf, plus two small drawers lower on the right side.

The most popular wood used for traditional Japanese furniture is zelkova (*keyaki*), prized for its flamelike grain and rich reddish-brown color. It was not generally used for *tansu* prior to the Meiji period (1868–1912), and even then, as was the case with rare woods of English and Continental furniture, it was often reserved for drawer faces or front panels.

The frame and the door panels are made of *keyaki*, although the top, sides, and back are of less expensive Japanese cedar (cryptomeria, or *sugi*). The entire *tansu* is finished with a refined lacquer (*kijiro*) that has a natural honey-reddish color. The style of this *tansu* and the reticulated iron fittings suggest that it was made in Yonezawa, a principal center for the production of *tansu* in Yamagata prefecture during the latter part of the Meiji period.
AGP

LITERATURE

Moes 1985, 91–92, cat. no. 47.

45

Kawakami Ryōka (Japanese, 1887–1921)

Wildlife Friends

Japan, Taishō period, c. 1918
Handscroll, ink, color, and gold on woven paper decorated with mica
8⅞₁₆ × 206 in. (21.4 × 523.2 cm.)

1993.4, Purchased with funds given by Mr. and Mrs. Willard G. Clark; Helen Babbott Sanders Fund

This handscroll depicts thirteen connected scenes of insects and frogs engaged in various activities associated with the cycle of life and death. Many of the scenes, including this one of cicadas amid decaying leaves, are accompanied by brief written references to essays, poetry, and ballads drawn from a wide range of sources, among which are the American writers Henry David Thoreau (1817–1862) and Walt Whitman (1819–1892).

In typical traditional Japanese-style painting (*Nihonga*), Kawakami Ryōka has integrated traditional Japanese pictorial elements with a humanistic sensitivity. With skillful brushwork, he has precisely painted in a boneless style themes from nature combined with an application of color in the manner of Shibata Zeshin (1807–1891), using lacquer and mica.

The subject matter may be viewed as a final flowering of a Japanese tradition of satirical representation observed in the well-known twelfth-century handscroll *Chōju giga*, or *Frolicking Animals*, a fragment of which is at present on long-term loan to the Brooklyn Museum of Art (L55.12). In Japan, artists often portrayed animals and insects to parody Buddhist subjects. In one scene, a frog seated on a lotus leaf, like the Buddha preaching, leads his companions at a drinking gathering under the autumn moon. Such images suggest references to older Japanese painting traditions, but Ryōka has infused them

Detail

with his personal interpretation.

The recent research of Japanese scholar Tanaka Atsushi has focused new attention on the artist. Born in Niigata prefecture, Ryōka spent most of his career as an artist in Tokyo; his last years were spent in Nakano, on the outskirts of Tokyo. The surviving eighteen works by the artist are primarily oil paintings of subjects from nature painted in a Western-influenced post-Impressionist style, most of which are recorded in a 1932 retrospective exhibition catalogue. The BMA handscroll, however, is considered especially important because it is the only extant work painted in *Nihonga* style and it is not included in the 1932 catalogue.

A box inscription by Saitō Yori (1885–1959) gives this handscroll the title *Yasei no tomo* (Wildlife friends), painted by Ryōka Sensei (my teacher, Ryōka). On the inside cover of the box, he wrote: "The painting of insects in the play, which I wrote and was published in *Bijutsu shinron* [New discourse on art], September 1927, is this very scroll," with his signature, seal, and the date 1928. The play was never performed but records the artist's act of painting a scroll like this singular work. *AGP/YL*

LITERATURE

Chiba 2002, 78–79, cat. no. 44.

46

Fukami Sueharu (Japanese, b. 1947)

Infinity II (Shinsho)

Japan, Kyoto, 1994

Porcelain with blue-green (*seihakuji*) glaze

6 × 47⅝ × 9½ in. (15.2 × 121 × 24.2 cm.)

1994.146a, b, Purchased with funds given by Alastair B. Martin

The Brooklyn Museum collection includes approximately 150 modern and contemporary Japanese studio ceramics, reflecting the diverse approaches and styles of more than 90 artists ranging from master potters to young emerging artists. Contemporary Japanese artists continue to explore new dimensions in the ceramic arts and are a primary focus of the Museum's current Japanese acquisitions.

Infinity II (Shinsho) is an exemplary work by the Kyoto artist Fukami Sueharu, who extends ceramics to the realm of conceptual sculpture. Fukami's reputation reached an international audience in 1985, when he received the Grand Prize at the Faenza International Ceramic Exhibition in Italy. Born to a potter's family, Fukami produces primarily porcelain pieces, ranging from utilitarian tableware made by the wheel technique to more expansive aesthetic statements in abstract form.

This sculpture typifies Fukami's current work, in which he uses a pressurized casting method that he has continued to develop since the late 1970s. To form the body, white liquid kaolin and petunse – the basic materials of porcelain – are poured into a mold. The clay body is then carved at every edge and rim. After an initial firing, the delicate process of glazing is followed by a refiring in an electric kiln.

Neither freestanding nor functional, Fukami's work is a pure vessel for his visionary expressions. Combining the blade-sharp edges and gently curved rims characteristic of Fukami's work, *Infinity II* reflects the counter-curves or waves of his recent monumental pieces. The flawless texture and alluring color of this work derive from Chinese, Korean, and Japanese green-glaze ware, a few examples of which are among the ceramics on view in the Asian Art galleries.

AGP

LITERATURE

Yoshinaga 1996, 97–99, fig. 79.

Brooklyn 1997, 44.

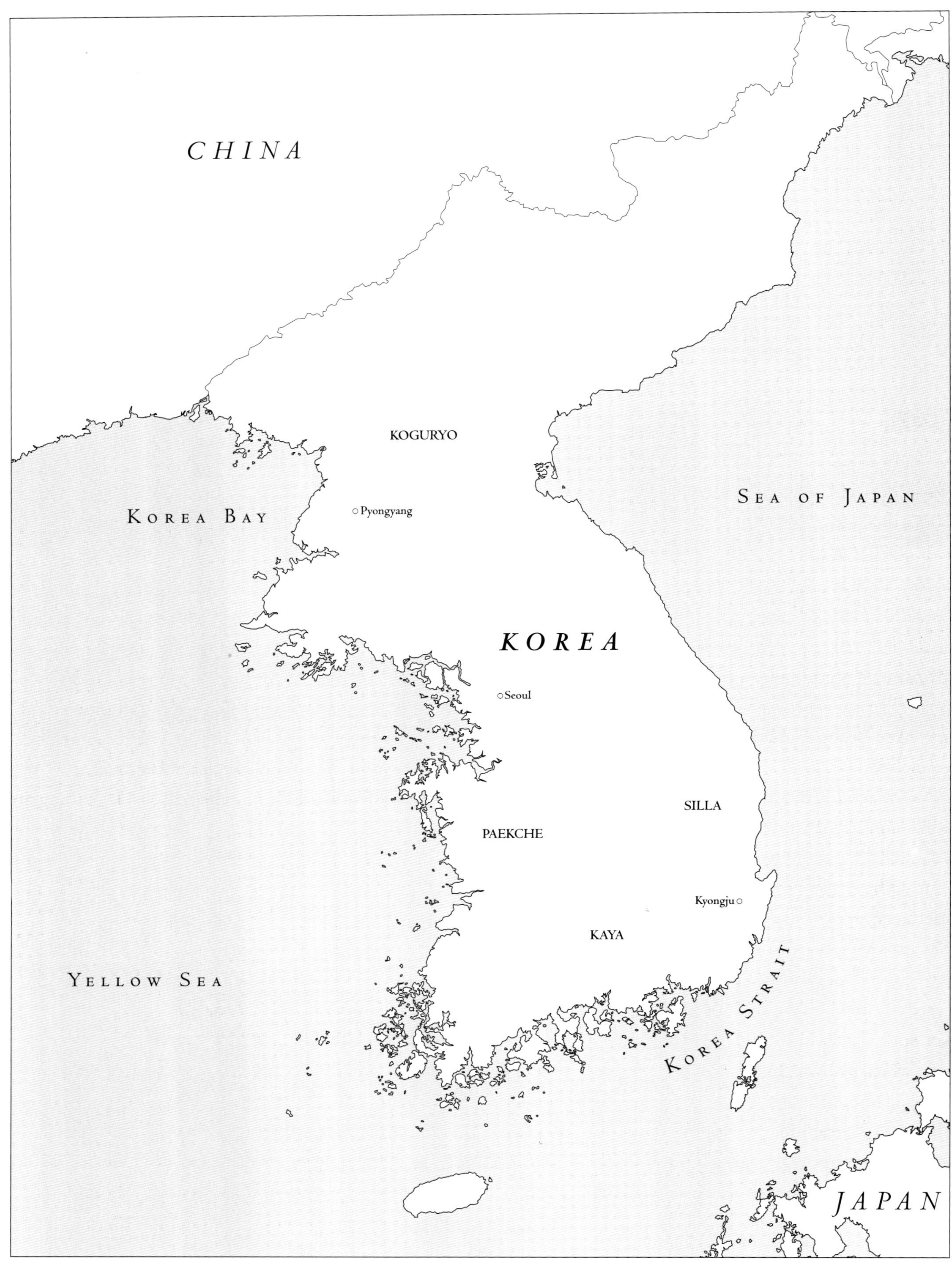
CHINA
KOGURYO
Korea Bay
Pyongyang
Sea of Japan
KOREA
Seoul
SILLA
PAEKCHE
Kyongju
KAYA
Yellow Sea
Korea Strait
JAPAN

Korea

The Brooklyn Museum of Art is one of the primary venues for the presentation of Korean culture in the United States. Of the twenty permanent Korean art collections in museums in the United States, the BMA's collection is not only one of the earliest, but also one of the finest. The collection of approximately eight hundred objects is the third largest in the country, following those of the Museum of Fine Arts, Boston, and the Asian Art Museum, San Francisco.

The collection consists of ceramics, paintings, textiles and costumes, furniture, sculptures, metal works, glass, arms and armor, and other decorative arts, dating from the Neolithic period to the early twentieth century. Its masterpieces include a rare Koryŏ-dynasty (918–1392) painting of the *Amit'a Triad* (see no. 50) and an exquisite Koryŏ-dynasty celadon ewer (see no. 49).

Of special note is the rich collection of Korean folk art, which grew from curator Stewart Culin's (1858–1929) interest in the popular culture of Korea. The Museum's groundbreaking research on this collection is an important contribution to the field of Korean art. Outstanding within this section is a small but significant group of nineteenth-century Korean games acquired by Culin in 1913.

Korean art is an important tradition of Asian art that has not been widely presented to American audiences. Traditionally, Korean culture has been viewed as linked to China and other East Asian cultures; currently, the collection is presented to emphasize Korea's unique traditions, culture, and arts. Before many other museums in the United States, the BMA put forth this view in two important special exhibitions. One hundred selections from the collection were assembled in 1987 in the special exhibition *Korean Art: The Brooklyn Museum.* Providing an overview of the history of Korean art and culture, this seminal exhibition celebrated the Museum's unique and important collection. The BMA was also among the first museums in the United States to focus on Korea's contemporary art. One of the earliest exhibitions in this field to be held in this country was *Korean Drawing Now*, organized at the Museum in 1981 by Gene Baro, then Curator of Prints and Drawings, together with the Korean Cultural Service.

The acquisition of Korean art continues to be a focus of the BMA. More than forty important Korean works of art have been acquired since the overview exhibition of 1987.

HW

47

Stoneware Vessel with High Pedestal

Korea, Kaya Federation, 5th–6th century
High-fired gray stoneware
H: 11½ in. (29.2 cm.); DIAM: 12 in. (30.5 cm.)

2000.41, Gift of Mr. and Mrs. Byung Kang

Utilitarian ceramic vessels were an important product of early Korean art. Among early ceramics of Korea, gray stoneware with a natural ash glaze was prominent. The Kaya Federation (42–562), which later became integrated into the Silla Kingdom (57 B.C.–A.D. 668), is known for its dark gray stoneware ceramics. Most of the extant relics of the Kaya are high-fired stoneware vessels; during this period, Korea was the second-most important producer of high-fired stoneware, after China. Such works influenced the production of the contemporaneous Sue ware, a type of ceramic ware that was introduced from Korea in the fifth century and used first as grave goods and later as household vessels.

Kaya high-fired stonewares ranged in shape from small cups to figurative sculptures and were integral to daily life as well as ritual ceremony. The various shapes reflect the use of the potter's wheel, which was introduced to Korean potters from China during this period. This vessel is an impressive example in its large scale and excellent condition. The form of a trumpet-shaped bowl set on a high pedestal provides clues to its function either as a food vessel or as a stand for a round-bottomed jar.

While the form and ornament of Kaya ceramics share many similarities with stoneware vessels produced in other regions in Korea during the Three Kingdoms period (57 B.C.–A.D. 668), the rectangular openwork on the pedestal and combed decorative bands on the body are unique to this type of stoneware. Also distinctive to Kaya ceramics is the use of a wood-fueled climbing kiln, which was first invented by the potters in the Kaya area. This type of kiln, which produced an intense and steady heat, was ideal for high-fired stoneware, such as this vessel.

HW

48

Standing Yakusa

Korea, Unified Silla period, 8th century
Bronze
7⅛ × 2 in. (18.1 × 5.1 cm.)

74.165, Frank L. Babbott Fund

Buddhism was first introduced to the Korean Peninsula through China during the Three Kingdoms period (57 B.C.–A.D. 668), reaching the Koguryŏ Kingdom in 372, the Paekche Kingdom in 384, and the Silla Kingdom in the mid-fifth century. Soon after its introduction, Buddhism spread widely throughout Korea and became the state religion with the Unified Silla period (668–935).

Religious statues for worship were actively produced from the Three Kingdoms period, the majority as small bronze sculptures. This Buddhist sculpture represents Yakusa, the Buddha of Healing who was also known as the Medicine Buddha (S: Bhaishajyaguru). Sickness and injury were so common in early Korean history that Yakusa was one of the most widely worshipped Buddhist deities.

The figure stands erect displaying identifying attributes: the left hand holds a small medicine bowl and the right hand expresses the gesture (S: *mudra*) of teaching, a gesture associated with standing Yakusas in eighth-century Korea. Also characteristic of eighth-century Buddhist sculptures are the thin delicate hands and the presence of two oval-shaped openings on the back of the body and another one on the back of the head. The openings on the body were for religious offerings, and the one on the head was for attaching a *mandorla* (aureole).

Active cultural exchange between the Unified Silla Kingdom and Tang-dynasty (618–907) China is reflected through Chinese influence on Korean Buddhist sculptures of the time. The full face of this figure is a stylistic element that originated in China.

HW

LITERATURE

Archives of Asian Art 1975–76, 100–101, fig. 8.
Moes 1987, 43, cat. no. 9.

49

Celadon Ewer

Korea, Koryŏ dynasty, first half of the 12th century
Stoneware with white and black slip decoration and blue-green glaze
H: 9⅞ in. (25 cm.); DIAM: 9½ in. (24.1 cm.)

56.138.1 a, b, Gift of Mrs. Darwin R. James III

Celadon ceramics of the Koryŏ dynasty (918–1392) are among the best-known works of Korean art. Celadons are high-fired, porcelaneous wares with a gray clay body covered with a translucent gray-green feldspathic glaze and are characterized by the luminous pale green color that results from the oxidized iron when both clay and glaze are fired in a reduction kiln.

Although the initial date of celadon production in Korea is varyingly set by scholars, it is generally accepted that Korean potters adopted celadon techniques from Song-dynasty (960–1279) China around the tenth and eleventh centuries. The subtle crackle and beautiful color of Korean celadon glazes have been praised in both Korean and Chinese texts. The twelfth-century chronicle *Xuanhe fenshi gaoli tujing* (Illustrated record of the Chinese embassy to the Koryŏ court during the Xuanhe era) documents the color of Koryŏ celadon as "the first-under-heaven," a synonym for the term describing the blue-green color of kingfisher feathers.

This Brooklyn ewer is one of the most celebrated Koryŏ ceramics, unique in its dynamic naturalistic form, superb glaze color, and meticulous detail. Only a few surviving examples employ this range of extraordinary technique. The lotiform body is carved with a design of overlapping lotus petals framing leaf sprays. A pulled handle in the form of a lotus stalk is elegantly tied at the top with reeds. The cover is in the shape of an inverted lotus blossom, while the knob of the lid recreates a lotus bud just beginning to unfurl. The cover and handle were originally joined by a chain, now marked by two loops, which are placed where a butterfly sitting on the cover would have connected with the insect's pupa on the handle. Dots of white slip accentuate the ornamental motifs. This decorative technique marks the earliest celadon wares of the twelfth century, just prior to the development of the slip inlay technique.

The donor was a descendant of the famous American missionary family of Horace Underwood, who established Yonsei University in Seoul in 1885. This ewer was possibly a gift of the Korean royal family to Mrs. Horace Underwood.

HW

LITERATURE

Brooklyn 1967, 162–63.
Moes 1987, 54–55, cat. no. 15.
Osaka 1992, 37, 139, cat. no. 24.
Woo 1999, 118.

50

Amit'a Triad

Korea, Koryŏ dynasty, 14th century
Hanging scroll, ink, color, and gold on silk
Overall: 95¼ × 40¼ in. (242 × 102.2 cm.);
image: 51¼ × 32¼ in. (130.2 × 82 cm.)

61.204.30, Gift of Professor Harold G. Henderson

Produced with a dazzling technical virtuosity, Koryŏ (918–1392) Buddhist paintings are renowned for their magnificent quality. Colors in dark tones, applied gold pigment, and meticulously expressed details characterize works of this period. Only about one hundred Koryŏ Buddhist paintings survive worldwide, with fewer than ten paintings housed in Korea. Over seventy percent of these works are in Japanese collections, most of them having arrived in Japan from the thirteenth through sixteenth centuries, and now owned by temples.

This impressive image, considered one of the premier Koryŏ paintings in the United States, depicts the Buddha Amit'a (S: Amitabha) accompanied by two bodhisattvas: Kwan'ŭm (S: Avalokiteshvara) on the right and Seji (S: Mahasthamaprapta) on the left. Amit'a, the ruler of the Western Paradise, is the main icon of the Pure Land Sect of Buddhism, an extremely popular cult in Korea during the Koryŏ dynasty. This Buddha was believed to carry the souls of newly deceased believers to the Western Paradise and is often shown with these two bodhisattvas.

Kwan'ŭm, a manifestation of Amit'a's mercy, is identified by a water sprinkler (S: *kundika*) held in his right hand and a small image of Buddha in his hair ornament. Seji, as the manifestation of Amit'a's spiritual wisdom, is recognized by a lotus stem in his hand and an image of a *kundika* in his hair ornament.

The position of Amit'a and the two bodhisattvas, standing diagonally on a lotus flower, suggests that they are on their way to this world to welcome the believers in one of the most popular iconographic representations of this subject. Considering that there are several Koryŏ examples of this painting with similar composition and scale, it is highly possible that a model for this type of painting existed earlier. In other images, Amit'a is generally seated on a throne flanked by two, four, or eight bodhisattvas.

HW

LITERATURE

Brooklyn 1967, 150–51.
Moes 1987, 48–49, cat. no. 11.
International Cultural Society of Korea 1989, 82.
Grove's 1996, vol. 18, 305.
Woo 1999, 120.

51

Attributed to Yi Chong (Korean, 1587–1607)

Scholar Contemplating a Cascade

Korea, Chosŏn dynasty, 16th century
Album leaf mounted as a hanging scroll, ink on silk
Overall: 45 × 16¼ in. (114.3 × 41.2 cm.); image: 11¼ × 10⅞ in. (28.6 × 27.6 cm.)

75.130, Designated Purchase Fund

Korean landscape paintings of the sixteenth century can be identified and associated with celebrated stylistic traditions in Chinese painting from the Song (960–1279) and early Ming (1368–1644) dynasties. Painters actively adopted such Chinese pictorial styles during the Koryŏ (918–1392) through the early Chosŏn (1392–1910) dynasties and developed into their own style through the mid-Chosŏn dynasty, around 1550–1700. Although a distinctively local style existed, most pre-eighteenth-century Korean landscape paintings were based on either Chinese paintings or Chinese painting manuals. It was only during the eighteenth century that Korean painters began to depict their own landscape with recognition of its special beauty.

The subject matter of this painting – a scholar contemplating a cascade – can be traced to a poem by the celebrated Chinese poet Li Bo (701–762) about the beauty of a famous cascade at Mount Lu. A scholar in his Chinese robe sits at the river's edge and looks over a cascade situated at the center of the painting. However, the figure is depicted in a rather small scale, suggesting that the landscape is a main theme. Strong and vigorous brushstrokes on the rocks remind us of the axe-cut brushstrokes often used by Southern Song (1127–1279) Ma-Xia School painters, who later influenced the Ming-dynasty (1368–1644) Zhe School style. Branches of the pine tree stylized in zigzag shapes suggest a close relationship of this painting with Zhe School paintings.

Yi Chong, the attributed artist of this painting, was the grandson of Yi Sang-jwa, the great Chosŏn court painter and master of Korean Zhe School painting.
HW

LITERATURE

Moes 1987, 92–93, cat. no. 37.
Brooklyn 1988, 91, cat. no. 58.

52

Kim Myoung-kuk (Korean, active first half of the 17th century)

Po-dae

Korea, Chosŏn dynasty, 17th century
Hanging scroll, ink on paper
Overall: 51¾ × 14⅜ in. (131.5 × 36.5 cm.);
image: 20½ × 10⅝ in. (52.1 × 27 cm.)

59.26.1, Gift of Mrs. Robert van Roejen, by exchange

The household god Po-dae, whose name can be literally translated as "cotton cloth bag," is always shown carrying a cloth bag on his shoulder. Believed to bring good fortune to a family, he was also said to be an incarnation of Mirŭk (S: Maitreya), the Buddha of the Future, and to have been a Chan (Zen) Buddhist monk who lived in China during the sixth century.

This painting is executed with bold, rough, and abbreviated brushwork characteristic of the artist's style. Kim Myoung-kuk, a court painter, was best known for this type of painting of eccentric figures based on Southern Song Chan paintings. Many of his paintings of Dalma (S: Bodhidharma; J: Daruma), an Indian supposed to have founded Chan Buddhism in China, also survive.

Kim's works have been widely appreciated not only in Korea but also in Japan. He went to Japan twice, in 1636 and 1643, while he was serving as a Chosŏn court painter. It was a common practice to include court painters in delegations to neighboring countries. Their duties were to paint official events of the delegation as a historical record and to record exotic scenery of the foreign countries they visited. During his free time, Kim created many figure paintings for his Japanese patrons. It was said that people who desired Kim's paintings would line up in front of his residence to request his work when he was staying in Japan.

Kim was also known for his love of alcohol and often painted while drunk. One name he frequently used to sign his paintings was "Drunken Old Man" (Chui-ong), written here in the lower-left corner.

HW

LITERATURE

Brooklyn 1967, 164–65.
Moes 1987, 96–97, cat. no. 39.

醉翁

53

Dragon Jar

Korea, Chosŏn dynasty, 18th century
White porcelain with iron-brown painted decoration under a clear glaze
H: 12⅜ in. (31.4 cm.); DIAM: 14⅝ in. (37 cm.)

86.139, Gift of the Asian Art Council

Produced from the late fourteenth century, porcelain became a major ceramic ware during the Chosŏn dynasty (1392–1910). Confucianism, the ruling philosophy of the Chosŏn dynasty, promoted a taste for simplified form and decoration. The white color of porcelain, influenced by Chinese porcelains, ideally reflected this minimalism.

Although the kilns producing Chosŏn porcelain were scattered throughout Korea, the royal kilns at Kwangju in Kyonggi province produced most of the court tablewares. To ensure that there was a sufficient supply of firewood, the site was relocated every ten years.

Unlike earlier celadons and *punch'ong* ceramics (of the fifteenth and sixteenth centuries), which were decorated with various techniques such as incising, carving, and inlay, porcelains were decorated only with underglaze painting. The pigments for the painted decoration were cobalt blue, iron brown, and copper red. In the early stage of porcelain production, cobalt blue was the most popular material for decoration. Korea imported the cobalt pigment from China, which had in turn imported it from the Islamic world. Since the cost of this precious material was great, most decoration with cobalt was reserved for court painters.

By the seventeenth century, as the relationship between China and the Islamic world deteriorated, the Chosŏn court experienced difficulties in importing cobalt from China and relied on indigenous sources of the mineral. In response to this dearth, potters began producing undecorated porcelains and substituted iron-brown pigment for cobalt blue. This jar is an outstanding example of seventeenth-century Korean folk ceramics with iron oxide decoration. It was intended as a food or wine vessel and served to protect its contents from evil spirits and to attract good fortune for its owner.

The dragon design possesses spontaneous, eccentric, and amusing qualities and exudes a sense of power and mystery. The use of iron oxide pigment here provides contrast to dragon motifs painted in underglaze cobalt blue on porcelain jars made for imperial use and Confucian temples. The dragons for these elite wares were depicted with a meticulous brushwork style based on Chinese models of the Ming dynasty (1368–1644). While powerful and majestic, the "official" dragon designs for the court and Confucian temples are not nearly as lively and dramatic as the "folk" dragons on iron-painted dragon jars.

HW

LITERATURE

Moes 1987, 54–55, cat. no. 15.
Brooklyn 1988, 90, cat. no. 57.
Brooklyn 1997, 39.
Woo 1999, 119.

54

Amit'a with Six Bodhisattvas and Two Arhats

Korea, Chosŏn dynasty, 18th century
Hanging scroll, ink and color on silk
31¾ × 35¼ in. (80.6 × 89.5 cm.)

86.260.2, Gift of Mr. and Mrs. Herbert Greenberg

Although it is traditionally thought that Buddhism was prohibited during the Chosŏn dynasty (1392–1910), when Confucianism was promoted as the state religion in Korea, Buddhism retained a tremendous influence on society and was especially popular with Korean women. Buddhist temples were sometimes built even in the palace, sponsored by the royal family. As a result, the production of Buddhist paintings for worship continued throughout the Chosŏn dynasty. However, with the loss of official patronage, painting declined in quality from the level achieved in the previous Koryŏ dynasty (918–1392). In Chosŏn-dynasty Buddhist paintings many detailed expressions were eliminated, images became formulaic, and much brighter mineral colors were applied.

Here, Amit'a (S: Amitabha), the Buddha of Infinite Light, is seated at the center flanked by bodhisattvas and monk disciples, or arhats. The two bodhisattvas standing closest to Amit'a on the first row are Kwan'ŭm (S: Avalokiteshvara) holding a water sprinkler (S: *kundika*) and Seji (S: Mahasthamaprapta) holding a blue-and-white bowl, remarkably, instead of his usual attributes of a lotus stem and a sutra. These two bodhisattvas are generally depicted together with Amit'a Buddha (see no. 50). The bodhisattva at the lower left is Chijang (S: Kshitigarbha), identified by a mendicant's staff and a wish-fulfilling ball (S: *cintamani*). He was believed to guide the souls from hell to the Western Paradise, where Amit'a resides. The bodhisattva at the lower right does not hold any attributes, but is probably Mirŭk (S: Maitreya), the Buddha of the Future, who is often paired with Chijang. The two monks standing behind Amit'a are the arhats Ananda and Kasyapa, the Buddha's favorite pupils.
HW

LITERATURE

Moes 1987, 76–77, cat. no. 29.

55

Three-Level Chest

Korea, Chosŏn dynasty, 19th century
Red and black lacquer on wood with zelkova burl panels and brass fittings
63⅛ × 44¾ × 29¾ in. (160.3 × 113.7 × 75.6 cm.)

34.530, George C. Brackett Fund

The wardrobe (*chang*) and chest (*nong*) are the primary types of furniture used to store clothes in the women's quarters in the Chosŏn (1392–1910) household. Under the influence of Confucianism, upper-class men and women in Chosŏn society were required to maintain separate living quarters in the same house. The men's quarters were usually located near the gate, whereas the women's quarters were located at the rear of the house. Since the men's quarters were designed for studying and formal gatherings and the women's quarters were designed for household activities, furniture in these quarters reflected their different uses.

Furniture decorated with red and black lacquer was normally restricted to royalty, and the use of these two colors suggests an imperial lineage for this wardrobe. The main frame and most of the moldings are in black lacquer, as are the five panels across the bottom. The edge of the overhanging top of the wardrobe, the frames of the upper and middle pairs of doors, as well as the moldings framing the openings for the lower two pairs of doors, the legs, and the stretcher are decorated in red lacquer.

The door panels, the front of the four small drawers across the top, and the remaining front panels are constructed from zelkova burl wood with an oil finish. In Korea, the complex, swirling grain of the zelkova burl suggests coiled dragons. Hence, the popular name for this decorative wood is "dragon wood" (*yong-mok*). The panels and drawers also bear decorations of flowers and birds in plants in openwork ornamental brass attachments. Korean chests were displayed prominently in the main room of the house. Chests in the women's quarters also displayed elaborate designs, showy woods, and ornamental fittings, as evident in this chest. However, since they were usually put against the wall, the sides and the back were nominally decorated. In the present chest, the side and the back panels are constructed from undecorated pinewood. *HW*

LITERATURE

Moes 1987, 166–67, cat. no. 78.

56

Garden Seat

Korea, Chosŏn dynasty, early 19th century
White porcelain with cobalt and iron decoration under a clear glaze
H: 18½ in. (47 cm.); DIAM: 19¾ in. (50.2 cm.)

86.260.3, Gift of Mr. and Mrs. Herbert Greenberg

Although most porcelain produced during the Chosŏn dynasty (1392–1910) functioned as utilitarian tableware, Korean potters did make various porcelain objects for other purposes, including ritual ceremony objects, scholars' objects, and even epitaphs. This garden seat demonstrates this diversity. Few similar seats survived; the Japan Folk Crafts Museum (Nihon Mingeikan) in Tokyo has one very comparable example.

In this work, a potter combined diverse decorative techniques: openwork, underglaze painting in cobalt blue and iron oxide pigments, and incised details. Openwork is considered to be one of the most difficult techniques, because it is hard to maintain the original shape of the object when fired at high temperatures over 1300°C. This technique was generally applied to non-utilitarian vessels such as water droppers, brush holders, and garden seats. On the other hand, images painted with cobalt blue, iron oxide, and copper red – frequently using all three pigments on one piece – were popular decorations on porcelain wares during the late Chosŏn period.

In addition, this garden seat is heavily decorated with three different ornamental bands: vine scrolls on the upper side; grapes and leaves in the middle; and bracket-shape windows and painted insects on the lower side. Grapes as a traditional symbol of abundance and fecundity give an auspicious meaning to the piece. Grapes and vines were also popular subjects in nineteenth-century ink paintings.
HW

LITERATURE

Moes 1987, 161, cat. no. 75.

57

Blue-and-White Dragon Jar

Korea, Chosŏn dynasty, 19th century
White porcelain with cobalt painted decoration under clear glaze
H. 20 in. (50.8 cm.); DIAM: 13 in. (33 cm.)

80.120.1, Gift of Dr. and Mrs. Stanley Wallace

Distinct from earlier celadons or *punch'ong* wares, which were decorated with complicated decorative techniques such as inlay and sgrafitto with white slip, Chosŏn-dynasty (1392–1910) porcelains were mainly embellished with painted patterns in iron brown, copper red, or cobalt blue. Cobalt blue was the most sought-after underglaze pigment. Since Korea had to import the mineral cobalt from the Middle East through China, the pigment was extremely precious. During certain periods when blue-and-white wares were very popular, the imperial Korean court was forced to regulate the use of this costly pigment.

This massive blue-and-white jar is decorated with two dragons and auspicious clouds – a long-beloved Confucian icon symbolizing Heaven and a virtuous king. In China and Korea, the image of a five-clawed dragon was usually reserved for royal use. The dragons painted on this jar have four claws on each foot, suggesting that this jar was intended for an elite but non-royal patron.

The best examples of this type of blue-and-white dragon jar date from the eighteenth century. Often they are decorated with five-clawed dragons, confirming that these jars were exclusively produced for the Chosŏn court. Eighteenth-century vessels are generally fuller in form, gradually expanding from the bottom to the shoulder. However, in the nineteenth century, this type of jar had a straighter profile with a high vertical neck and an abruptly downward tapering body, as can be seen here.
HW

LITERATURE

Moes 1987, 154, cat. no. 69.

58

Spirit Shrine

Korea, Chosŏn dynasty, dated June 1811
Hanging scroll, ink and color on paper
67$\frac{5}{16}$ × 56$\frac{5}{8}$ in. (171 × 144 cm.)
86.25, Designated Purchase Fund

Spirit shrine paintings were intended for ancestor worship during the Chosŏn dynasty (1392–1910). Memorial services for ancestors, conducted throughout the year on the "memorial day" of each ancestor as well as on the lunar New Year and Harvest Moon Day, were among the most important family events in Korean Confucian households. Most Chosŏn households were equipped with ancestral shrines: small structures, usually located in the garden, which contained the memorial tablets for ancestors. However, families who were unable to afford ancestral shrines instead used spirit shrines such as the example here, which were pictorial representations of ancestral shrines. Middle-class families would also use spirit shrines as temporary substitutes.

In this example, the anonymous artist has created the image of an actual building. An ancestral shrine is prominently placed at the center of a landscape and surrounded by a gateway, stone walls, and a pair of auspicious pine trees. Other traditional symbols identify the auspicious nature of this place: cosmic comma-shapes (*tae-gŭk*) mark the entry gate, and floral-decorated vases hold flowering branches of peonies.

Most spirit shrine paintings were executed in a folk art style that generally emphasized flat patterns and bright colors, such as red, yellow, green, and blue. The size or scale of objects in the image is often exaggerated; for instance, a flower vase might be larger than a front gate.

This spirit shrine painting is very unusual since it commemorates royal ancestors. The inscription on the tablet in the center of the shrine reads "Peace for previous King and Queen [unnamed]," suggesting that the painting was used at an official ancestor-worship ceremony. The name of the building is given on the white rectangular panel above the entrance, and the ink inscription in the lower-right corner includes a date that translates as June 1811. This is the only recorded dated spirit shrine painting.

In Korea, folk paintings have recently gained scholarly recognition of their place in the history of Korean painting. Their aesthetic qualities were first recognized by private collectors in Korea and by foreign museums. The Brooklyn Museum of Art has been actively collecting Korean folk paintings since the mid-1970s.
HW

INSCRIPTION
Inscribed, in the center: "Peace for previous King and Queen [unnamed]"; and in the lower-right corner: "the sixth month of the sixteenth year of the Chia-ching era [1811]"

LITERATURE
Moes 1987, 86–87, cat. no. 34.

國魂殿
先王先后列位仙駕

59

Mountain Spirit

Korea, Chosŏn dynasty, 19th century
Hanging scroll, ink and color on silk
Overall: 43¼ × 34½ in. (109.8 × 87.6 cm.);
image: 34 × 24½ in. (86.3 × 62.2 cm.)

84.145, Designated Purchase Fund

Koreans have worshipped mountains as supernatural spirits since ancient times. Initially, the mountain itself was represented as a divine image; this identity was later transferred to the image of a tiger, a powerfully symbolic animal and inhabitant of the high terrain of Korea. Eventually, the deity of the mountains was symbolized as an old man accompanied by a tiger. This figure was known in the Shamanist pantheon as the Mountain Spirit, or *Sanshin*.

As a Shamanist deity, the Mountain Spirit embodied abundance and fertility. When integrated into Buddhism, he became the patron spirit who would deliver babies and protect them from misfortune. Most Korean Buddhist temples have a separate shrine containing images dedicated to the local Mountain Spirit.

In this image, the Mountain Spirit is mounted on a tiger in three-quarter view and wears a red Chinese official robe. Two nymphs stand in the background. They are depicted in a slightly smaller scale to emphasize the prominence of the deity at the center, a common pictorial practice in Korean folk painting to express hierarchy. This painting is executed in bright reds, yellows, greens, and blues, and with little modeling and use of perspective – attributes typical of folk paintings depicting this subject matter.

HW

LITERATURE

Moes 1987, 78–79, cat. no. 30.
International Cultural Society of Korea 1989, 83.
Woo 1999, 120.

60

Tiger and Magpie

Korea, Chosŏn dynasty, 19th century
Hanging scroll, ink and color on paper
Overall: 62½ × 22⅜ in. (158.8 × 56.9 cm.);
image: 34¼ × 16½ in. (87 × 42 cm.)

1996.123.2, Bequest of Mrs. Carl L. Selden

Tiger and magpie paintings are among the most delightful works of all Korean folk art. While other folk paintings served a practical or secular function, tiger and magpie paintings functioned to repel evil spirits. A work of this nature would have been displayed in Chosŏn (1392–1910) households at New Year's Day to protect the family against evil throughout the coming year. In Korean mythology, the tiger was believed to be the most powerful and spiritual creature among all animals with apotropaic powers. However, the depiction of Korean tigers in paintings and other applied arts is primarily humorous. Pine trees and magpies are usually included in folk paintings of tigers, with the pine tree as a symbol of longevity and the magpie as a symbol of joy or good news. Together, they create an even greater auspicious wish for the coming year.

In this image the tiger is seated on his haunches while the magpie chatters at him from the safety of the pine tree. Although the overall brushwork is not meticulous, as in other Chosŏn folk paintings, the depiction of the tiger's fur is impressively realistic, possibly qualifying this painting as one of the exemplary tiger and magpie paintings of the Chosŏn dynasty. This painting is neither signed nor dated, another characteristic of Korean folk painting.

HW

LITERATURE

Moes 1987, 128, cat. no. 54.

61

Chang Seung-ŏb (Korean, 1843–1897)

Geese and Reeds

Korea, Chosŏn dynasty, 19th century
Hanging scroll, ink and color on satin
Overall: 79 × 18¾ in. (200.5 × 47.5 cm.);
image: 51 × 12½ in. (129.7 × 34.5 cm.)

1998.181, Gift of Leighton R. Longhi and Rosemarie Longhi

The artist Chang Seung-ŏb is considered Korea's leading bird-and-flower painter of the mid- to late nineteenth century. His work is best known for showing the transition between traditional and modern painting in Korea. Geese and reeds (K: *lo-an*; C: *luyan*), one of the artist's favorite subjects, demonstrates the prevalence of wordplay in Korean art. *Lo-an*, the Korean word for "geese and reeds," is also a homonym for "peace and abundance in old age" (see also no. 22). Here, yellow chrysanthemums, another symbol for old age, accentuate the auspicious meaning of the painting.

The artist has depicted two geese dynamically approaching reeds and yellow chrysanthemums occupying the lower half of the painting. Chang's brushwork was admired for its power and liveliness, yet it is very well controlled.

The artist's seal on the lower-right corner is similar to that on another work by the same artist, located in the Ho-am Museum of Art, Seoul (Chung-ang 1985, cat. no. 137). Because Chang never learned how to write Chinese characters, the inscriptions on his paintings were always done by others and frequently the paintings bear no signature at all. As most of his paintings were executed on paper, the satin support of this one is an unusual format, possibly created for a wealthy patron.

HW

South and Southeast Asia

The Brooklyn Museum of Art's South and Southeast Asian collections include works from nations defined by their geographical proximity to the Indian subcontinent, ranging in date from prehistory to the present. The South Asian collection consists of works from India and Pakistan, Bangladesh, and their Himalayan neighbors of Tibet, Nepal, and Bhutan, spanning more than five thousand years of production from archaeological finds to everyday popular arts. The Southeast Asian collection represents works from Myanmar (Burma), Thailand, Laos, Cambodia, Vietnam, Malaysia, Indonesia, Singapore, Brunei, and the Philippines. Southeast Asian art at the Museum focuses on individual cultures and objects, largely reflecting the wide reach of the religions historically originating in South Asia – Hinduism and Buddhism.

Throughout all of these cultures, basic religious tenets constitute an overarching theme. The objects that have been selected for this catalogue were largely

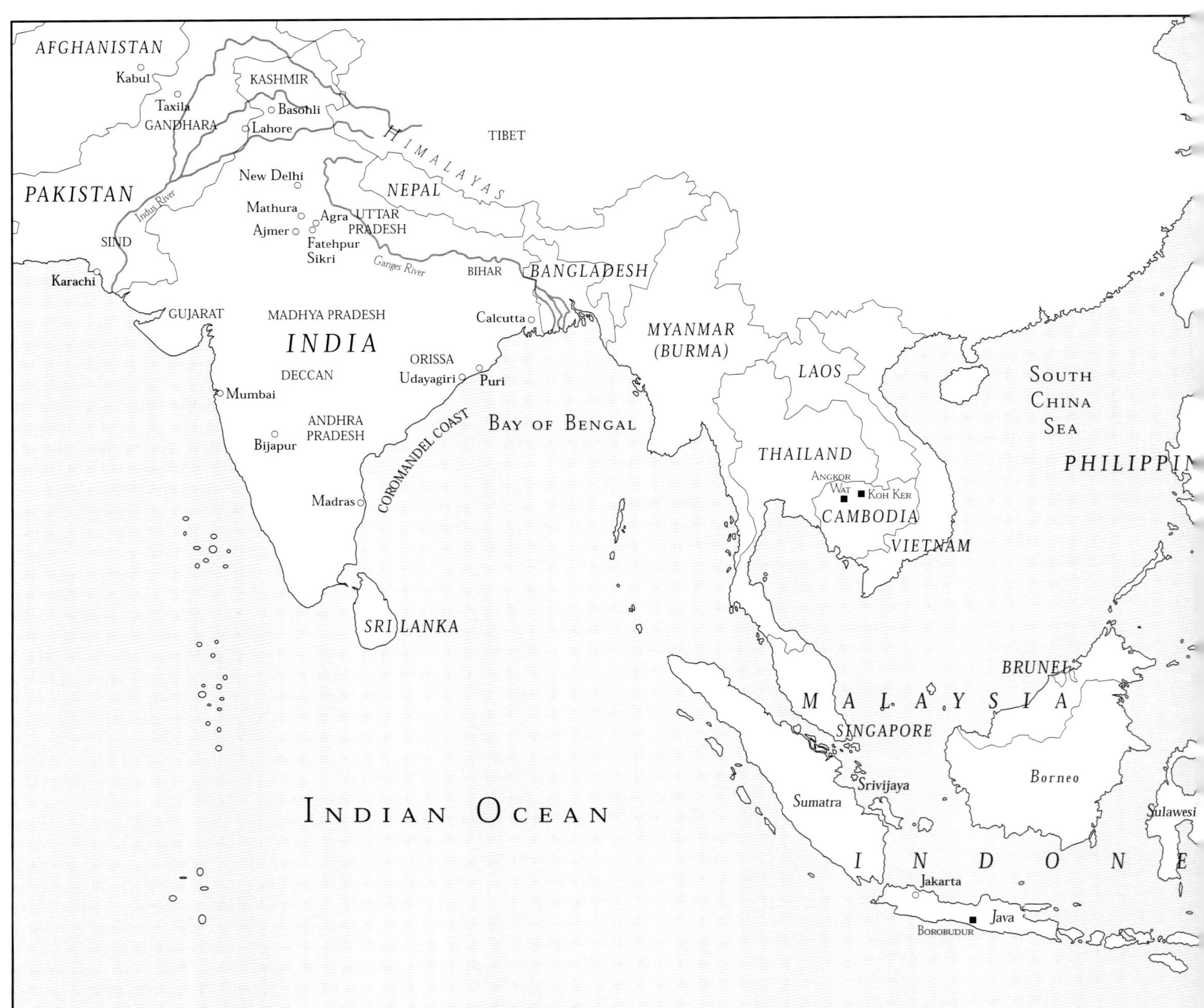

created as religious icons or embellishments for the walls of religious buildings.

These religious ideas and cultural values shaped many of the important artistic traditions in this part of the world and were ultimately based on Indic religious traditions. Although we have described local or regional stylistic and cultural associations for these objects, they are not strictly homogeneous traditions, but belong to a larger network of religious and secular thought.

Outside of the religious sphere, courtly traditions, such as Mughal (1526–1756) decorative arts produced in India, are also a strength of the BMA collection, and popular arts, such as terracottas and Kalighat paintings from eastern India, are equally valued. The depth of the BMA collection provides a fuller sense of society, culture, and the meaning of art in everyday life in South and Southeast Asia because of the institution's history of acquiring utilitarian objects of high craftsmanship and popular art, as well as the arts of the reigning elites.

AGP

62

Standing Female

Pakistan, Sirkap or Charsadda, Kushan period, 1st century
Red molded terracotta
H: 6⅞ in. (17.5 cm.)

88.194, Gift of Georgia and Michael de Havenon

Several standing female figures like this one have been found at Taxila and Sirkap, in present-day Pakistan. All were formed by a double-mold process, some with additional elements such as a headdress with applied ornaments. With slender upper bodies, prominent bare breasts, slightly protruding bellies, and relatively heavy hips and thighs, they may have functioned as fertility symbols. They stand with legs together in a stiff pose, the arms usually reaching downward away from the body.

Stylistic comparisons suggest that the Brooklyn figure is from Sirkap or Charsadda. It documents the prevalence of the Hellenistic tradition in Indo-Parthian culture in the northwestern region of India during the Kushan period (c. 50–320). The type of modeling of the facial features shown here is generally regarded as Hellenistic, and the figure recalls naked Aphrodite figurines of the third to second century B.C., a comparison that may extend to the religious nature of the subject. Most aspects of the figure are uninterrupted by surface detail, save for the hair and a long braid at the back, which accentuates the asymmetrical composition created by applied elements.

The Kushan period is marked in terracotta art by a proliferation of figural sculptures in a variety of types, forms, and sizes. From this northwestern region, a mixture of Indian religious motifs and a sense of plasticity derived from Hellenistic sources are often found in such terracotta specimens as Buddha images or unidentified male images with mustaches or beards and Western costumes.

AGP

LITERATURE

Poster 1986, 15, 117, cat. no. 51.

63

Nagaraja

India, Mathura, Kushan period, 1st–2nd century
Red sandstone
45⅛ × 18 × 10⅜ in. (114.5 × 45.8 × 26.4 cm.)

67.202, Frank L. Babbott Fund and A. Augustus Healy Fund

Monumental sculpture is one of the central cultural legacies of the Kushan period (c. 50–320) in northern India. Images were meant to convey a religious purpose and often represent the principal deities of the Hindu or Buddhist religion. A cobra hood rising at the back of this anthropomorphic image identifies it as the Nagaraja, or serpent king, one of the mythical early converts to Buddhism.

In spite of a badly weathered surface, the standing Nagaraja is a powerful presence. Nagas were semi-divine nature spirits with human faces, serpent tails, and necks expanding into cobra hoods. During this era, Naga worship was itself a powerful religion, but by the Kushan period, Naga temples came to be more associated with Buddhism. The red sandstone quarried at Sikri is typical of the Mathura region, an important trade and religious center, where Naga temples have been documented at the site of Sonkh. Although many comparable images can be found, Stanislaw Czuma cites a Nagini (female Naga) in the Cleveland Museum of Art as the closest parallel in scale and style (Czuma 1985, 85, cat. no. 26).

This sculpture exemplifies the Mathura style by representing a fleshy human form with erect stance and broad shoulders. Carved in the round, the massive figure symbolizes the paradigmatic heroic god-king, or deva-raja. The figure wears a prominent turban wrapped with pearls or beads, surmounted by a flourish of folds imitating an open cobra hood. He is nude except for a revealing dhoti, or lower garment, which is gathered between his legs and held by a belt. An immense swath of fabric is flamboyantly tied, extending from the figure's left hip, where part of the left hand remains. His round face and facial details of open eyes and a slightly smiling mouth typify the Kushan style. He is unadorned except for a garland and ear plaques. The arching cobra and its open hood are carved in relief on the back of the sculpture. The very top of the cobra hood and the lower extremities of the deity are now void.

AGP

LITERATURE

Czuma 1977, 89–91, 105, figs. 6–7.
Czuma 1985, 83–84, cat. no. 25.

64

Seated Buddha Torso

India, Andhra Pradesh, Iksvaku period, late 3rd century
Pale green limestone
16¾ × 15 in. (42.5 × 38.1 cm.)

86.227.24, Gift of the Ernest Erickson Foundation, Inc.

This figure's position, hand gestures, and attributes, and the two deer in the center of the throne, are emblematic of the scene of the historical Buddha's First Sermon in the Deer Park at Sarnath. The image is probably from Nagarjunakonda, in the Guntur district of the modern state of Andhra Pradesh, one of the greatest art centers in ancient India. Buddhist artistic activity at Nagarjunakonda enjoyed the patronage of the Iksvaku rulers, mostly their queens and princesses, who succeeded the Satavahanas at the end of the second century and ruled until early in the fourth century.

The greenish limestone used in this sculpture is typical of the stone sculptures of Nagarjunakonda. This Buddha, with his head missing, is seated in a half-lotus position known as a *satamaparyanka asana*. The left hand on his lap forms a gesture of contemplation (*dhyana mudra*), and the broken right hand must once have displayed the gesture of protection (*abhaya mudra*). The wheel on the sole of the Buddha's foot refers to the Wheel of Law, which he set in motion. Two seated lions with their heads turned back flank the deer on the front of the throne and are associated with royal and heroic virtues.

AGP

LITERATURE

Los Angeles County Museum of Art 1950, 22, cat. no. 34.
Asia Society 1962, 42–43, cat. no. 26.
Katz 1963, 57, cat. no. 95.
Pal 1984, 195, cat. no. 78.
Poster 1987, 148–49, cat. no. 66.
Brooklyn 1988, 100–101, cat. no. 66.
Stone 1994, 50, 66, fig. 109, 174.
Brooklyn 1997, 45.

65

Vishnu's Battle with the *Rakshashas*

India, Uttar Pradesh, Gupta period, 5th century

Red terracotta relief

12¼ × 14¾ × 4½ in. (31 × 37.5 × 11.5 cm.)

73.124, Gift of Dr. Bertram H. Schaffner

Vishnu, the Hindu Preserver of the Universe, rises on his eagle mount Garuda, shown in anthropomorphic form with his wings outspread. Vishnu is four-armed and holds a bow in his upper-left hand and a conch held to his lips with his lower left; the two right hands are now missing. An attendant, who also holds a bow in his outstretched arm, accompanies the deity. The presence of the bow and conch may represent the *Uttarakanda* section, or Chapter Six, of the *Ramayana* epic in which Vishnu battles the demonic *rakshashas*. The demons are not visible in this narrative panel, but the text tells us that Vishnu disperses his adversaries with his arrows, using his conch to strike awe and terror as he rides on Garuda.

This panel is crafted in the regional style of Mathura, particularly with the modeling of the figures, the curled hair in the Gupta period (320–647) style – here articulated by stamped circles over the wiglike headdresses – and with the circular punch marks over the wing and in the lower-right corner. As in other terracotta reliefs of the Gupta period, the hands are summarily modeled, but the heads are fully rendered in high relief with arched brows, pierced eyes, and structured cheekbones, all of which lend expression to the group.

AGP

LITERATURE

Poster 1973, cat. no. 52.
Pal 1978b, 81, no. 28.
Banerjee 1985, 86–88.
Huntington and Huntington 1985, 216, fig. 10.38.
Poster 1986, 154–55, cat. no. 92.

66

Green Tara

India, Orissa, Cuttack Hills, 8th century
Weathered gneiss
67⅜ × 26 × 17 ½ in. (171.2 × 66 × 44 cm.)

60.138, Carll H. de Silver Fund and Ella C. Woodward Memorial Fund

This imposing stone sculpture, which has been in the Museum's collection since 1937, depicts Tara, the Buddhist goddess of compassion. The Sanskrit word *tar,* meaning "to cross over," refers to Tara's role as a guiding light for Buddhist practitioners. In particular, Tara helps living beings to "cross over" from a world of suffering, sickness, and death to a state of transcendental peace and enlightenment. Like most Indian divinities, Tara wears the diaphanous garments, jewelry, and elaborate headdress of a royal figure. Her divine status is indicated by the rectangular lotus pedestal on which she stands, the halo behind her head, and the small kneeling devotee at the lower left. Her right hand is extended in the gesture of giving and her broken left hand most likely offered freedom from fear.

There are many manifestations of Tara, but the most popular are the Green Tara and White Tara. In a 1966 essay, BMA Associate Curator Lois Katz identified this image as Green Tara, based on the partially closed lotus in the upper-right section of the sculpture, an attribute unique to this manifestation of the goddess. Another of Green Tara's iconographic features is the miniature Buddha Amoghasiddhi, embodying wisdom, which she wears in her headdress (abraded in the Brooklyn Tara). The four-armed figure at the bottom right is Ekajata, who is frequently depicted as an attendant to Green Tara. Green Tara is a particularly popular divinity because of her ability to protect her followers from harm and danger.

Stylistically, the Brooklyn Tara can be dated to the eighth century and attributed to a particular area known as the Cuttack Hills, in the Indian state of Orissa. Careful visual comparison of the Brooklyn Tara with documented eighth-century sculptures from the Cuttack Hills provides ample evidence for this attribution. Stylistic similarities include a massive quality and robust physique, a distinctive oval shape of the face, heavy-lidded eyes, and soft, tubular limbs.

It is worth noting that the eighth century was a florescent period for Buddhism in Orissa. The early rulers of the Bhaumakara dynasty (8th–10th century) were devout Buddhists, and the religion continued to prosper even under later Hindu rulers. The Cuttack Hills region was the site of several large Buddhist monasteries during this period, and Orissa played a major role in the development of Mahayana and Tantric Buddhism. As one of only a handful of Orissan Buddhist sculptures in the United States, the Brooklyn Tara is an important visual document of a crucial period in Indian Buddhism.

TB

LITERATURE

Archives of the Chinese Society of America 1961, 37, fig. 4.
Katz 1966–67, 113–28.
Brooklyn 1967, 124–25.
Newman 1984, 40–41, fig. 35.
Behera and Donaldson 1998, 117.

67

Seated Tara

Eastern India, Bihar, Pala dynasty, 9th century
Black schist
30¼ × 15½ × 7¼ in. (76.9 × 39.4 × 18.5 cm.)

1995.136, Purchased with funds given by Dr. Bertram H. Schaffner

From the eighth to the eleventh century, the eastern region of the Indian subcontinent was ruled by a group of kings known as the Palas (8th–12th century), who were renowned as generous patrons of art and culture. During this time, Buddhism flourished at great monastic universities, and numerous foreign pilgrims came to visit the many sites associated with the Buddha's birth and preaching. They encountered the aesthetic and cultural traditions of the Pala kingdoms, and this cultural exchange had important influence on Buddhist art in other regions of Asia, as is evidenced in the artistic and iconographic developments in China, Indonesia, Burma, Tibet, and Nepal.

This imposing ninth-century image of the Buddhist divinity Tara marks the eminence of the Pala artisans. Her image is especially cherished in Buddhist art, as she represents a beacon on the Buddhist path to enlightenment. Her divinity is manifold and she is also celebrated for her maternal qualities and her wisdom. In this image she is associated with the bodhisattva Amoghasiddhi (the follower of Buddha depicted as the "all-accomplishing insight" attained by Buddha during his enlightenment), and like him, she is associated with the color green. Her right hand is extended in the gesture of gift bestowing (*varada mudra*), and in her left hand she holds the stalk of a closed blue lotus.

The two lions on the base of the throne are copied from the earliest Buddhist iconography of the Maurya period (322–185 B.C.), nearly a millennium before the creation of this sculpture. Two small devotees worship the goddess at her feet and the two musicians in the upper portion witness her beauty.

Often, Pala sculptures were created as independent steles to be set into shrines or niches as part of the larger architectural arrangement of brick temples. This stele has a rounded upper portion that helps to date the image to the ninth century, after which the pointed stele was more commonly used. Tara's voluptuous figure and full circular breasts emphasize her earthly quality and typify the style of the early Pala period. The fashion of the period is demonstrated in the lavishly incised textiles of her upper garment and the delicate jewelry that adorns her. Many of these sculptures were almost certainly painted, which undoubtedly enhanced their visual effect. This image can be associated with the Bihar district of Gaya because of the deep and highly detailed carving, including the flame motif on the border of the halo and the posture of the figure.

The Sanskrit inscription around the halo is a formulaic Buddhist invocation carved in the local *devanagari* script and used on many Pala images: "Invoke the presence of the Dharma, the universal truth taught and embodied by the . . . [god or goddess in the image]." *SM/AGP*

LITERATURE

Pal 1978c, 90–91, cat. no. 53.

68

Agni

Northern India, probably central Madhya Pradesh,
c. early 10th century
Sandstone
32½ × 10 in. (82.5 × 25.4 cm.)

77.199, Gift of Bernice and Robert Dickes

A rare subject in detached stone sculpture, the Hindu divinity Agni is represented as a potbellied, two-armed male deity. Here he has an elliptical aureole of flames (*jvalas*) emanating from his shoulders and marking his divine nature as the keeper of fire. He is bearded and his hair is tied in a high chignon with jeweled hair ornaments. Clothed in a tightly fitting dhoti, he wears the sacred thread (*yajnopavita*), necklaces, and a draped linked girdle. Only the head and torso of the figure remain; the arms are void below the shoulders and the legs are broken off below the knees. As one of the guardians of the four directions, Agni would be placed at the southeastern direction of a structural temple. But the divinity plays many roles in Hindu culture and religion and can even be traced to pre-Hindu Vedic culture, where he was the sacred keeper of the sacrificial fire.

Although the provenance of this piece is unknown, the softly modeled torso with ornamentation in high relief corresponds to tenth-century stone reliefs from central Madhya Pradesh in northern India. Vishakha Desai and Darielle Mason note comparable examples in sculptures found at Ashapuri, such as a standing Shaiva ascetic figure from the Bhutanatha temple.

Agni's youthful face and idealized facial features play contrast to the naturalism of the sagging, protruding belly. Such refined and expressive characteristics indicate the work of an anonymous craftsman who, under the supervision of a temple leader, would follow strictly codified rules of scale and iconography in the creation of this Hindu divinity.

The earliest stone image of Agni is from Mathura and dates to the Kushan period (c. 50–320). In their 1993 publication, Desai and Mason confirm the identification of this sculptural figure as Agni.

AGP

LITERATURE

Archives of Asian Art 1979, 86, fig. 4.
Desai and Mason 1993, 152, cat. no. 7.
Brooklyn 1997, 46.

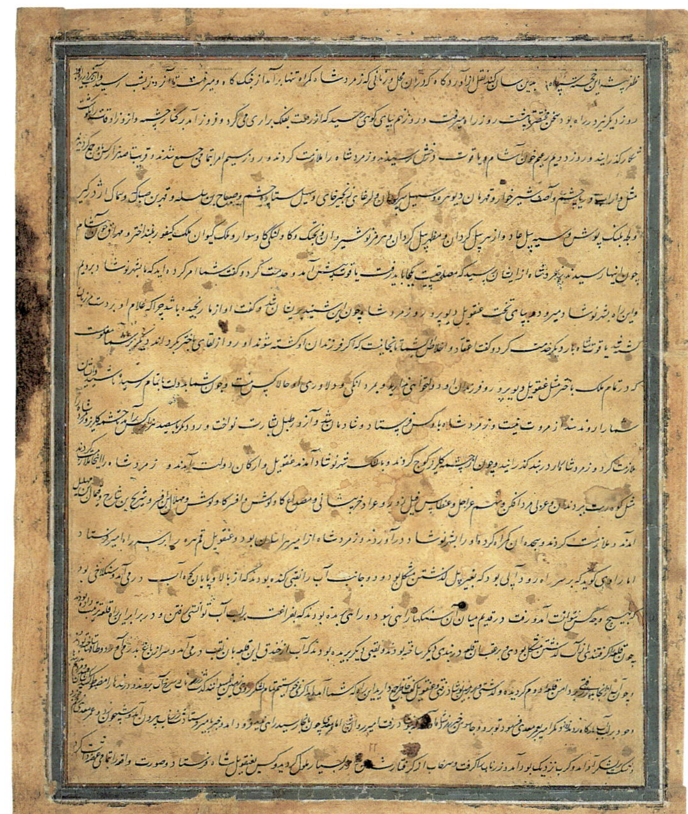

Reverse

69

Zumurrud Shah Takes Refuge in the Mountains

Folio from the *Hamzanama*
India, Akbar period, c. 1570
Opaque watercolor and gold on cotton cloth
Overall: 31 × 25 in. (78.8 × 63.5 cm.); image: 26¾ × 20⅛ in. (68 × 51.1 cm.)

24.48, Museum Collection Fund

The *Qissa-i Amir Hamza* (Story of Amir Hamza), or *Hamzanama* as it is commonly known, recounts the picturesque exploits of Hamza, the uncle of the Prophet Muhammad. The Mughal emperor Akbar (r. 1556–1605), who enjoyed these stories so much that he personally recited them in the harem, ordered his artists to prepare an illustrated copy of the *Hamzanama* on a scale never seen before – 1,400 paintings on sheets of paper backed with cloth measuring a yard square. Literary sources record that though more than fifty painters busied themselves with the colossal undertaking, it took fifteen years to complete. A date of 1564–65 on one painting early in the manuscript helps fix the starting date of the project at 1557, shortly after the thirteen-year-old Akbar acceded to the throne.

The large size of the paintings allowed them to be used in a manner different from most Mughal manuscripts. Rather than forming part of a bound volume that an individual would cradle and peruse, these paintings were held up for display to a larger audience while a storyteller expanded on the story summarized on the reverse of the preceding folio. The painters, several of whom collaborated on such paintings, chose among the many narrative possibilities of the complicated stories. Here they bypassed such colorful episodes as a hero trapped alive in a coffin, a romantic ruse that led to the conquest of a fort, a host of battles, and the seizing of an enemy's treasury. Instead, they elected to depict Hamza's arch-rival, the giant Zumurrud Shah, after he fled the battle and reached the foot of a towering mountain, where he regrouped his allies. The artists substituted a domestic spirit for the martial one described in the text as they filled the area around the giant with such extraneous genre elements as villagers herding bulls and women tending their children. The four folios held by the BMA are treasures of the Indian painting collection.

JS

LITERATURE

Brooklyn 1967, 128–29.
Khandalavala and Chandra 1969, 70, 78, 111.
Chandra 1989, 41, fig. 1.
Faridany-Akhavan 1989, 99, pl. 22.
Seyller 1993, 502–5.
Chandra 1994, 62, 64.
Poster 1994, 68, cat. no. 23.
Seyller 2002, 130–31, cat. no. 39.

70

Wall Hanging (*Kalamkari*)

India, Madras region (Pulicat?), c. 1610–20
Painted resist and mordants, dyed cotton
108¼ × 37¾ in. (275 × 96 cm.)

14.719.2, Museum Expedition 1914, Museum Special Fund

This painted textile originally formed part of a seven-panel wall hanging in the collection of the Brooklyn Museum. Its large size and composition of repeating arches and columns suggest that the work was intended for use within a setting of monumental architectural elements. It recalls the raja's palace of Chandragiri, a sixteenth- to seventeenth-century capital of the southern Indian kingdom of Vijayanagar. It was most likely made at Pulicat, a port and textile-producing center on the Coromandel Coast under the control of Chandragiri. Stylistically, the piece relates to wall paintings in the few surviving monuments of Vijayanagar, which historical sources describe as portraying "all the ways of life of the men who have been here even down to the Portuguese, from which the king's wives can understand the manner in which each one lives in his own country" (Gittinger 1982, 92). As with such wall paintings, this hanging may have been intended for the harem.

On four or five registers within the arch of each panel, distinct figure types are portrayed. The panel selected here depicts men and women in European dress. The cut of the men's billowing trousers, their neck and wrist ruffs, and their tall hats closely resemble late sixteenth- and early seventeenth-century European dress. However, the patterns of the cloth from which the clothes are made derive from native Indian textiles. Despite their European dress, the women may be Indian, for until the 1620s, English and Dutch traders in India took local women as their wives and mistresses. The artist may have looked to Western prints for such motifs as the nursing mother in the lower register. Although the activity here cannot be precisely identified, the seated figures are offering and receiving jewels, and may refer to the significant jewel trade that was carried out in the ports of the Coromandel Coast.

The present work is a *kalamkari*, a painted cloth or textile in which the design is achieved by applying dye with a pen, or *kalam*, rather than by printing or stamping. For centuries India has been famous worldwide for fine woven and dyed textiles. The region of southern India produced textiles that combined the techniques of block printing and wax resist with hand-painted details in colors that included red, violet, brown, blue, yellow, green, and violet-black. These textiles eventually developed into the important trade items calico and chintz.

Because of the fragile state of repair of the hanging at the time of acquisition in 1914, the Museum Conservation Department divided the seven panels and mounted them separately. This panel is one of three that were restored and featured in the 1982 special exhibition *Master Dyers to the World*, organized by the Textile Museum in Washington, D.C.
AGP

LITERATURE

Brooklyn 1967, 132–35.
Gittinger 1982, 89–108, cat. no. 81.
Lawrence 1989, 22, fig. 2.
Poster 1994, 15, fig. 1.

71

Stalling Elephant

India, Deccan, Bijapur, mid-17th century
Opaque watercolor, ink, and gold on paper
6½ × 4⅞ in. (16.5 × 12.4 cm.)

2002.38, Gift of Dr. Bertram H. Schaffner in honor of his 90th Birthday

The painting depicts two mahouts who guide their elephant to take a bow. The younger mahout holds an elephant goad in his right hand and leans forward, touching his forehead with his left hand. The elephant bows with outstretched forelegs and curled trunk. The older mahout, with long mustache and light beard, sits farther back on the elephant and holds onto a saddlecloth cord with his thumb and forefinger to balance the movement of the elephant.

Stalling Elephant is a masterwork of the Deccani Indian tradition of paper marbling, which flourished briefly during the seventeenth century. There are approximately twenty-seven published examples of figurative marbling in public and private collections that have been linked to the Deccan (Weimann 1983). This particular example represents one of the most complex and sensitive manipulations of the paper marbler's art. The elephant, riders' costumes, and saddlecloths are made from four different patterns of combed marbling on a single page. Such a feat was possible, as Christopher Weimann has demonstrated (Weimann 1983), by employing a complex, multi-stage technique, in which stencils were used to cover areas that were not to be marbled. After the marbling was accomplished, the riders' faces and shawls, the elephant's bells and cords, and the tree and birds in the sparely decorated background were painted and accented with gold. The figures in this work show strong Mughal influence, reflecting the artistic environment of the Deccan, then a melting pot that included Persian, Turkish, and northern Indian, primarily Mughal, traditions.

The seal along the upper left edge of the work is smudged and incomplete because the painting has been trimmed down. It was described previously as illegible (Poster 1994, 105). With the help of Dr. John Seyller, however, a date, A.H. 1105 / A.D. 1693–94, and regnal year, 2, were deciphered.

AF

LITERATURE

Poster 1994, 105, cat. no. 58.
Weimann 1983, 135–37.

72

Siddha Lakshmi with Kali

Folio 34 from *Tantric Devi* series
India, Punjab Hills, Basohli, c. 1660–70
Opaque watercolor, gold, silver, and peacock blue-green beetle wing cases on paper
Overall: 8⅝ × 8½ in. (21.9 × 21.6 cm.); image: 7⅛ × 6 11/16 in. (18 x 17 cm.)

84.142, Gift of Mr. and Mrs. Robert L. Poster in honor of Dr. Bertram H. Schaffner

Shimmering and radiant against a rich sienna background, the goddess Lakshmi, as Bhadrakali, is seated at the center of this painting on a large open lotus. She is exquisitely dressed in a gold sari and lotus crown with a silver-rayed halo and ornaments detailed with applied beetle wing cases. She raises a gold fluted vessel to her lips in her right hand and holds the stem of a lotus bud in her left. Dark-skinned with gaping mouth and fangs and the attributes of Shiva (crescent moon and the third eye on the forehead), dressed in a bright orange full skirt detailed with stylized gold flowers, Kali, the Goddess of Time, stands to her right holding a wine beaker. The goddess Lakshmi's lotus pedestal rises out of a pond represented by a semicircular arc banked by a strip of grass. Two sprouting lotus leaves and an overall pattern of tiny lotus petals are in the pond at the lower part of the page. The sky is indicated by a narrow cloud band at the top of the page, which has a wide red border with silver rules marking an inner border.

The seated goddess has a golden-yellow skin color, typical of Lakshmi, Vishnu's consort, in Indian iconography. She is seated on a lotus and holding a lotus stalk in her right hand and her crown is decorated with lotuses; the lotus is also associated with Lakshmi, and never with the goddess Kali. The terrifying goddess Kali is always depicted in Indian sculpture and painting as scantily dressed and sometimes topless, as is the case with the attendant here. But the main figure is dressed in the formal attire of a full skirt, *choli*, and scarf. All of these attributes confirm the fact that the seated figure is Siddha Lakshmi and the standing companion is Kali. A verse in Takri script inscribed on the verso also supports the identification.

Although the subject may be related to a Shaivite theme, the introduction of the lotus crown, the golden garment, and the lotus seat of the principal goddess may reflect a new interest in Vaishnava religious attributes. Recent scholarship has brought to light the rise of Vaishnava cults in Basohli during the mid-seventeenth century under Raja Sangram Pal (r. 1635–c. 1673).

In other paintings of this now-dispersed series illustrating the manifestations of the Great Goddess, she is often shown savoring the potent liquor she demands for nourishment, as here, or trampling the corpses of those she has vanquished. The series has been called *Tantric Devi* because the text inscribed in the local *takri* script of the Punjab Hills on the reverse of each page illustrates an unidentified manuscript in praise of tantric goddesses such as Bhadrakali, Bhima, and Shyama.

The Hill states of Kulu and Mankot had close political ties to the court of Basohli, and the highly stylized mode of Basohli painting became the prototype for the painting styles that emerged in those states. Many paintings from the same series have been discussed in the relevant literature: two paintings are in the Chandigarh Museum and one is in the collection of the National Museum, New Delhi. Six leaves were acquired in 1918 by the Lahore Museum and one is held by the Sri Pratap Singh Museum, Srinagar. There are single unpublished examples in the Museum of Fine Arts, Boston, and the Los Angeles County Museum of Art. This page is one of a second group of twelve pages, acquired by an American traveling in Amritsar in 1922, which came to light in 1979 and was subsequently dispersed.

AGP

INSCRIPTION

Inscribed, at top right: "Siddha Lakshmi with Kali."
On reverse: "One should [let one] meditate thus in the lotus of his heart on Siddha Lakshmi, goddess of remembrance, Bhadrakali [all epithets of Siddha Lakshmi] who is young, with a face resembling the rising moon and crown bedecked with the crescent moon. Whose priceless graceful form is clad in a yellow dress, seated on an eightfold [cosmic] lotus, accompanied by Kali, drinking draughts of liquor." (Trans. Sonali Mitra, Poster 1994, 236)

LITERATURE

Pal 1983, 278, pl. 4.
Poster 1994, 236–38, cat. no. 191.
Poster 1995, 66, fig. 10.
Dehejia 1999, 262, cat. no. 31.

३४

73

Silver-Gilt Rosewater Sprinkler

India, Mughal dynasty, early 17th century
Silver with ring-punched decoration
H: 11⅝ in. (29.5 cm.)

2001.5, Gift of Georgia and Michael de Havenon in honor of Layla S. Diba on her retirement as Hagop Kevorkian Curator of Islamic Art

Rosewater sprinklers, or *gulabpash*, served an important Mughal (1526–1756) court ceremonial role in the welcoming of guests, and they continue to be used for auspicious occasions in India today. This beautiful silver-gilt engraved and openwork rosewater sprinkler is made from two interlocking sections: a graceful tapering neck capped by a floral bud and a round bulbous body decorated in reserved and engraved floral bouquets and palmettes resting on a splayed foot with openwork floral panels.

The Brooklyn Museum sprinkler is from the same family collection as another silver-gilt rosewater sprinkler once owned by the first earl of Denbigh and engraved with the coat of arms of William, second earl of Desmond and third earl of Denbigh. Through European documentation, we can date much of India's precious materials in circulation during the seventeenth and eighteenth centuries. From Sir Thomas Herbert's *Travels in Persia, 1627–29*, we know that the first earl of Denbigh traveled to Surat, India, in 1631. Both pieces are believed to have been acquired by the first earl during this trip. It is extremely rare to find rosewater sprinklers and silver-gilt pieces of such an early date and quality, and this piece expands the BMA's presentation of metalwork from the early seventeenth century, when contact between India and the West was encouraged.

AF

LITERATURE

Pal 1989, 148, 245 n. 47.

74

Ivory Throne Leg

India, Orissa, 17th century
Ivory with traces of color
15½ × 4⅛ in. (39.4 × 10.5 cm.)

1992.83, Gift of the Asian Art Council

The indigenous craft traditions of eastern India long predate the arrival of the Mughals in India in the mid-sixteenth century, when the emperor Akbar (r. 1556–1605) succeeded in annexing the northern part of the subcontinent. Carved ivory components for furniture were common in eastern India from early times, with a few examples of furniture most likely intended for royal use. A multitude of connections exists between furniture design and the architecture of Orissa, an area of staunch Hindu orthodoxy. A dedicatory inscription on the Jaganatha Temple at the seacoast town of Puri records the gift of eight sets of carved ivory thrones to the king's personal deity during the reign of King Purushottamdeva (r. 1467–97).

The Orissan ivory throne leg belongs to a set of four, now dispersed. It displays a range of qualities that add to our current understanding of the rich diversity of syncretic idioms that flourished in the ancient regions of India. The carving in high relief depicts a rearing mythical lion (*vyala* or *shardula*) bearing a long beaked nose with flaring nostrils, a deeply carved toothy grin, and luxuriant fur carved in cascading ringlets. Enormous strength emanates from the elongated proportions of the lion, enhanced by minutely carved details, such as a delicate landscape with animals emerging from a rocky mountain on the reverse side. The lion is a typical motif for the throne of divinity and a symbol of royal authority.

Most of the complete throne legs of the seventeenth century are attributed to Mughal manufacture, but specific ornamental details indicate a contrary provenance for this refined work. The meticulous carving and ingenious compression of miniature elements present a layering of detail and balance of form that reflect its Orissan counterparts in other media. The mannered stylization of the rearing animal, including the configuration of a head turned backward, provides a pose that is strangely contorted, yet not menacing. The hunting scene combined with such mannerisms is an earmark of Orissan ivory throne legs.

AGP

LITERATURE
Archives of Asian Art 1993, 110, fig. 8.

75

Attributed to Ghasi

Maharana Jawan Singh of Mewar Receiving the Governor General of India, Lord William Cavendish Bentinck, February 8th, 1832

India, Rajasthan, Udaipur

Opaque watercolor, gold, and silver on cloth

74 7/16 × 50 3/8 in. (189 × 128 cm.)

2002.34, Gift of the Alvin E. Friedman-Kien Foundation, Inc., in honor of Dr. Bertram H. Schaffner's 90th Birthday

This unusually large painting on cotton is visually striking and of great historical importance, for it depicts a meeting from the 1832 Ajmer *darbar*, considered to be the first major gathering of Rajput rulers and the British governor general. A *darbar* is an official audience between rulers that includes a series of strictly regulated ceremonial meetings heralded by gun salutes and punctuated by an exchange of *nazar* (gifts). The Ajmer *darbar*, which was initiated by the governor general Lord William Cavendish Bentinck, began on January 17, 1832, and concluded the following month. The BMA painting contains a treasure trove of visual details from the meeting on February 8 that corroborate and expand on the contemporary historical accounts of the *darbar*.

In the painting, Maharana Jawan Singh of Mewar (r. 1828–38) receives Lord Bentinck before a royal red *darbar* tent and enclosure. Jawan Singh, identified here by his gold nimbus and gold *patka* (sash), as well as his ceremonial sword and shield, and Lord Bentinck, who is formally attired in an orange coat, share a seat on a throne made especially for the occasion. The red royal tent's double awning, edged in emerald green and elaborately decorated with a pattern of gilded floral vine scrolls, forms a natural backdrop for the stage-like presentation of this ceremony and its principals, Jawan Singh and Bentinck. The cast of characters, primarily Mewar nobles (*thakars*) and British officials, unfolds in neatly delineated rows around the perimeter of the pristine white-cotton carpet that is center stage.

It is noteworthy that both Rajput and British officials are seated on European-style chairs. Dr. Joachim Bautze suggests that the introduction of chairs was a sign of British predominance since the Rajputs did not use chairs (Bautze 1998, 161). It also may be observed that the white-stockinged feet of nearly every figure within the royal tent enclosure were probably not an oversight on the part of the artist. The single figure depicted with his shoes on is Jawan Singh, whose gold footwear lends a certain edge of power to the maharana. His position of prominence is further denoted by his dress and adornment, and by the ceremonial peacock feather fans (*morchals*) held by his attendants. Jawan Singh's gifts to the British include multi-colored bolts of cloth laid out on the white carpet before the stepped platform.

The painting has a well-documented provenance, having long been in the collection of Dr. William K. Ehrenfeld. There is extensive commentary on the painting by Bautze, the leading expert on historical Rajput painting, who attributes this example to the court artist Ghasi (Bautze 1998). This artist is known for his clearly delineated *darbar* paintings that visually reflect the ceremonial attention to protocol and hierarchy.

AF

LITERATURE

Bautze 1998, 158–63, cat. no. 40.
Ray 2002, 105–9, cat. no. 64.

76

Narasimha Avatara

Eastern India, Calcutta, Kalighat, c. 1910
Watercolor, ink, and silver on paper
Sheet: $17\frac{1}{4} \times 11$ in. (43.5×28 cm.)

1997.145, Gift of Dr. Bertram H. Schaffner

The Hindu deity Vishnu assumes the half man–half lion form in his incarnation as Narasimha to destroy the immortal demon Hiranyakashipu, the father of his devotee Prahalad. In a well-known episode of Hindu mythology, Prahalad's unwavering faith in Vishnu is tested by Hiranyakashipu, whose powers of immortality make him invincible in day or night, on earth or in heaven, indoors or outdoors, and indestructible by any weapon, man, or beast. On Prahalad's beckoning, Vishnu descends from heaven in the form of Narasimha. By appearing at dusk, through a pillar at the threshold of the house, he challenges Hiranyakashipu's invincibility and cleverly annihilates the demon with his claws.

This image was produced at Kalighat in Calcutta, a Hindu temple site dedicated to the worship of the goddess Kali. Kalighat paintings were made for commercial sale to pilgrims who visited the temple. The Kalighat school of painting flourished from the mid-nineteenth century until the early part of the twentieth century. In a departure from the conventional technique in traditional Indian miniature paintings of layering bold pigment, these images display the blossoming of a new graphic quality. The artists emphasized form with fluid ink outlines and a strong graduated palette of transparent watercolors, and imbued their figures with a renewed vigor through calligraphic brushstrokes of black ink and color, which appear brighter on the machine-made paper. In many Kalighat images, the figure of Narasimha is composed in a theatrical setting. The god is portrayed in this painting with bent legs and arched forearms, a pose popular in classical Indian dance.

Although the Kalighat artists mainly depicted religious subjects, they also incorporated into their oeuvre secular and political themes. They often illustrated the tenuous relationship between the Calcutta elite and the British rulers. By adapting this iconographic representation of Narasimha to portray the demon as an English gentleman with a mustache and Western shoes, the artist reveals a subtle commentary on contemporary Calcutta society.

SM

77

Brahmanical Triad

Kashmir, early 8th century
Green chlorite
$7\frac{1}{8} \times 6\frac{1}{4}$ in. (18.1 × 15.8 cm.)

78.209, A. Augustus Healy Fund and the Asian Art Acquisition Fund

Brahma and Vishnu, each with his personified attributes, are depicted here flanking the central image of the god Shiva, who appears in the form of the *lingam*, the phallic symbol of Shiva. The three deities constitute the principal divinities of Brahmanism. Traditionally, Brahma is considered to be the Creator, whereas Vishnu is the Preserver and Shiva, the Destroyer. The Kashmir relief is one of only two known representations of the three gods in one icon.

At the left the four-armed Brahma is shown as an ascetic brahmin priest with matted locks and large hoop earrings, wearing monastic robes and carrying a staff and water pot in his left hands. Unfortunately, the attributes of his right hands are damaged and thus unidentifiable. Two geese (*hamsa*) are shown at his feet. At the center is the *lingam*. To the right stands four-armed Vishnu, accompanied by a female at his right, symbolizing the mace, and a male to his left, representing the Wheel of Law, or a discus. He also carries a conch and lotus in his upper hands. A diminutive image of the earth goddess Bhudevi is shown between his feet. Such details and the placement of Shiva at the center of the icon may indicate that this was the object of a Shaivite cult, although in Kashmir, the source of this icon, Vishnu was customarily considered the supreme deity, and Brahma and Shiva were worshipped as different aspects of Vishnu.

AGP

LITERATURE

Pal 1973–74, 33–34, fig. 1.
Archives of Asian Art 1980, 118, fig. 5.
Kramrisch 1981, 9, cat. no. 8.
Poster 1982, 261–62, fig. 5.

78

Standing Vishnu

Nepal, 9th–10th century
Copper alloy
H: 9½ in. (24.1 cm.)

80.278.1, Gift of Cynthia Hazen Polsky

The Hindu divinity Vishnu figures prominently in Nepalese art. Usually depicted with four arms as seen here, he can be shown in any one of his ten incarnations. In early images, such as this bronze, he is represented standing, wearing a crown and adorned with jeweled earrings, necklaces, armlets, bracelets, and girdle and wearing a stylized flamed halo. In his hands he holds the requisite attributes: the flaming wheel (*chakra*), lotus, conch, and mace, which is missing from the upper left hand. The graceful rendering of the dhoti, patterned with an incised stripe-and-dot pattern, and the sash at his waist, holding the sacred thread (*yajnopavita*) extending from his left shoulder, accentuate the hieratic posture of the figure. These are stylistic aspects associated with Nepalese images of the Licchavi period (300–879/880).

The Vishnu also represents the earliest phase of bronze casting in Nepal. The copper content of the bronze provides a rich orange-brown coloration to the piece that is typical of such early pieces. This figure compares to several other magnificent images of standing deities, dating from the seventh to eleventh century, many of which also appear on rectangular bases. While details of clothing and jewelry compare in form, it is the suave naturalistic modeling of the figures that is the keynote of Nepalese art.

AGP

79

Folios from a *Gandavyuha* Manuscript

Nepal, 12th century
Colors on palm leaf
2 × 21⅝ in. (5.1 × 54.9 cm.) each

86.227.136, .137, Gift of the Ernest Erickson Foundation, Inc.

The earliest evidence of the preparation of illuminated manuscripts in eastern India and Nepal dates to around 1000. These early works, principally intended to bestow spiritual merit on a Buddhist patron and his family, were made of palm leaves, with the text written in Sanskrit and illuminations painted in small rectangular panels on both sides. Such manuscript illumination became increasingly refined over the next two centuries.

These two leaves are from a dispersed, undated manuscript, of which leaves are known in the Cleveland Museum of Art, the Los Angeles County Museum of Art, the Virginia Museum of Fine Arts, Richmond, the Seattle Art Museum, and the San Diego Museum of Art. The manuscript was formerly identified as the *Astasharika Prajnaparamita*, or the Sutra of Perfect Wisdom. However, in the 1978 study *The Arts of Nepal*, Pratapaditya Pal re-identified other leaves from the manuscript as the popular Sanskrit Mahayanist text *Gandavyuha*, often called "The Pilgrim's Progress of Buddhism." Pal has attributed the style to twelfth-century Nepal (Pal 1978a, 46–49). While expounding the basic function of spiritual teachers in Mahayana philosophy, the text describes the pilgrimage of Sudhana, a merchant's young son, and his encounters with a series of guides, teachers, hermits, monks, bodhisattvas, deities, and animals in a forest. The popularity of the text is indicated by the prominence of more than forty *Gandavyuha* panels carved in relief in the ninth-century temple at Borobudur, the chief Buddhist monument in central Java.

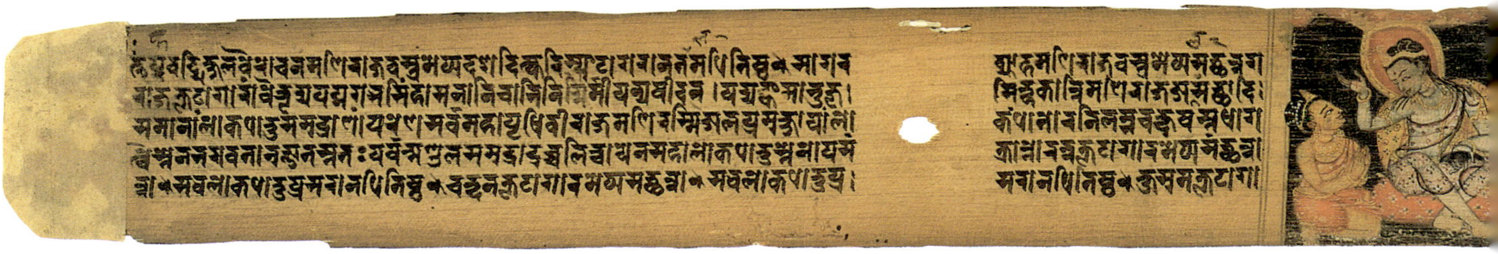

86.227.136

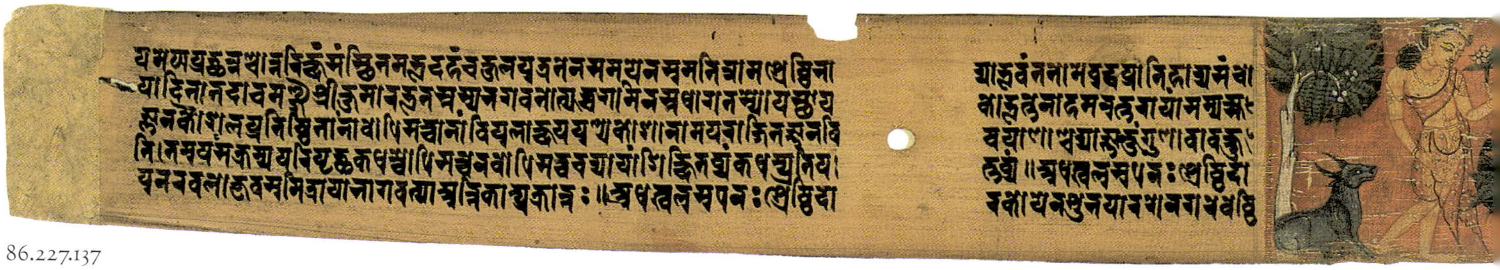

86.227.137

Like the other known *Gandavyuha* leaves, the two palm leaves from the Erickson Collection are sumptuously decorated. The Sanskrit text, which appears on both sides of the leaves, is divided into three sections by two holes for the threading of the pages. A square panel in the center of the obverse side of each page depicts figures in an abbreviated fashion, their profiles outlined in black against an uncluttered background. This style is closely related to the contemporaneous Pala tradition (8th–12th century) in eastern India, but the simple figural style of the narrative here is more lyrical, graceful, and lively. The folio painted on a blue background (86.227.136) depicts an unidentified seated divinity representing a divine teacher. He holds a text in his left hand and lectures to a kneeling figure of Sudhana. The folio painted on a red background (86.227.137) depicts Sudhana standing, wearing a yellow garment and holding a lotus in his left hand. A reclining deer is shown to his right, and a forest setting is suggested by the large green leaves of two banana trees. Neither illustration appears to bear any immediate connection to the text it accompanies.

AGP

LITERATURE

Katz 1963, 63–64, cat. no. 118a–b.
Poster 1987, 170–71, cat. nos. 118–19.
Poster 1994, 16, fig. 2.

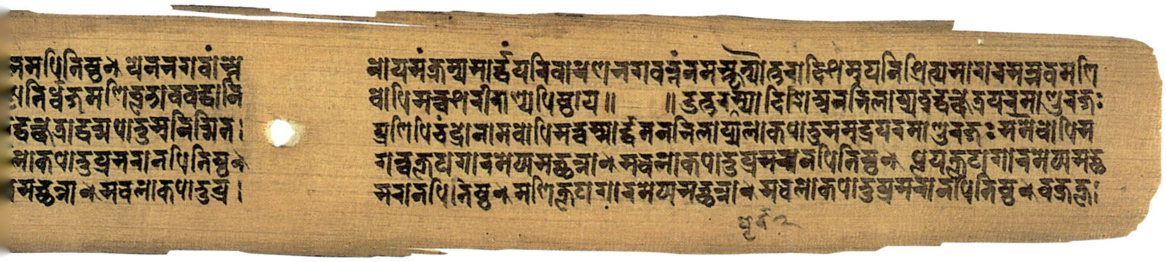

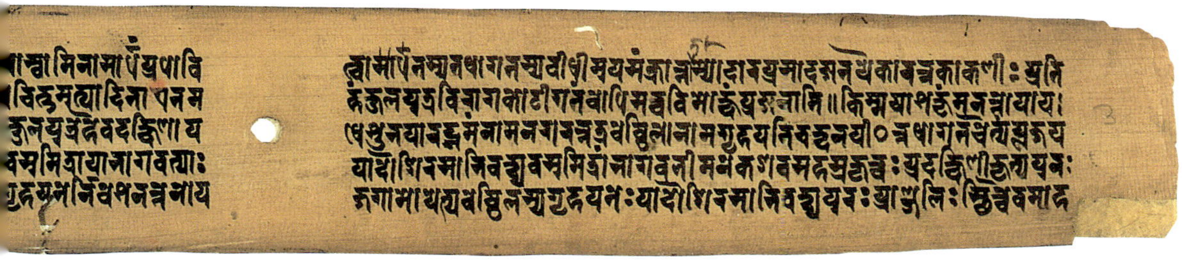

80

Seated Maitreya

Tibet, 13th–14th century
Gilt copper alloy
9½ × 7½ in. (24.1 × 19.1 cm.)

67.80, Charles Stewart Smith Memorial Fund

This wonderfully preserved image of Maitreya is shown making the teaching gesture of setting in motion the Wheel of Law. The image is identified as Maitreya, the Buddha of the Future, by the *stupa* (relic container) in his headdress and by the flanking lotus also surmounted by a *stupa*. The artist has emphasized the hieratic pose of the figure and the stereotyped gesture of the hands while at the same time conveying the Maitreya's authority and withdrawal to meditation by the figure's facial expression and down-turned eyes.

Although the spiked snail curls of this figure are seen in some Buddha images from western Tibet, the abstract patterning of the folds of the monastic garment, pulled taut over his outstretched knees, is more typical of Nepalese workmanship. Although such differences make attribution and dating of the piece difficult, it is known that Nepalese craftsmen were often employed in Tibet to produce bronze statuary. This piece has been cited by Ulrich von Schroeder as exemplary of Sino-Tibetan artistic exchanges, or of the Chinese influence on Tibetan art, because of its eastern Tibetan, or Kham and Amdo, stylistic elements, although few works remain in situ for sculptural documentation or comparison.
AGP

LITERATURE

Pal 1969, 145, cat. no. 45.
Beguin 1977, 177, no. 184.
Schroeder 1981, 342, fig. 87A.
Poster 1982, 263, fig. 8.
Brooklyn 1988, 107, cat. no. 71.
Brooklyn 1997, 48.
Pal 1997, 13, fig. v.
Singer and Denwood 1997, 13, fig. v.

81a

Manuscript Cover with the Five Tathagatas

Tibet, c. 1200
Wood with red color and gold
9⅝ × 27½ × 1⅛ in. (24.5 × 70 × 2.8 cm.)

1997.59.1, Gift of the Asian Art Council

81b

Upper Cover from an Unidentified Manuscript

Tibet, c. 13th century
Wood with color and semi-precious stones
7⅛ × 28½ × 1 in. (18 × 72.4 × 2.5 cm.)

1997.59.2, Gift of the Asian Art Council

81c

Upper Cover from an Unidentified Manuscript

Tibet, c. 14th century
Wood with color
10⅞ × 27½ × 1⅜ in. (27.6 × 70 × 3.5 cm.)

1997.59.3, Gift of the Asian Art Council

The Museum collection of Tibetan art consists of sculpture, painting, and ritual objects. In recent years, a corpus of manuscript covers has come to light, and these three works exemplify the range and style of these works. Made of wood and decorated with low-relief carving, polychrome, and gilt, these three Tibetan book covers present a fabulously rich and graphically powerful statement of the function and meaning of the book and the written word in Tibetan Buddhism.

Books in Tibet are sacred ritual objects, used by Buddhist monks in communal worship and the choral reading of texts. The subjects of the texts are translations of Indian sutras, or Buddhist texts. The book covers continue the traditional format of Indian books wherein stacks of loose leaves are contained between wooden covers.

Even without the manuscripts they once protected, these covers convey a wonderful story. Moreover, their brilliant decoration hints at the complex subject included within. The earliest example (no. 81a) depicts the five Dhyani Buddhas or Tathagatas (Transcendent Ones), carved in wood and highlighted with polychrome and gilding. From left to right, the Buddhas are Akshobhya, Ratnasambhava, Vairochana, Amitabha, and Amoghasiddhi. Each divinity wears a high crown and sits within an arch over paired animals. At the base is the auspicious *kirttimukha*, or "face of glory."

The second manuscript cover (no. 81b) is decorated with a painted surface of intersecting lines forming three diamond shapes, contrasted with a trapezoidal form and enhanced by the appliqué of three semi-precious stones of coral and turquoise. The patterns of the jewel encrustation and the arrangement of three diamond shapes suggest a stylized representation of the "Three Jewels of Buddhism," which are the Buddha, the Dharma (the doctrine or the scriptures), and the Sangha (assembly of saints), often represented in the hierarchical form of a ritual mandala.

In the third example (no. 81c) the wonderfully preserved images of twelve dancing female divinities are set against a red ground. In contrast to the more hieratic posture of the Buddhas in the second book cover, these goddesses are lively figures with their long black tresses and flowing scarves suggesting movement. The twelve females are *dakinis*, enlightened female divinities who embody and bestow transcendental wisdom. Their dynamic poses reflect the fluidity and energy found in Pala manuscript illustrations of the thirteenth and fourteenth centuries. Ornate floral scroll motifs executed in a highly refined style decorate the borders of this manuscript cover. The painting style here derived from Nepal and eastern India, but the cover itself was executed in Tibet. Its large size reflects the new tradition of using paper for manuscript illumination. In earlier times, palm leaves were used in India and Nepal until paper began to be used by the Tibetans.

AGP

LITERATURE

Rossi and Rossi 1996, cat. nos. 5, 18.

81a

81b

81c

82

Portrait of the Great Thangpa

Tibet, last quarter of the 13th century
Opaque watercolor and gold on cotton
20⅛ × 14⅞ in. (51.5 × 37.9 cm.)

1991.86, Gift of the Asian Art Council

The tradition of Buddhist portraiture in Tibet dates at least to the eleventh century. The central figure of this thangka (ritual painting) is Thangpa Chenpo (1142–1210), a leading ascetic monk of his time and founder around 1180–85 of the Tagklung monastery, one of central Tibet's seven most important and wealthiest Buddhist centers. A register beneath his throne may depict scenes from his life, and the border cartouches contain images of deities, guardians of the faith and the four directions, and teachers, marking the lineage of the central figure in a diagrammatic arrangement.

A Sanskrit inscription, painted in gold Tibetan script on the reverse of the thangka, gives the names of each of the figures represented and a long auspicious encomium to the abbot, who was known in the *Blue Annals* (the chief document of Tibet's early history) as a paradigmatic ascetic. Veneration of this monk is demonstrated by the replication of his portrait in many other contemporaneous versions. The number of portraits suggests a special ritual use.

The thangka is executed in gouache technique with brilliant mineral pigments and gold on an extremely fine cotton ground. The images are defined by an assured flowing line augmented by colors, with a solid red background isolating most of the figures. This style is based on an eastern Indian tradition, formed during the Pala dynasty (8th–12th century), whereas a Central Asian influence is seen in the abstract treatment of the elements of a landscape. These combined regional styles became the hallmark of the Karma Kagyu School of painting, named for one of the Tibetan Buddhist sects, which features these particular deities and teachers.
AGP

LITERATURE

Archives of Asian Art 1992, 100, fig. 2.
Brooklyn 1997, 49.

83a, b

Two Kneeling Figures

Thailand, Dvaravati period, c. 7th–8th century
Stucco

83a
11 × 5¼ × 4 in. (27.9 × 13.3 × 10 cm.)
86.227.161, Gift of the Ernest Erickson Foundation, Inc.

83b
10½ × 5¼ × 4 in. (26.7 × 13.3 × 10 cm.)
86.227.162, Gift of the Ernest Erickson Foundation, Inc.

These two extraordinary kneeling figurines, originally part of a frieze, exemplify the Dvaravati stucco tradition of the seventh and eighth centuries. Their kneeling posture suggests the typical repetition of idealized figures adoring a central Buddha image in architectural decorations. Each figure faces his right, presenting a three-quarter profile, and sits with his body resting gracefully on his left foot while his right leg is drawn up as a support for his right elbow. His eyes are downcast and his head slightly bowed, in a pose of respect.

The jewelry on the left figure (no. 83b) is clearly represented as a necklace, a large round earring worn in his left ear, upper-arm bands on his left arm, and a bracelet on his left wrist. Each figure wears a skirt, or dhoti, looped around the waist with a flamboyant pleated end between the legs. Their torsos are attenuated and delicately modeled. Although extensively repaired or possibly made up from a number of fragments, the figures are consistent in form, posture, and attire with stucco bas-reliefs excavated at Nakhon Pathom, a site in central Thailand. The attenuated body of the left figure, although in a seated pose, is comparable to other stucco fragments.

The head on the left figure shows a complex headdress and head ornaments and contrasts with that of the other figure (no. 83a), which exhibits the remains of snail shell-styled curls, the possibility of a cranial protuberance (*ushnisha*), and elongated earlobes – attributes associated with Buddha images. Both heads had been broken off their bodies and then replaced. The facial features particularly show a strong Indian influence.

AGP

LITERATURE

Poster 1987, 164–65, cat. nos. 112–13.

84

Seated Divinity

Indonesia, Central Java, 9th century

Volcanic stone

26¾ × 17$\frac{5}{16}$ × 25$\frac{9}{16}$ in. (68 × 44 × 65 cm.)

87.188.9, Gift of Georgia and Michael de Havenon

The ancient art of Java features religious icons that adorned Hindu and Buddhist temples. This beautifully preserved fragment of a male figure can be identified as Hindu by its posture and royal attire, and by the sacred thread, which takes the form of a serpent.

Although this is a fragment, certain attributes of the ascetic manifestation of the Hindu deity Shiva are recognizable, such as the long strands of hair that rest on the shoulders. Possibly the yogic form of Shiva carrying the serpent on his right shoulder, the figure is shown seated on a decorated cushion with his left hand resting in his lap. He is heavily ornamented with jewels and the sacred thread. Stylistic motifs of interest include the taut realism of the torso and the snake encircling it, as well as the subtle reference to the layering of two long garments that end just above the anklet.

Although the statue's original location within a temple is unknown, similar examples have been found in the main shrines, the side chapels, or on exterior walls of temples.

AGP

85

Torso of a Male Divinity

Cambodia, Khmer, c. 978–1010

Sandstone

48¾ × 21½ in. (124 × 54.5 cm.)

1991.131, Purchase gift of Dr. Bertram H. Schaffner

The Khmer empire was one of the most powerful political and cultural powers of mainland Southeast Asia from the ninth through thirteenth centuries. The empire was based in Cambodia and had its capital at Angkor. Khmer influence reached an apex in the eleventh century, when the Khmer borders extended well into modern-day Vietnam, Laos, and Thailand. Large figures served as the major icons of Khmer temples and often appeared in the cella of a chapel or in an important wall niche. This sculpture may have been associated with one of the hundreds of temples built in the form of symbolic heavenly mountains by the Khmers throughout this area.

Although the Khmer kings adopted Hinduism as the state religion, they also supported Buddhist projects. Both religions had been brought to Cambodia by traders and missionaries from India. Khmer temple art borrows many of its forms from Indian prototypes, especially the royal cult of the "god-king," or *deva-raja,* in which the ruler is a living representation of the god.

This imposing torso of a *deva-raja* is presented as a perfected version of the human form, with a polished surface and geometric proportions. Although it is difficult to determine its identity with certainty, it probably represents the Hindu god Shiva.

The Khleang style of the torso is named for the Prasat Khleang, two shrines within the royal precincts of Angkor Thom, a huge enclosure whose construction spanned several hundred years, beginning from the tenth century. This was one of the formative Angkor styles, which blossomed after the capital was transferred to Angkor from Koh Ker in 978. Although very little sculpture survives at the Khleang or the two other major Angkor monuments associated with this style – the pyramidal temples Ta Keo and the Phimeanakas – the monuments suggest an active stylistic development throughout the late tenth through early eleventh centuries. The monumentality and the quality of this torso suggest that it comes from the precincts at Angkor and foreshadows the classical Angkor Wat style of the twelfth century.

AGP

LITERATURE

Archives of Asian Art 1993, 110, fig. 7.

Brooklyn 1997, 47.

86

Head and Torso of a Buddha

Thailand, Sukhotai period, 14th century
Bronze
38 × 22½ × 11 in. (96.5 × 57.2 × 28 cm.)

88.94, Purchased with funds given by the Charles Bloom Foundation, Inc., in memory of Mildred and Charles Bloom

Over the past decades the Brooklyn Museum of Art has acquired many important Buddhist images from such Southeast Asian regions as Thailand, Cambodia, Sri Lanka, and Myanmar. Although the collection now contains a group of sculptures representative of the variety of stylistic and iconographic norms of these regions, none can compare with the impressive bronze *Head and Torso of a Buddha*. Although fragmentary, it is considered to be one of the finest examples of monumental Sukhotai bronze casting outside of Thailand. It was during the Sukhotai period (1250–1378) that a national style of Thai sculpture emerged. The heroic proportions of the figure reflect this style, demonstrating that statuary made in the later period of Thai art could still be enormously expressive. Such life-size bronze images exemplify the dexterity and assurance of the Sukhotai artisans. The quantity of such works indicates the existence of a significant number of wealthy commissions and patrons, although few sculptures of this quality are extant.

The sacred attributes, including raised spiral curls, cranial protuberance (*ushnisha*), elongated earlobes, downcast eyes, and three lines on the neck, indicating beauty (*vallis*), identify this figure as a Buddha. As in Indian prototypes for such Buddha images, the expansive chest is partially covered by a transparent garment covering only the left shoulder and ending in a narrow shawl flap. The right side of his chest is unclothed in the fashion typical of the period. The figure belongs to the so-called Lion-type group, named for the image of the Buddha as Shakyasinha, the "Lion of the Shakyas," referring to the royal lineage of the historical Buddha, Shakyamuni.

With the flame finial and arms missing, we cannot fully confirm the identification of the figure as Shakyamuni, who is often shown with his hands in the earth-touching pose or clasped in his lap holding a begging bowl. The stylized modeling and proportions, classic of the period of the fourteenth century, are heroic. The breadth of the shoulders in relation to the size of the head, the depression of the navel, the length of the earlobes, and the modeling of the torso are features that exaggerate aspects of the figure's physiognomy. The casting of the bronze is unusually refined, with each element, snail curl, or curve of drapery exquisitely defined, and the patina is an evenly modulated dark green that is exceptionally well preserved.
AGP

LITERATURE

Archives of Asian Art 1990, 74, fig. 6.

The Islamic World

The Brooklyn Museum of Art is home to a small but distinguished collection of Islamic art. Established by Stewart Culin (1858–1929), Curator of Ethnography from 1903 to 1929, the Islamic collection embodies art and culture from vastly diverse geographical areas from Spain to India and Central Asia to North Africa, as well as export Chinese art for the Persian market. It has expanded to more than seventeen hundred objects from acquisitions and gifts, most notably through the generosity of curator Charles K. Wilkinson (1897–1974) and of the Ernest Erickson Foundation.

The full wealth of artistic production is represented in the collection with objects executed in a variety of media, dating from the eighth and ninth centuries through the twentieth century. The Islamic Galleries present Islamic culture chronologically, focusing on the

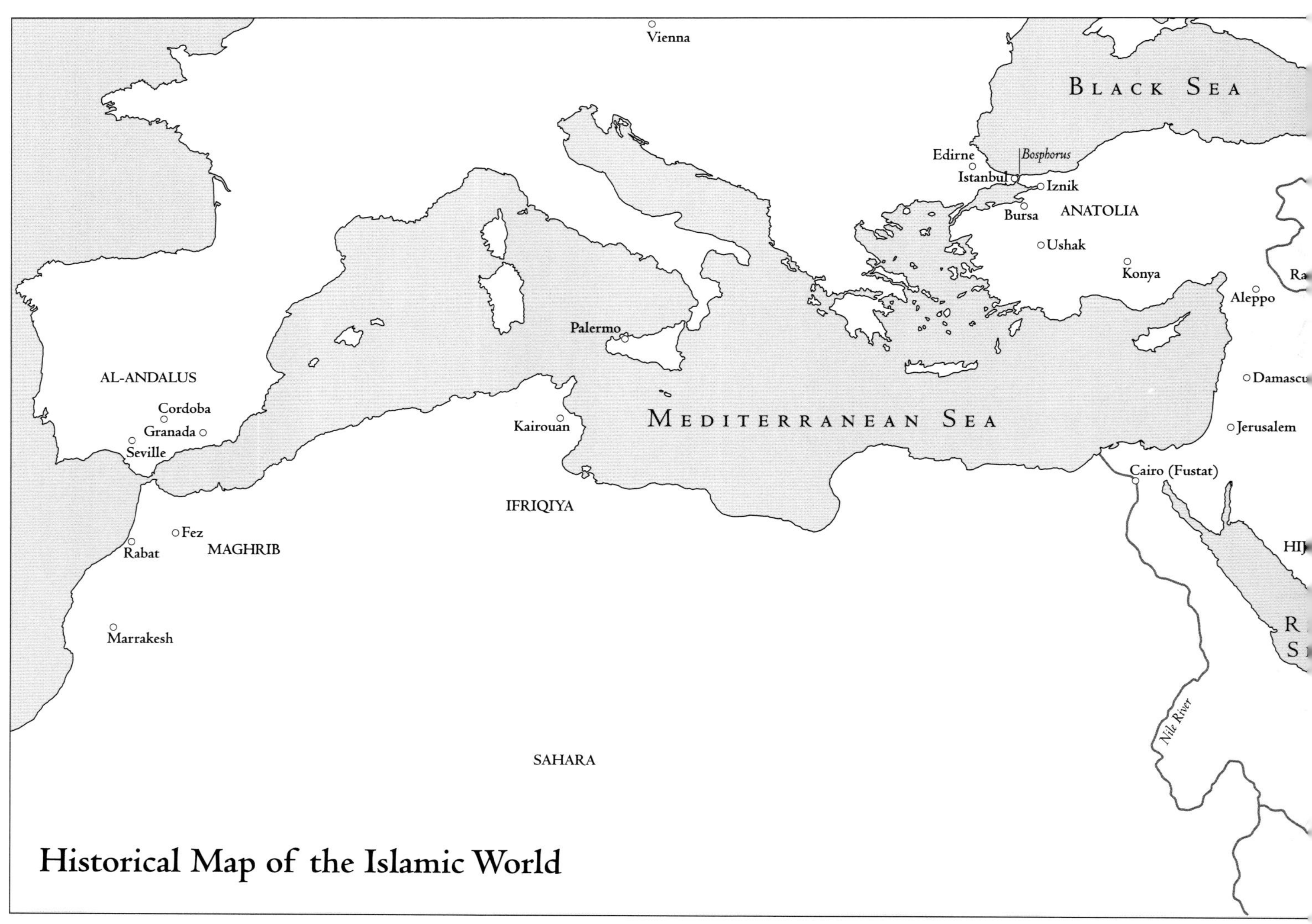

Historical Map of the Islamic World

art of Syria, Iraq, and Iran from the earliest period of Islam, to Islamic art in Egypt, North Africa, Central Asia, and Turkey, and the twentieth-century art of Iran. Mughal art of India is an area shared with the South Asian art collection.

Well represented in the collection are medieval Islamic ceramics and tilework from the tenth through fifteenth centuries; Ottoman Turkish carpets, textiles, and manuscripts; the arts of Safavid and Qajar Persia (Iran) from the sixteenth through twentieth centuries, including miniatures, oil paintings and calligraphy, ceramics, lacquerwork, carpets, textiles, and costumes; and Northern African textiles, costumes, and jewelry. The Museum has one of the world's preeminent collections of Qajar art outside of Iran.
AF

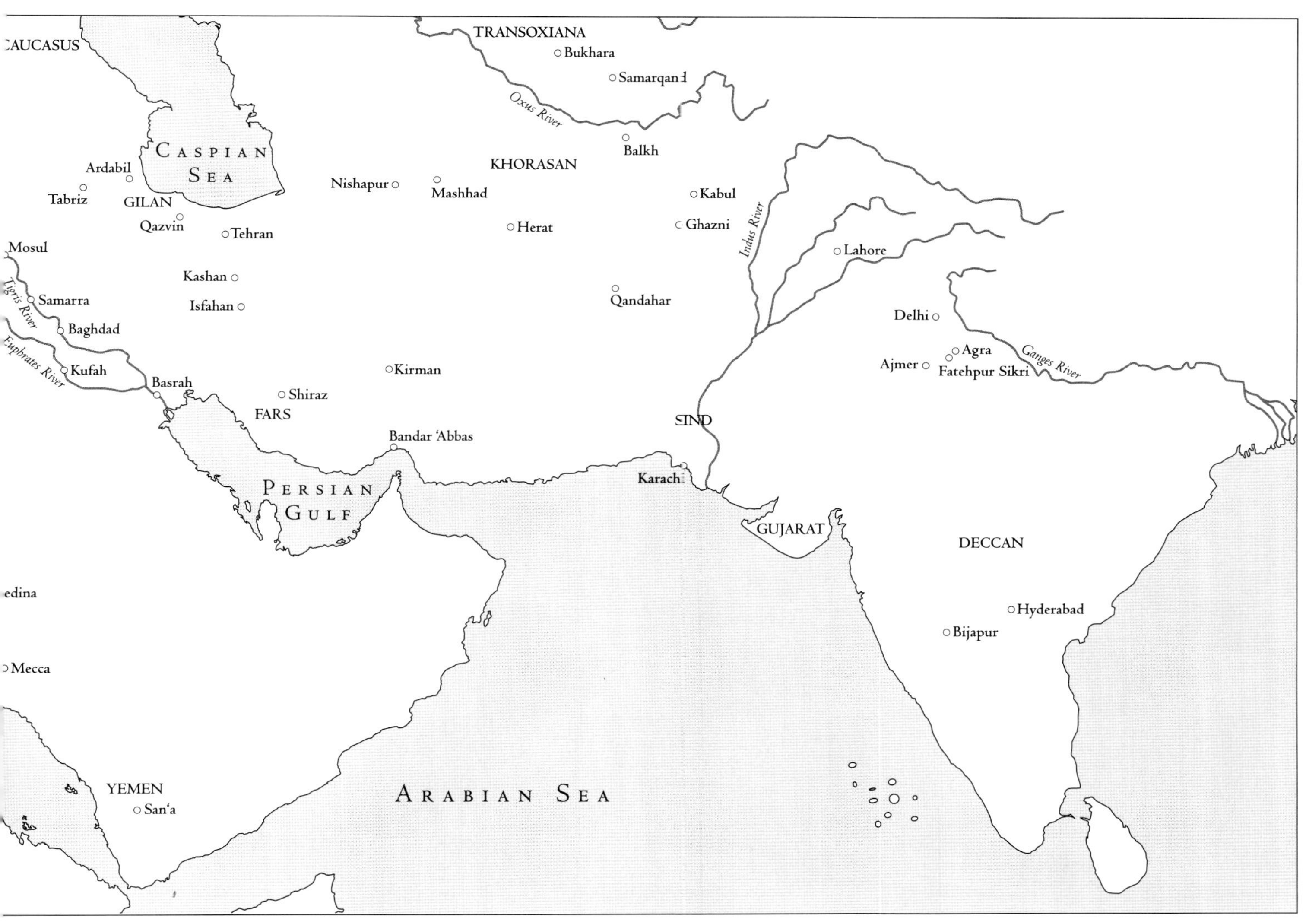

87

Silk *Tiraz* Fragment of Caliph Marwan II

Tunisia, Umayyad dynasty, mid-8th century
Silk, compound twill weave
3⅛ × 20⅞ in. (8 × 53 cm.)

41.1265, Gift of Pratt Institute

Early Islamic textiles are extremely rare today; this fragment of a silk *tiraz* and its associated pieces in other collections together constitute the earliest dated Islamic textile known. At the beginning of the Islamic era in 622, both the Byzantine and Sassanian empires produced magnificent textiles. This tradition continued under the Umayyads (661–750), the first Islamic dynasty. At this time, a *tiraz* was a textile band bearing an inscription, sometimes an armband on a ceremonial robe bestowed by a caliph as a badge of honor. Royal textile manufactures also known as *tiraz* flourished throughout the Islamic empire; the inscription on this fragment locates its *tiraz* of production in Ifriqiya, an ancient name for present-day Tunisia.

This exquisite small fragment is one of several pieces. When this textile was first studied by Florence Day in 1941, four fragments were known. In 1997, the Brooklyn Museum of Art, with the support of the government of Tunisia, undertook a collaborative study of this fragment. At that time, the scholar Sheila Blair established the existence of two additional fragments in the Pushkin Museum, Moscow.

A reconstruction of these fragments reveals that the textile comprised a field design of rows of pinwheels interspersed with smaller rosettes and a border of hearts and pearl shapes in stripes. Between the field and border an embroidered inscription was added that reads: "The servant of God, Marwan, Commander of the Faithful. Of what was ordered. [to be made by] al-R. [or al-Z.] in the *tiraz* of Ifriqiya." This inscription confirms that the textile was produced during the reign of an Umayyad ruler named Marwan. Two rulers bore this name: Marwan I (r. 684–85) and Marwan II (r. 744–50). Owing to the brevity of Marwan I's reign, and the lack of any supporting evidence connecting this *tiraz* to him, scholars have attributed the production of this textile to the reign of Marwan II.

The work was purchased with some Coptic textiles from Egypt by Frederic B. Pratt from the dealer Dikran Kelekian around 1910 or later and was donated to the Museum in 1941 by the Pratt Institute, Brooklyn.
LSD

LITERATURE

Day 1952, pl. vi.

88

Earthenware Bowl with Kufic Inscriptions

Northeastern Iran or Uzbekistan, Samanid period,
late 9th–early 10th century
Buff earthenware with white engobe, black slip, and transparent colorless glaze
H: 4 9/16 in. (11.5 cm.); DIAM: 14 in. (35.5 cm.)

86.227.19, Gift of the Ernest Erickson Foundation, Inc.

Produced in northeastern Iran, in the province of Khorasan or in Transoxiana (present-day Uzbekistan) under the Samanid period (819–1005), this bowl with its bold inscription in kufic script exemplifies the elegance and perfect harmony of "black-on-white wares" unearthed in the cities of Nishapur and Samarqand. The words written in black on a white ground are elegantly and rhythmically spaced around the inner rim. Clarity of design is achieved through the use of a white engobe (a thin wash of slip, or fluid clay, and pigment used as a ground) to cover the buff earthenware, on which the inscription is painted in brownish pigment mixed with slip. By adding slip to the pigments, the potters prevented them from running.

By 875, the Samanids had established an autonomous state, controlling a vast and important area of the eastern Islamic world. In 900 they were granted the governorship of Khorasan by the Abbasid caliph in Baghdad. Although the Samanids often looked to their imperial past for inspiration, it is unlikely that this bowl was produced for an imperial patron. The inscription reads: "Peace is that which is silent and only his speech will reveal the [?] of the man with faults." This suggests that it was probably made for a humbler individual, perhaps a wealthy merchant. The inscriptions on these vessels are the first extant examples of Arabic proverbs to appear in the Islamic world (Ettinghausen and Grabar 1987, 230). Like those on similar ceramics, the inscription is aphoristic in nature, advising the owner against harmful or impetuous actions or decisions.

ME

LITERATURE

Katz 1963, 25, pl. 10.
Volov 1966, 133, figs. 1, 3.
Ferber 1987, 205, pl. 146.
Brooklyn 1988, 112, pl. 75.
Brooklyn 1997, 50.

1995.51b (detail)

89

Leaf from a Blue Vellum Qur'an

North Africa, Tunisia or Egypt,
late 9th–early 10th century
Gold and silver leaf on indigo-dyed vellum
Overall: 11 3/16 × 15 in. (28.4 × 38 cm.)

1995.51a, b, Gift of Beatrice Riese

This hitherto unrecorded double-sided leaf comes from one of the finest Qur'an manuscripts known. It contains fifteen lines of kufic script in gold ink on blue-dyed vellum (hence its identification as a "Blue Qur'an"). As with most Qur'ans from the eighth through tenth centuries, it is distinguished by its use of horizontal format, vellum, and kufic script. Noted for its refined angular forms, thick extended strokes, and stark quality, the kufic script was the first script to develop in the Islamic world and was predominantly used during the early Islamic period.

On the two sides of this leaf (recto, 1995.51a; verso, 1995.51b), as with all pages from the dispersed "Blue Qur'an," the voweling and diacritical marks are omitted and ornamentation is kept to a minimum. This allows for an uninterrupted progression and bold movement of the letters from right to left. The text of this page is from Chapter Four of the Qur'an – *Surat al-Nisa'* or "Chapter on Women." One of the interesting features of this Qur'an is that the binding marks appear on the left side of each page, indicating that the manuscript was paginated in reverse. Jonathan Bloom has noted that this may have resulted from the rearrangement of the text by illiterates at a later date (Bloom 1991, 173).

No more than three or four Qur'ans on colored vellum are known. The majority of early Qur'an manuscripts are executed in brown or black ink with red voweling and diacritical marks against a white ground. The use of gold lettering makes this page an especially

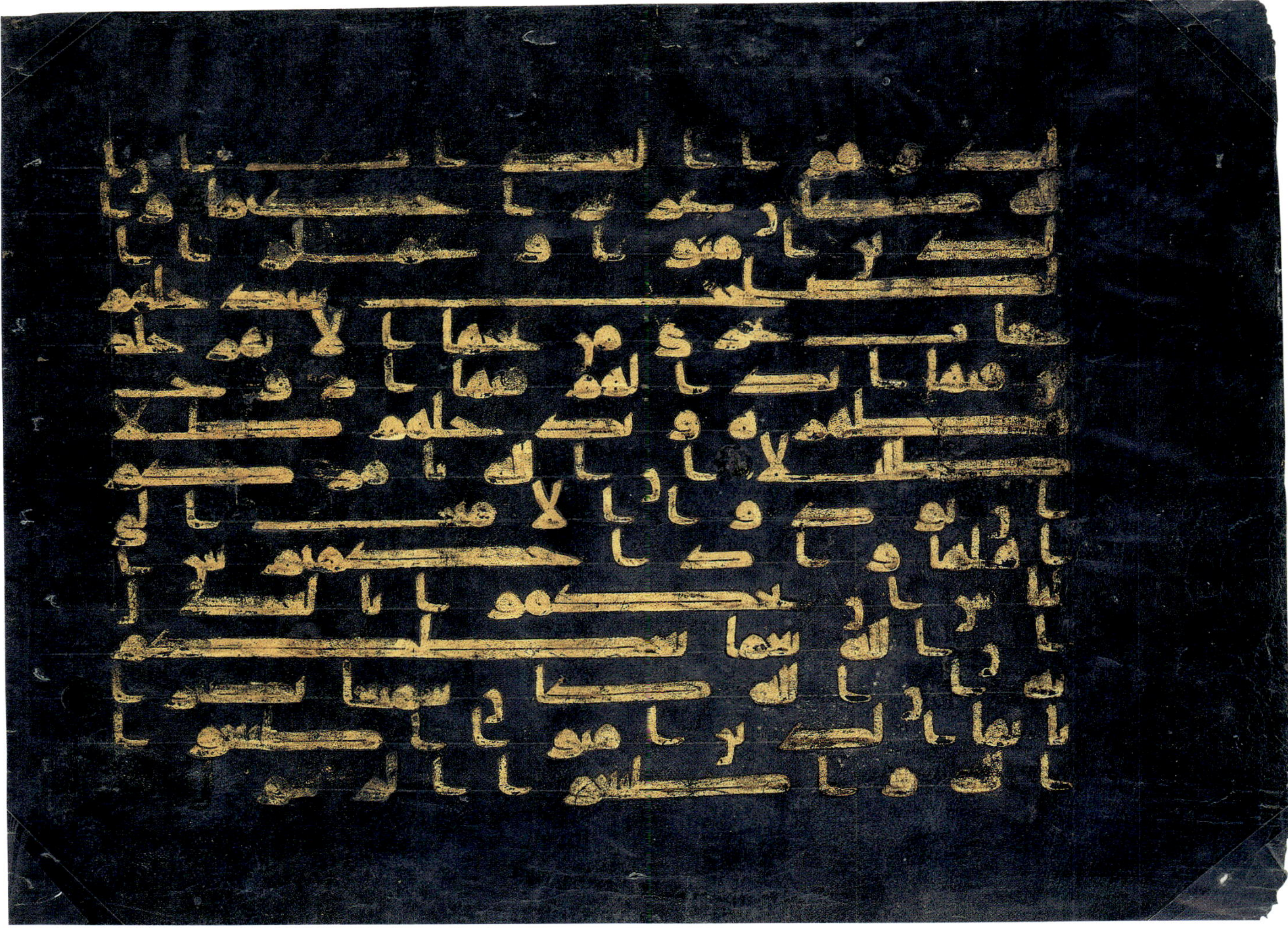

1995.51a

rare example of its type. The transcription of the Qur'an in gold ink adds to its stately presence and suggests that it was commissioned either by the caliph himself or a wealthy and pious patron such as a governor. The prototype for writing in gold ink on blue vellum or parchment probably came from the Christian Byzantine Empire, since official Byzantine documents and manuscripts were often written on blue or purple vellum with gold or silver ink. Bloom assigns the "Blue Qur'an" manuscript to the early years of Fatimid rule in Kairouan, in present-day Tunisia, and contends that many lavishly decorated Byzantine official documents of this kind were sent to the Fatimid caliphs (909–1171) in North Africa. His research also reveals that the Byzantines sent embassies with luxurious gifts to the Fatimid court. It would, therefore, be logical to assume that since the Fatimid rulers were in search of prestige and legitimacy for their new state, they would find it desirable to commission such lavish manuscripts to further their cause.

Firm evidence is lacking regarding the origin, exact date, and patron of the dispersed manuscript. However, recent study and analysis establish that all the pages that are said to come from the "Blue Qur'an" come from one manuscript now at the National Institute of Art and Archaeology in Tunis, undoubtedly produced in the Muslim West during the tenth century (Bloom 1991, 171). David James adds that the manuscript conforms to one mentioned in the inventory of manuscripts contained in the library of the Great Mosque of Kairouan in A.H. 693/A.D. 1293 (James 1980, 22). Thus it is likely that the Brooklyn Qur'an leaf was produced on caliphal order in the late ninth to early tenth century in Kairouan and was intended as a donation to a religious shrine or a diplomatic gift.

ME

90

Earthenware Bowl with Kufic Inscription

Syria, Fatimid dynasty, 11th–12th century
Earthenware with turquoise glaze and luster overglaze painting
H: 3 in. (7.6 cm.); DIAM: 9½ in. (24.1 cm.)

2000.40, Gift of the Asian Art Council; purchased with funds given by the Mark and Anla Cheng Kingdon Foundation and an anonymous donor; Museum Expedition, 1913–1914, Museum Collection Fund, by exchange

This bowl in pristine condition is distinguished by its superb turquoise glaze, fine potting, and graceful calligraphic inscription in olive green luster. The side walls are ornamented with a purely decorative band of pseudo-kufic, while the center exhibits a motif that reads "*baraka*," or "blessings." The elegant yet sumptuous decoration is reminiscent of that found on early Abbasid (750–1258) blue-and-white ceramics or Samanid (819–1005) ceramic production of the ninth and tenth centuries. The style of writing, known as floriated kufic after the vegetal ornamentation of the letters, however, dates this work to the eleventh to twelfth century.

This bowl belongs to a group of luster-painted, glazed, and incised wares found at Tell Minis in Syria that exhibit a rare combination of the finest qualities of the cream and gold luster-painted Fatimid (909–1171) wares of Egypt and superb turquoise glazed ceramics of Seljuk Persia (1038–1194). Wares from this group first appeared in 1960 and have since entered major museum and private collections including the David Collection in Copenhagen, the Victoria and Albert Museum, London, and the Metropolitan Museum of Art in New York.

The lustrous sheen of this bowl exemplifies the statement of Abu'l-Qasim, the author of the Persian ceramic treatise *Arayis al-Javahir* (c. 1300), that lusterware is surely like alchemy, the transformation of base metals into gold.

LSD

91

Jug with *Naskhi* Inscriptions

Northeastern Iran, first half of the 13th century
Brass inlaid with silver, chased and engraved decoration
H: 5½ in. (14 cm.)

86.227.123, Gift of the Ernest Erickson Foundation, Inc.

This jug is typical of the inlaid brass vessels produced in the province of Khorasan in northeastern Iran in the late twelfth and early thirteenth centuries. It is one of six fine medieval Iranian metal objects donated to the Brooklyn Museum of Art by the great collector, connoisseur, and active board member Ernest Erickson (1893–1983). Current research has suggested that owing to a shortage of silver in this region, medieval Iranian metalworkers resorted to using more economical materials such as brass and bronze for the body of vessels and silver and copper for inlaid decoration.

The decoration is divided into six horizontal registers of varying widths containing epigraphic, figural, and geometric ornamentation. The top panel encircling the neck of the jug consists of a band of inscription in Arabic in human-headed *naskhi* script that reads: "Glory, success, dominion, safety, happiness, care, and long life to the owner." This register is followed by a band of cheetahs, dogs, and rabbits chasing each other. The main decorative band around the bulbous body consists of the twelve signs of the zodiac in roundels superimposed on a ground of geometric interlace. The final register on the foot of the jug consists of another band of human-headed *naskhi* that reads: "Glory, success, happiness, safety, intercession, and long life to the owner." The tips of the vertical letters end in human heads, whereas the descending letters end in legs and feet.

The creative treatment of the epigraphy on this vessel celebrates the playfulness and sense of humor of the medieval Iranian metalworkers. Zodiac imagery is a universal theme in Islamic art and appears on a wide range of objects. Originally derived from the representations of the constellations developed by Greek astronomers, this imagery embodies apotropaic properties. Together with the aphoristic inscriptions on this jug, the signs of the zodiac were intended to protect the owner from harmful powers.

ME

LITERATURE

Katz 1963, 36.
Ferber 1987, 233, pl. 177.

92

Loom Width of Silk Fragment

Inner Mongolia or Western China, 13th–14th century
Silk, tabby weave, with gilt paper brocading
18 × 22 in. (45.7 × 55.8 cm.)

1992.81, Gift of the Asian Art Council

This hitherto unpublished textile fragment belongs to a small group of silk brocades of the medieval period that have been found in Tibetan monasteries. A green brocade of the finest quality, it is complete, with both selvages intact. The pattern, woven with the aid of gilded translucent paper strips, is divided into three rows and consists of four lobed medallions with confronting birds on either side of a vertical motif. Although the birds appear to be parrots, their massive legs and sharp claws lead us to believe that they are more likely birds of prey, perhaps falcons. The interstitial designs include a four-petaled floral motif on a ground filled with a meandering cloud design. A characteristic feature of the group is the synthesis of eastern Iranian–style animals with birds and Chinese-inspired secondary motifs.

The stylistic features and use of gold paper strips have been deciding factors for the attribution and dating of this example (Watt and Wardwell 1997, 123). The type of gold thread in the textile – gilded strips of paper wrapped around a silk core – is generally considered a Chinese technique, which made its way to Chinese Turkestan and parts of Central Asia during the Mongol period, while the motif of aligned medallions and roundels enclosing pairs of animals was current in silks of the eastern Iranian world in the twelfth and thirteenth centuries.

The exact place of manufacture of this textile has yet to be determined. It has been attributed to Inner Mongolia or eastern Turkestan under Mongol rule, since entire colonies of craftsmen, who had been captured by the Mongols in northern China, resettled in distant cities of this region and brought with them the weaving techniques and decorative repertoires of their homelands (Watt and Wardwell 1997, 127). The high level of technical expertise of this silk leads us to believe that it was probably a product of an imperial workshop. The eclectic iconography and heraldic representation of the bird design, as well as the presence of Arabic pseudo-inscriptions on comparable fragments, indicate that textiles from this group may have been intended for a Muslim clientele. In fact, gold brocades such as this were traded in great quantities with the Ilkhanid (1256–1353) and Mamluk (1250–1517) empires as well as Europe. Other fragments of this textile are found in the David Collection in Copenhagen and in the AEDTA Foundation Collection in Paris.
ME

93

Bahram Gur at the House of Baharam the Jew

From the "Second Small *Shahnama*" of Firdawsi
Iraq, Baghdad; or Iran, Shiraz or Tabriz, Ilkhanid period, 1300–1340
Opaque watercolor, ink, and gold on paper
Overall: 6⅝ × 5¼ in. (16.8 × 13.3 cm.); image: 1 9/16 × 4 13/16 in. (4.1 × 12.2 cm.)

86.227.130.1a, b, Gift of the Ernest Erickson Foundation, Inc.

This illustrated folio is from a dispersed manuscript of the *Shahnama* (Book of Kings), the Persian national epic, versified by the poet Firdawsi (940–c. 1020) in the early eleventh century. It belongs to a group of three *Shahnama* manuscripts commonly referred to as the "Small *Shahnamas*," produced during the reign of the Ilkhanid rulers of Iran (1256–1353) in the first half of the fourteenth century. Second in the group, this manuscript is known as the "Second Small *Shahnama*." These are considered to be the earliest surviving manuscripts of the *Shahnama* and therefore are key documents for the study of the history of Persian painting. Lacking colophons, dedications, dates, and indications of place of production, the manuscripts have been grouped together on stylistic grounds. Their place of production and date have always been subject to debate, with attributions ranging from Baghdad and Tabriz to Shiraz and western India between 1300 and 1340.

There are three leaves from the dispersed "Second Small *Shahnama*" manuscript in the Islamic collection at the Brooklyn Museum of Art. The illustrations are noted for their minute size, lavish use of gold leaf for the background and secondary motifs, minimal landscapes, and thick application of colors. Despite the small scale of the paintings, the artist(s) depicted the various elements of each painting with precision, providing a glimpse of life during the late Ilkhanid period. The small size and portable nature of these manuscripts suggest they were well suited to the nomadic lifestyle associated with the Ilkhanids.

Many of the paintings from this group of manuscripts are lively and charged with energy. The painting *Bahram Gur at the House of Baharam the Jew* is among the simpler and more tranquil compositions. It depicts the king Bahram Gur, who has asked Baharam for a night's lodging, settling in for the night. The text reveals that Baharam has consented to this favor, provided that Bahram Gur clean up after his horse and pay for any damages incurred.

ME

LITERATURE

Katz 1963, 34, cat. no. 56.
Simpson 1979, 380, fig. 43.
Ferber 1987, 239, cat. no. 182.

94

Attributed to Sultan 'Ali Mashhadi (Persian, 1442–1519)

Folio of Poetry

From the *Divan* of Sultan Husayn Mirza
Afghanistan, Herat, Timurid dynasty, c. 1490
Opaque watercolor and gold on indigo blue ground, with découpage and gold-flecked border
Overall: 8⅞ × 5¼ in. (22.5 × 13.3 cm.)

45.4.3, Ella C. Woodward Memorial Fund

These four couplets of poetry in fine *nasta'liq* script were not written with a pen. Instead, the letters were meticulously cut from colored papers and pasted onto the dark blue paper. This technique, known as *qit'a*, or découpage, is used on this leaf and other leaves of this dispersed manuscript of the *Divan* (Anthology) of Sultan Husayn Mirza (r. 1470–1506). Although we do not have concrete proof, this page has been attributed to the great master of calligraphy Sultan 'Ali Mashhadi on technical and stylistic grounds (Welch 1979, 170).

A great-great-grandson of Timur (r. 1370–1405), Sultan Husayn Mirza ruled over the northeastern Iranian province of Khorasan from 1470 until his death in 1506. He was not only a patron of the arts, but also a poet of considerable talent. Along with his closest friend, Mir 'Ali Shir Nava'i (1440–1501), also a poet of great distinction, he was responsible for establishing Chaghatay Turkish as a major literary language (ibid.).

The verses on this folio, from a *ghazal*, or sonnet, composed by Sultan Husayn Mirza himself, have been translated from Chaghatay Turkish into English by Professor Wheeler M. Thackston:

> O Husayni, when I cast a glance at the fiery countenance,
> fire catches in my eyes from the blow of the pain
> of separation.
> In me there are a hundred entreaties every moment; in
> him/her is nothing but disdain. Every moment I die a
> hundred deaths; that beauty is unconcerned.
> Say not that in your mournful heart is the melancholy
> over his/her tress, for in my mad heart is that
> same melancholy.
> My religion and Islam have been lost to love's plunder.
> Say not that I have only become mad for him/her.

The word for "melancholy" (*sawda*) in the lines above also means "blackness," which accords with the blackness of the beloved's tress of hair.

Other folios of calligraphic découpage from this manuscript are found in the Sadruddin Aga Khan Collection, the Freer Gallery of Art, Washington, D.C., the Los Angeles County Museum of Art, and in an album made for the Ottoman Sultan Murad III (r. 1574–95) now in the National Library of Austria (Vienna, Österreichische Nationalbibliothek Cod. Mixt. 313).
ME

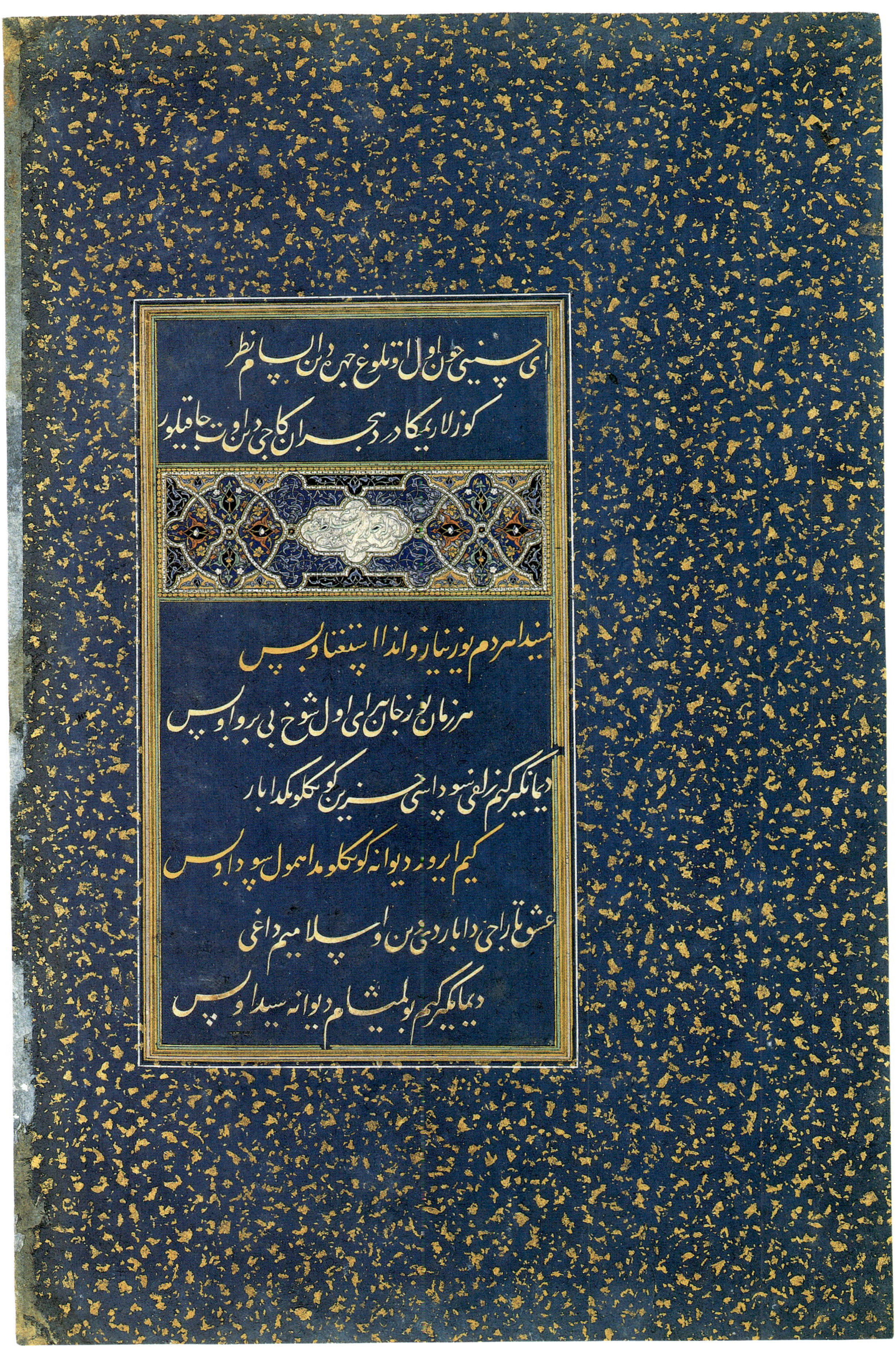

95

Mamluk Carpet

Egypt, last quarter of 15th–early 16th century
Wool pile, asymmetrical knot
$78\frac{1}{4} \times 51\frac{1}{4}$ in. (198.7 × 130.2 cm.)

43.24.3, Gift of Mr. and Mrs. Frederic B. Pratt

Mamluk carpets are known for their dazzling visual effect produced by jewel-like tones, geometric forms, and radiating designs. Notable for their use of quality materials and high level of technical mastery and craftsmanship, these carpets are among the earliest preserved intact.

In this example, the pattern consists of a central octagon on a ruby-red ground, which moves outward to spandrels filled with three-petaled flowers. Cypress trees and papyrus plants resembling tiny umbrellas fill the tripartite rectangular bands above and below. Within the medallions at the rim are swirling floral motifs nearly identical to those in the carpet's border. The overall combination of jewel tones of red, green, and blue, and the silky sheen of the fine wool are perhaps an allusion to the opulent rubies, emeralds, and sapphires found in the Mamluk court treasuries (Bier 1991, ii).

Produced under the patronage of the Mamluk sultans of Egypt (1250–1517), these carpets seem to represent the culmination of a sophisticated tradition of carpet weaving. However, the origins of this tradition remain a matter of conjecture. One of the leading authorities on Islamic carpets, Charles Grant Ellis, relates these to Mongol carpets, of which none survive, whereas another scholar, Esin Atıl, sees closer stylistic affinities with Turkmen and eastern Anatolian carpets (Ellis 1974, 49; Atıl 1981, 226).

Mamluk carpets demonstrate some curious characteristics, namely the pervasive use of wool (a material that does not appear to have been produced in Egypt) and the use of the asymmetrical (Persian or Senneh) knot, rather than the symmetrical (Turkish or Ghiordes) knot seen in Turkish rugs imported by the Egyptians at this time (Middleton 1996, 9). Although we do not know exactly where these carpets were produced, Islamic and European documents mention Cairo as an important center for carpet weaving. Owing to their popularity both locally and in Europe, these carpets continued to be produced until the mid-sixteenth century, even after the fall of the dynasty.

Through their use of faceted stars and compartmentalized designs, Mamluk carpets fit perfectly into the larger repertoire of Mamluk aesthetic taste and design. A similar treatment of geometric forms, compositions, and colors appear in stained glass, metalwork, woodwork, mosaic floors, manuscript illumination, and leather bindings of the Mamluk period.

ME

LITERATURE

Erdmann 1961, pl. 7, fig. 12.

96

Ushak Medallion Carpet

Turkey, Ushak region, Ottoman dynasty, first half of the 16th century
Wool pile on wool foundation, symmetrical knot
160 × 73 in. (406.4 × 185.4 cm.)

43.24.2, Gift of Mr. and Mrs. Frederic B. Pratt

This beautiful large-scale Ottoman medallion carpet was woven in the Ushak region of western Anatolia, home to one of the longest commercial weaving traditions. Ushak medallion carpets were used in Ottoman court settings and were also highly prized in European collections.

The focal point of this carpet is the burgundy-red central medallion surrounded by a dark indigo ground enlivened with a cream-colored peony blossom scroll. Intricately designed corner medallions also frame the central medallion, which is often repeated in this type of carpet. The curvilinear designs of the medallions and floral vine scrolls in the carpet mark a departure from earlier Turkish carpets with geometric designs such as Lottos or Holbeins (so named for the frequent appearance of such carpets in European still lifes and portraits by these artists). Ushak medallion carpets reflect the use of a paper cartoon, which would have been provided by the Ottoman court design studio, the *nakkaşhane*. The close parallels between the motifs and design presentation of Ushak medallion carpets and arts of the book produced during the third quarter of the fifteenth century suggest an earlier dating for this class of carpets. Ushak medallion carpets are also seen in European paintings, starting in the mid-sixteenth century.

The Brooklyn Museum Ushak medallion carpet is remarkable for the brilliance of its colors and its excellent condition, although this carpet, which is more than thirteen feet long, has been cut down. The design of the carpet is quite similar to an example in the Thyssen-Bornemisza collection, Lugano (Beattie 1972, pl. 14).
AF

LITERATURE

Brooklyn 1997, 51.

97

Spherical Hanging Ornament

Turkey, Iznik, Ottoman dynasty, third quarter of the 16th century
Underglaze painted composite body, brass mount
DIAM: 12 in. (30.3 cm.)

43.24.8, Gift of Mr. and Mrs. Frederic B. Pratt

The Brooklyn Museum of Art has a fine representative collection of Islamic ceramics. One outstanding example is a large spherical hanging ornament from Ottoman Turkey (1281–1924). The sixteenth century marked the culmination of Ottoman Turkish imperial power and patronage of the arts, particularly under the ruler Sultan Süleyman the Magnificent (r. 1520–66). In the second half of the sixteenth century, Ottoman ceramic production at Iznik (ancient Nicaea) reached maturity. Floral motifs of carnations, tulips, roses, and hyacinths were painted in lively compositions using a distinctively successful palette of vibrant cobalt blue, turquoise, emerald green, and a new pigment often called "sealing-wax red." As seen in the Brooklyn hanging ornament, the thickness of this pigment provides texture and allows motifs to stand in relief under a transparent glaze.

Created by the designers of the imperial workshops, or *nakkaşhane*, the design on this spherical hanging ornament is a harmonious combination of naturalistic floral motifs, stylized arabesques, and palmettes characteristic of the height of Iznik production (mid-16th century). The absence of decoration on one side, the directional orientation of the design, and the metal brackets on the top and bottom provide clues to the purpose of such objects. They were intended to hang on chains suspended from the ceilings and domes of mosques and other religious structures and to be viewed only from a distance or directly underneath (Travelstead 1982, 237; Atıl 1987, 271–72; Atasoy and Raby 1989, 224, 228). Thus, they were considered to be integral elements of a decorative program for a mosque interior.

Large spheres, such as this example, were often paired with mosque lamps (Atıl 1987, 271). In both Christian and Muslim sanctuaries in the Middle East it remains common practice to hang spherical ornaments of glass, metal, or ceramic. The symbolism of these spheres, which they would share with such objects as the ostrich egg sometimes depicted hanging in a niche above the head of the Madonna in fifteenth-century Italian paintings, may be that of the orb of heaven (Blair and Bloom 1991, 96). Painted eggs and egg-shaped ceramic vessels were also hung in Middle Eastern churches and are known to be symbols of fertility.

A possible prototype for the Brooklyn hanging ornament is an ornament of the same shape dating to the 1550s in the Benaki Museum in Athens, presumably found on the grounds of the Haram in Jerusalem in the nineteenth century and associated with Sultan Süleyman's refurbishment of the Dome of the Rock (Carswell 1998, 68). However, the design, composition, and coloration, particularly the extensive use of sealing-wax red, places it in the 1570s to 1580s. Similar hanging ornaments are found in the MAK – Austrian Museum of Applied Arts/Contemporary Art, Vienna, the David Collection, Copenhagen, and the Victoria and Albert Museum and the British Museum in London.
ME

LITERATURE

Travelstead 1982, 237, fig. 1.
Soustiel 1985, 333, fig. 357.
Blair and Bloom 1991, 54, 95, fig. 31a.
Brooklyn 1997, 50.

98

Riza-yi 'Abbasi (Persian, active 1585–1635)

Hunters at a Stream

Iran, Isfahan, Safavid dynasty, c. 1625
Ink and wash color on paper
Overall: 13⅜ × 8⅞ in. (33.9 × 22.5 cm.); image: 8½ × 5½ in. (20.9 × 14 cm.)

35.1027, Frank L. Babbott Fund

This single-page album drawing by the Safavid (1501–1732) master Riza-yi 'Abbasi exemplifies the artist's distinctive calligraphic style and ingenious draftsmanship. The composition depicts an old bearded hunter on horseback fording a stream while his horse stops for a drink of water. The rider, carrying bows and arrows, tilts his head down in a moment of repose. To his left a young man with a musket sits on a rock outcrop holding a cup of water from the stream with both hands. Above, to the right of the old man, another young hunter with a musket and a dead bird hanging from its muzzle observes the scene below from behind a rocky hill. Here, Riza combines the perfection and sinuosity of line with tints of delicate pastel shades and Chinese decorative accents. The palette of wash colors and the flowing lines convey a sense of transience and otherworldliness.

Sheila R. Canby, the leading authority on Riza-yi 'Abbasi, contends that this drawing embodies several layers of meaning pertaining to age and time (Canby 1990, 83; Canby 1996, 136). The juxtaposition of polarities such as age and youth and traditional and modern is particularly striking in this work. The beardless young hunters with large modern muskets, wearing European caps, have successfully shot a bird of prey, while the tired old horseman wears a turban, still hunts with a bow and arrow, and remains empty-handed (Canby 1996, 136). By the second half of the seventeenth century under the reign of Shah 'Abbas I (r. 1588–1629), modern European weapons, such as the musket, had become commonplace, gradually replacing the traditional bow and arrow. Canby believes that the contrasts of age and time in this painting are an indication of the artist's nostalgia for Iran's bygone days (Canby 1990, 84).

Although the drawing contains an elaborate inscription and a signature, revealing that Riza produced it for his son Muhammad Baqir, it is not dated. However, its association with other signed and dated works by Riza in the 1620s has aided in dating this work to around 1625. *ME*

LITERATURE

Blochet 1930, 48, no. 137.
Kühnel 1939, 1887, pl. 917a.
Diez 1944, 161, pl. 94.
Stchoukine 1964, 110, 193.
Rice 1965, 249, no. 243.
Brooklyn 1967, 120–21.
Eng 1970, 456, pl. 138.
Canby 1990, 82–84, fig. 14.
Canby 1996, 135–36, 196, cat. no. 99.

99

Attributed to Muhammad Zaman (Persian, active 1649–1704)

A Blue Iris

Iran, Isfahan, Safavid dynasty, A.H. 1074–75/A.D. 1663–64
Opaque watercolor and ink on paper
Overall: 13⅛ × 8⅜ in. (33.3 × 21.3 cm.);
image: 7½ × 4⅜ in. (19.1 × 11.1 cm.)

86.23, Hagop Kevorkian Fund and Middle Eastern Special Fund

Illustrated manuscripts were the principal format of Persian painting from the fourteenth century onward. By the seventeenth century, however, single-page paintings – either detached or mounted in albums – were introduced. Floral studies were among the favored subjects, and in the course of the century, paintings such as this one increasingly showed the influence of European traditions of naturalism. These traditions were transmitted primarily through the intermediary of prints, which were readily available to artists and designers in the royal capital of Isfahan, where this painting was probably produced.

The iris depicted in this watercolor is delicately and realistically painted, with every vein in the petals of the flower and striation of the leaves painstakingly rendered. The shading from lavender to deepest purple and the curling of the petals reflect the artist's familiarity with European painting. The image is mounted within three illuminated margins of black, green, and salmon painted with elegant arabesque and floral designs typical of seventeenth-century albums of calligraphy and painting. The work is inscribed with "Ya Sahib al-Zaman" (O Lord of Time), the allegorical signature of Muhammad Zaman ibn Haji Yusuf Qumi (active 1649–1704), the leading exponent of European-style painting in the latter half of the seventeenth century at the court. Zaman executed a number of works of European religious and allegorical subjects, floral studies, and illustrated manuscripts in a markedly Europeanizing style. This work is among his earliest known paintings.

Some scholars have argued that Zaman traveled to Italy and that his style was formed there, while others believe that Zaman never traveled abroad and that his style can be satisfactorily explained by exposure to Dutch prints. During this period there was significant interest at the court in European painting. Dutch artists were active in Isfahan, and merchants and missionaries trained Persian painters and designers through the copying of herbals and allegorical prints. This blue iris epitomizes the hybrid style that evolved out of the diversity of cultural traditions that characterized Isfahan during the Safavid period (1501–1732).

LSD

LITERATURE

Grube 1972, 197, pl. 173.
Ferber 1987, 110, pl. 74.
Diba 1996, 106, fig. 86.

100

Khusraw Discovers Shirin Bathing

From *Pictorial Cycle of Eight Poetic Subjects*
Iran, Shiraz, Zand dynasty, mid-18th century
Oil on canvas
36 × 35 in. (91.4 × 88.8 cm.)

1997.108.7, Bequest of Irma B. Wilkinson in memory of her husband, Charles K. Wilkinson

In the eighteenth century the Zand dynasty (1750–94) reigned in southern Iran and presided over a revival of the arts, which had suffered a severe decline after the fall of the Safavid Empire (1501–1732) to Afghan raiders in 1732. The capital of Shiraz was embellished with new palaces and mansions, which were decorated with life-size portraits of Zand rulers and court and lyrical narrative paintings depicting themes from Persian poetry and literature.

This painting depicts an episode from the love story of the Sassanian (226–640) ruler King Khusraw and the Armenian Queen Shirin, a well-known subject in the works of the celebrated poets Nizami (1141–1209) and Amir Khusraw Dihlavi (c. 1253–1325) and a favored subject of Persian manuscript painting. This work is one of a group of eight paintings in the Museum's collection that constitutes the only extant cycle of wall paintings from an eighteenth-century Shiraz mansion. Collectively they provide valuable evidence of the original architectural setting and narrative program of the period. These oil-on-canvas paintings were cut to fit small niches located in the upper walls of a reception room of an urban residence or pleasure or hunting pavilion. Persian painting is primarily known for its achievements in the art of the illustrated manuscript. However, a centuries-old tradition of monumental wall painting was revived in the capital of Isfahan in the seventeenth century. This cycle of paintings represents one of the few surviving works of the eighteenth century in a Western museum that document the later evolution of Persian painting.

Although the paintings are neither signed nor dated, they exhibit particularly close affinities with illustrated manuscripts of the 1780s produced in Isfahan and Shiraz and with paintings of related subjects signed or attributable to the Zand court painter Mirza Baba (active 1789–1810) painted in 1794. The treatment of these paintings is simpler than that of manuscript painting: the scale of the figures is larger and the number of figures and degree of ornamental patterning are reduced. They exemplify a popular style of painting produced for the wealthy elite and considerably broaden the repertoire of Zand painting.

In contrast to many paintings of this period, the provenance of these works is well documented. Charles K. Wilkinson (1897–1974), Curator of Near Eastern Art at the Brooklyn Museum of Art from 1969 to 1974, acquired them from the renowned archaeologist Ernst Herzfeld. These paintings are shown in a photograph of Herzfeld's study in Tehran taken in the 1930s.
LSD

LITERATURE
Diba 1998, 161, fig. 29d.

101

Attributed to Muhammad Hasan (Persian, active 1808–40)

Prince Yahya

Iran, Qajar dynasty, c. 1835–36
Oil on canvas
67 × 35 in. (170.2 × 88.9 cm.)

72.26.5, Gift of Mr. and Mrs. Charles K. Wilkinson

An inscription in a cartouche in the upper left-hand corner of this painting identifies the sitter as "His Highness Prince Yahya" (b. 1817), the forty-third son of the second ruler of the Qajar dynasty, Fath 'Ali Shah (1797–1834). In hope of maintaining political centralization, shahs often appointed their sons as governors of the various provinces of the empire. As a youth, Prince Yahya was appointed governor of the province of Gilan, on the Caspian coast.

In this painting, Prince Yahya appears to be in his teens, probably not more than seventeen or eighteen years of age. This speculation helps date the painting to around 1835–36. Here, Prince Yahya is seated in a traditional frontal pose. His jeweled crown and pearl-embroidered red robe correspond to his rank and title. In addition to the regalia, he bears the order of the Lion and Sun, probably given to him by the shah in recognition of his services to the court. A still life in the foreground includes a jewel box and a watch fob and two jewel-encrusted bottles set on a carpet. Such objects were probably in circulation at court and allude to the pervasive consumption of European luxury goods among Qajar royalty.

Life-size paintings, like this one, were originally created as integral elements of preconceived architectural programs and were intended to fit into specific niches in palaces and pavilions. This painting was not meant to be an individualized portrait of a prince, but an icon of power, placing the prince in full regalia within the complex hierarchy of the Qajar court. According to Layla S. Diba, the delicate rendering of the physiognomy and the distinct treatment of the rug and the wood balustrade closely resemble the work of Muhammad Hasan (Diba 1998, 195).
ME

LITERATURE

Ekhtiar 1989a, ill. (unpag.).
Ekhtiar 1989b, 47, fig. 1.
Brooklyn 1997, 52.
Diba 1998, 194–95, pl. 47.

102

Lutf 'Ali Suratgar Shirazi (Persian, active 1802–71)

Mirror Case

Iran, Shiraz, Qajar dynasty, A.H. 1262/A.D. 1845
Opaque watercolors with gold pigment, crushed metallic pigment, and leather detailing on lacquer-varnished pasteboard with metal flecks and mirrored interior
7½ × 6¼ in. (19.3 × 15.8 cm.)

36.940, Gift of Mr. and Mrs. Frederic B. Pratt

Reflecting the experimental spirit of the later Qajar period (1785–1925), this mirror case by the eminent master of flower painting Lutf 'Ali Suratgar Shirazi is noted for its striking eclecticism, combining rose and nightingale (*gul-o-bul-bul*) imagery with figures in Western European costume. The front of the object is inscribed with the artist's signature.

Two of the three painted surfaces (front and back) of this mirror case display the rose and nightingale theme. The inner surface (see interior view), however, depicts a composition in which eight religious and secular figures in European costume are grouped together without scale or thematic connection against a landscape of lakes and waterfalls. These figures include an aristocratic gentleman in seventeenth-century English costume seated on a stool with a whippet, an apostle figure with two children and a pensive female kneeling before him, a veiled Madonna figure, and a young girl with distinctly Persian features dressed in English or French costume of the nineteenth century holding a bouquet. Blending post-Renaissance Western European subjects and stylistic conventions with native Persian idioms, this mirror case is indeed a collage of artistic traditions.

The juxtaposition of the rose and nightingale and Western-inspired imagery is a recurring tendency in later Qajar lacquer painting. Demands of the foreign tourist market for such objects, as well as a genuine interest in experimentation with European styles and conventions, earned painters of the mid-nineteenth century the epithet "*farangisaz*," or Europeanizer.

Originating in manuscript illustration as a decorative motif and evolving into an independent painting genre, the rose and the nightingale decorative theme culminated in the eighteenth and nineteenth centuries under Zand (1750–94) and Qajar rule. During this period, it enjoyed immense popularity owing to its universal appeal and its inherent earthly and divine messages. Lutf 'Ali's sensitive rendition of the rose and the nightingale on the outer cover of this mirror case serves as evidence of his skillful hand and mastery over the technique of lacquer painting. He uses minute metallic flecks in the background of the *gul-o-bul-bul* design, giving the surface a distinctive sense of warmth and a subtle shimmer. The imagery represented also reflects changes resulting from shifting Persian tastes, as well as Iran's increasing interaction – cultural and artistic – with Europe. The product is a new hybrid style, which is either directly based on European models, particularly Dutch and Flemish flower painting, or filtered through Mughal Indian intermediaries.

ME

LITERATURE

Ekhtiar 1989a.
Ekhtiar 1989b, 49, figs. 4a–b.

Front

Back

Interior

Bibliography

Addiss 1980
Addiss, Stephen. *Katachi: Form and Spirit in Japanese Art*. Exh. cat. Albuquerque: Albuquerque Museum, 1980.

Akanuma 1977
Akanuma Taka, ed. *Ninnami Hozen*. Nihon tōji zenshū (Japanese ceramics collections), vol. 30. Tokyo: Chūō Kōronsha, 1977.

Anninos 2000
Anninos, Tony. "Tibetan Leather Boxes." *Arts of Asia* 30, no. 1 (January–February 2000): 101–17.

Archives of Asian Art 1974–75
"Arts of Asia Acquired by North American Museums, 1973–1974." *Archives of Asian Art* 28 (1974–75): 113–28.

Archives of Asian Art 1975–76
"Arts of Asia Acquired by North American Museums, 1974–1975." *Archives of Asian Art* 29 (1975–76): 98–119.

Archives of Asian Art 1976–77
"Arts of Asia Acquired by North American Museums, 1975–1976." *Archives of Asian Art* 30 (1976–77): 103–26.

Archives of Asian Art 1979
"Arts of Asia Acquired by North American Museums, 1977–1978." *Archives of Asian Art* 32 (1979): 84–100.

Archives of Asian Art 1980
"Arts of Asia Acquired by North American Museums, 1979." *Archives of Asian Art* 33 (1980): 116–31.

Archives of Asian Art 1981
"Arts of Asia Acquired by North American Museums, 1981." *Archives of Asian Art* 34 (1981): 96–97.

Archives of Asian Art 1990
"Arts of Asia Acquired by North American Museums, 1989." *Archives of Asian Art* 43 (1990): 72–88.

Archives of Asian Art 1991
"Arts of Asia Acquired by North American Museums, 1990." *Archives of Asian Art* 44 (1991): 103–16.

Archives of Asian Art 1992
"Arts of Asia Acquired by North American Museums, 1991." *Archives of Asian Art* 45 (1992): 99–111.

Archives of Asian Art 1993
"Arts of Asia Acquired by North American Museums, 1992." *Archives of Asian Art* 46 (1993): 108–20.

Archives of Asian Art 1994
"Arts of Asia Acquired by North American Museums, 1993." *Archives of Asian Art* 47 (1994): 86–100.

Archives of the Chinese Art Society of America 1953
"Chinese Art Recently Acquired by American Museums." *Archives of the Chinese Art Society of America* 7 (1953): 84–86.

Archives of the Chinese Art Society of America 1960
"Oriental Objects Recently Acquired by American Museums." *Archives of the Chinese Art Society of America* 14 (1960): 65–78.

Archives of the Chinese Art Society of America 1961
"Oriental Objects Recently Acquired by American Museums." *Archives of the Chinese Art Society of America* 15 (1961): 35–46.

Asia Society 1960
Masterpieces of Asian Art in American Collections. Exh. cat. New York: Asia Society, 1960.

Asia Society 1962
The Art of India: Stone Sculpture. Exh. cat. New York: Asia Society, 1962.

Atasoy and Raby 1989
Atasoy, Nurhan, and Julian Raby. *Iznik: The Pottery of Ottoman Turkey*. Ed. Yanni Petsopoulos. London: Alexandria Press, in association with Thames and Hudson, 1989.

Atil 1981
Atıl, Esin. *Renaissance of Islam: Art of the Mamluks*. Exh. cat. Washington, D.C.: National Museum of Natural History and Smithsonian Institution Press, 1981.

Atil 1987
———. "The Royal Kilns." In *The Age of Sultan Süleyman the Magnificent*. Exh. cat. Washington, D.C.: National Gallery of Art and New York: Abrams, 1987.

Banerjee 1985
Banerjee, P. "A Terracotta Panel from Bhitargaon." *Roopa Lehka* 57 (1985): 86–88.

Bautze 1998
Bautze, Joachim K. *Interaction of Cultures: Indian and Western Painting 1780–1910: The Ehrenfeld Collection*. Alexandria, Va.: Art Services International, 1998.

Beattie 1972
Beattie, May. *The Thyssen-Bornemisza Collection of Oriental Rugs*. Castagnola: Villa Favorita, 1972.

Beguin 1977
Beguin, Gilles. *Dieux et demons de l'himalaya: Art du bouddhisme lamaïque*. Paris: Secrétariat d'État à la Culture, Éditions des Musées Nationaux, 1977.

Behera and Donaldson 1998
Behera, K. S., and Thomas Donaldson. *Sculpture Masterpieces from Orissa: Style and Iconography*. New Delhi: Aryan Books International, 1998.

Berliner and Handler 1995
Berliner, Nancy, and Sarah Handler. *Friends of the House: Furniture from China's Towns and Villages*. Exh. cat. Salem: Peabody Essex Museum, 1995.

Bier 1991
Bier, Carol. *Beyond the Pyramids: Geometry and Design in the Carpets of Egypt, 1450–1750*. Exh. brochure. Washington, D.C.: Textile Museum, 1991.

Blair and Bloom 1991
Blair, Sheila S., and Jonathan M. Bloom. *Images of Paradise in Islamic Art*. Exh. cat. Hanover: Hood Museum of Art, Dartmouth College, 1991.

Blochet 1930
Blochet, Edgar. *Catalogue de la Collection Demotte.* New York, 1930.

Bloom 1991
Bloom, Jonathan M. "The Early Fatimid Blue Koran Manuscript." *Graeco-Arabica* 4 (1991): 171–78.

Brindle and White 1982
Brindle, John V., and James J. White. *Talking in Flowers: Japanese Botanical Art.* Exh. cat. Pittsburgh: Hunt Institute for Botanical Documentation, Carnegie-Mellon University, 1982.

Brinker and Lutz 1989
Brinker, Helmut, and Albert Lutz. *Chinese Cloisonné: The Pierre Uldry Collection.* Trans. Susanna Swoboda. Exh. cat. New York: Asia Society, 1989.

Brooklyn 1967
The Brooklyn Museum Handbook. Brooklyn: The Brooklyn Museum, 1967.

Brooklyn 1988
Masterpieces in The Brooklyn Museum. New York: The Brooklyn Museum, in association with Abrams, 1988.

Brooklyn 1991
The Guennol Collection. Vol. 3. Brooklyn: The Brooklyn Museum, 1991.

Brooklyn 1997
Brooklyn Museum of Art. Brooklyn: Brooklyn Museum of Art, in association with Scala Books, 1997.

Cahill 1962
Cahill, James. *The Art of Southern S'ung China.* New York: Asia Society, 1962.

Canby 1990
Canby, Sheila R. "Age and Time in the Work of Riza." In *Persian Masters: Five Centuries of Painting,* ed. Sheila R. Canby. Bombay: J. J. Bhabha for Marg Publications, 1990.

Canby 1996
———. *The Rebellious Reformer: The Drawings and Paintings of Riza-yi 'Abbasi of Isfahan.* London: Azimuth Editions, 1996.

Carswell 1998
Carswell, John. *Iznik Pottery.* Eastern Art Series. London: Published for the Trustees of the British Museum by British Museum Press, 1998.

Chandra 1989
Chandra, Pramod. "The Brooklyn Museum Folios of the *Hamza-nama.*" *Orientations* 20, no. 7 (July 1989): 39–45.

Chandra 1994
———. "The Brooklyn Museum Folios of the *Qissa-i Amir Hamza (Hamza-nama).*" In Poster 1994, 61–66.

Chiba 2002
Chiba Mizuo et al., eds. *Kawakami Ryoka to iu gaka ita – Yorozu Tetsugoro, Kishida Ryusei, Kawakami Ryoka ga mukiatta shizen, fukei ten* (There was once a painter named Kawakami Ryoka: Nature and landscape as envisioned by Yorozu Tetsugoro, Kishida Ryusei, and Kawakami Ryoka). Towacho and Chigasaki: Yorozu Tetsugoro Memorial Museum and Chigasaki City Museum, 2002.

Chiba City Museum of Art 1996
Shukufuku sareta Shiki. Kinsei Nihon kaiga no shosō (Celebrated four seasons: An aspect of Japanese paintings from the 16th to the 19th centuries). Exh. cat. Chiba: Chiba City Museum of Art, 1996.

China Institute in America 1971
Early Chinese Gold and Silver. Exh. cat. New York: China House Gallery, China Institute in America, 1971.

China Institute in America 1972
Dragons in Chinese Art. New York: China House Gallery, China Institute in America, 1972.

Christie's 2001
Christie's, New York. *The Falk Collection I: Important Chinese Ceramics and Works of Art, Thursday, 20 September, 2001.* New York: Christie's, 2001.

Chung-ang 1985
The Beauty of Korean Art. Vol. 18. Seoul: Chung-ang Daily Newspaper, 1985.

Czuma 1977
Czuma, Stanislaw. "Mathura Sculpture in the Cleveland Museum Collection." *The Bulletin of the Cleveland Museum of Art* 64, no. 3 (March 1977): 83–114.

Czuma 1985
———. *Kushan Sculpture: Images from Early India.* Exh. cat. Cleveland: Cleveland Museum of Art, in cooperation with Indiana University Press, 1985.

Day 1952
Day, Florence E. "The Tiraz Silk of Marwan." In *Archaeologia Orientalia in Memoriam Ernst Herzfeld,* ed. George C. Miles, 39–62. Locust Valley, N.Y.: J. J. Augustin, 1952.

Dayton Art Institute 1984
Chinese Gold and Silver in American Collections: Tang Dynasty, A.D. 618–907. Exh. cat. Dayton: Dayton Art Institute, 1984.

de Lippe 1978
de Lippe, Aschwin. *The Art of India: Stone Sculpture.* Amsterdam, New York, Oxford: North Holland Publishing Company, 1978.

Dehejia 1999
Dehejia, Vidya. *Devi: The Great Goddess – Female Divinity in South Asian Art.* Exh. cat. Washington, D.C.: Arthur M. Sackler Gallery, Smithsonian Institution, in association with Ahmedabad: Mapin Publishing and Munich: Prestel Verlag, 1999.

Desai and Mason 1993
Desai, Vishakha N., and Darielle Mason, eds. *Gods, Guardians, and Lovers: Temple Sculptures from North India, A.D. 700–1200.* Exh. cat. New York: Asia Society, in association with Ahmedabad: Mapin Publishing, 1993.

Diba 1996
Diba, Layla S. "The Rose and the Nightingale in Persian Art." *Arts of Asia* 26, no. 6 (November–December 1996): 100–12.

Diba 1998
Diba, Layla S., and Maryam Ekhtiar, eds. *Royal Persian Paintings: The Qajar Epoch, 1785–1925.* Exh. cat. New York: Brooklyn Museum of Art, in association with London: I. B. Tauris, 1998.

Diez 1944
Diez, Ernest. *Die Iranische Kunst*. Vienna: Wilhelm Andermann Verlag, 1944.

Dunn 2001
Dunn, Michael. *Traditional Japanese Design: Five Tastes*. Exh. cat. New York: Japan Society, distributed by Abrams, 2001.

Ekhtiar 1989a
Ekhtiar, Maryam. *The Art of Qajar Iran* (checklist of The Brooklyn Museum's holdings with an annotated bibliography). New York, 1989.

Ekhtiar 1989b
———. "The Qajar Visual Aesthetic: Highlights from The Brooklyn Museum Collection." *Orientations* 20, no. 7 (July 1989): 46–53.

Ellis 1974
Ellis, Charles Grant. "Is the Mamluk Carpet a Mandala: A Speculation." *Textile Museum Journal* 4, no. 1 (December 1974): 30–50.

Eng 1970
Eng, Robert. "Riza-i 'Abbasi: A Safavid Miniature Painter." Unpublished master's thesis, Hunter College, (1970): 65–105.

Erdmann 1961
Erdmann, Kurt. "Neuere Untersuchungen zur Frage der kairener Teppiche." *Arts Orientalis* 4 (1961): 65–105.

Eskenazi 2002
Eskenazi, Giuseppe. *Two Rare Chinese Porcelain Fish Jars of the 14th and 15th Centuries*. London: Eskenazi, 2002.

Ettinghausen and Grabar 1987
Ettinghausen, Richard, and Oleg Grabar. *The Art and Architecture of Islam: 650–1250*. Pelican History of Art. London: Penguin Books, 1987.

Fane and Poster 2000
Fane, Diana, and Amy G. Poster. *The Guennol Collection: Cabinet of Wonders*. Exh. cat. Brooklyn: Brooklyn Museum of Art, 2000.

Faridany-Akhavan 1989
Faridany-Akhavan, Zahra. "The Problems of the Mughal Manuscripts of the *Hamza-Nama*, 1562–77: A Reconstruction." Ph.D. diss., Harvard University, 1989.

Ferber 1987
Ferber, Linda, et al. *The Collector's Eye: The Ernest Erickson Collection at The Brooklyn Museum*. Exh. cat. Brooklyn: The Brooklyn Museum, 1987.

Finlay 1996
Finlay, John R. "Returns to the Past: Chinese Art in The Brooklyn Museum." *Arts of Asia* 26, no. 6 (November–December 1996): 68–79.

Fitzhugh and Dubreuil 1999
Fitzhugh, William J., and Chisato O. Dubreuil, eds. *Ainu: The Spirit of a Northern People*. Exh. cat. Washington D.C.: Arctic Studies Center, National Museum of Natural History, Smithsonian Institution, in association with University of Washington Press, 1999.

Fontein and Wu 1973
Fontein, Jan, and Wu Tung. *Unearthing China's Past*. Exh. cat. Boston: Museum of Fine Arts, distributed by New York Graphic Society, 1973.

Getz 1912
Getz, John. *Catalogue of the Avery Collection of Ancient Chinese Cloisonnés*. Exh. cat. Brooklyn: [Museum of the Brooklyn Institute of Arts and Sciences], 1912.

Gittinger 1982
Gittinger, Mattiebelle. *Master Dyers to the World: Technique and Trade in Early Indian Dyed Cotton*. Exh. cat. Washington, D.C.: Textile Museum, 1982.

Goodwin 1988
Goodwin, Shauna. "The Realm of Beauty: A Cherry Blossom Picnic Screen in The Brooklyn Museum." *Orientations* 19, no. 6 (June 1988): 40–49.

Grabar 1992
Grabar, Oleg. *The Mediation of Ornament*. Princeton: Princeton University Press, 1992.

Grove's 1996
Turner, Jane, ed. *The Dictionary of Art*. New York: Grove's Dictionaries, 1996.

Grube 1972
Grube, Ernst J. *Islamic Paintings from the Eleventh to the Eighteenth Century in the Collection of Hans P. Kraus*. New York: H. P. Kraus, 1972.

Guth 1995
Guth, Christine. "The Cult of Kannon Among Nineteenth-Century American Japanophiles." *Orientations* 26, no. 2 (December 1995): 28–34.

Hashimoto 1968
Hashimoto Sumiko. *Keppatsu to kamikazari* (Hairdos and hair ornaments). Nihon no bijutsu (Japanese art), vol. 23. Tokyo: Shibundō, 1968.

He 1996
He, Li. *Chinese Ceramics: A New Comprehensive Survey from the Asian Art Museum of San Francisco*. New York: Rizzoli, 1996.

Hisamatsu 1987
Hisamatsu Yumiko. "On Kaiho Yusho's Drying Fishnet Screens in the Imperial Household Collection," *Bijutsushi* 121 (1987): 1–20.

Huntington and Huntington 1985
Huntington, John, and Susan Huntington. *The Art of Ancient India: Buddhist, Hindu, Jain*. New York: Weatherhill, 1985.

International Cultural Society of Korea 1989
Mi guk park mul guan so jang Han kook mun hwa ja/The Korean Relics in the United States. Seoul: International Cultural Society of Korea, 1989.

Itō H. 1984
Itō Hiroshi. *Yūjo* (Courtesans). Kinsei fūzoku zufu (Illustrated premodern customs and manners), vol. 7. Ed. Kirihata Takeshi et al. Tokyo: Shōgakkan, 1984: 77–95.

Itō Y. 1990
Itō Yūko. "Yūjo monogatari emaki" (The Scroll of courtesans' life). *The Annual Collection of Essays and Studies, Faculty of Letters, Gakushuin University* 37 (1990): 151–85.

James 1980
James, David. *Qur'ans and Bindings from the Chester Beatty Library*. London: World of Islam Festival Trust, 1980.

Japan Ceramic Society 1956
Tōsetsu 39, no. 6 (1956): 50.

Jiang 1987
Jiang Feng, ed. *Zhongguo meishu cidian* (Dictionary of Chinese art). Shanghai: Shanghai Cishu Chubanshe, 1987; Taipei: Shiung Shih Art Books, 1989.

Katz 1963
Katz, Lois. *Asian Art: From the Collections of Ernest Erickson and the Erickson Foundation, Inc.* Exh. cat. Brooklyn: The Brooklyn Museum, 1963.

Katz 1966–67
———. "The Brooklyn Tara: A Rediscovery." *The Brooklyn Museum Annual* 8 (1966–67): 113–28.

Kennedy 1990
Kennedy, Alan. *Japanese Costume: History and Tradition.* Paris: A. Biro, distributed by Rizzoli International, 1990.

Khandalavala and Chandra 1969
Khandalavala, Karl, and Moti Chandra. *New Documents of Indian Painting: A Reappraisal.* Bombay: Prince of Wales Museum of Western India, 1969.

Kobayashi 1979
Kobayashi Tadashi, ed. *Edo shomin no kaiga: Fūzoku-ga to ukiyo-e* (Painting of people during Edo: Genre painting and Ukiyo-e). Nihon bijutsu zenshū (Japanese art collections), vol. 22. Tokyo: Gakushū Kenkyū-sha, 1979.

Kobayashi 1981
———. "Sakura no yūraku e byōbu" (*Cherry Blossom Viewing Picnic* screen). *Kokka,* no. 1041 (1981): 32–40.

Kobayashi and Kano 1992
Kobayashi Tadashi and Kano Hiroyuki, eds. *Edo no kaiga 1: Kanō-ha to Fūzuka-ga* (Edo painting 1: Kanō school and genre painting). Nihon bijutsu zenshū (Japanese art collections), vol. 17. Tokyo: Kōdansha, 1992.

Kokka 1942
"*Drying Fishnets,* Ascribed to Yusho Kaihoku." *Kokka,* no. 625 (December 1942): 375.

Koyama 1959
Koyama Fujio. *Céramique ancienne de l'Asie: Chine, Japon, Corée, Asie du Sud-Est, Proche-Orient.* Trans. Daisy Lion-Goldschmidt. Tokyo: Bijutsu Shuppan-sha and Fribourg: Office du Livre, 1959.

Krahl 1998
Krahl, Regina. "Bright as Silver, White as Snow: White Wares of North and South China." In *Bright as Silver, White as Snow: Chinese White Ceramics from Late Tang to Yuan Dynasty: Examples from the Kai-yin Collection,* ed. Lo Kai-Yin, 13–24. Exh. cat. for Denver Art Museum. Hong Kong: Yungmingtan, 1998.

Kramrisch 1981
Kramrisch, Stella. *Manifestations of Shiva.* Exh. cat. Philadelphia: Philadelphia Museum of Art, 1981.

Kühnel 1939
Kühnel, Ernest. "History of Miniature Painting and Drawing." In *A Survey of Persian Art: From Prehistoric Times to the Present,* ed. Arthur Upham Pope and Phyllis Ackerman, 1829–97. London: Oxford University Press, 1938–39.

Kuo 1992
Kuo, Jason C. *Word as Image: The Art of Chinese Seal Engraving.* Exh. cat. New York: China House Gallery and China Institute in America, distributed by University of Washington Press, 1992.

Lawrence 1989
Lawrence, Deirdre E. "Culin: Collector and Documentor of the World." *Orientations* 20, no. 7 (July 1989): 20–27.

Lee, G. 1955
Lee, George. "A Chinese Bronze Vessel." *The Brooklyn Museum Bulletin* 17, no. 1 (Fall 1955): 2–4.

Lee, S. 1953
Lee, Sherman. "Two Early Chinese Ivories," *Artibus Asiae* 16, no. 4 (1953): 264.

Lee and Ho 1968
Lee, Sherman, and Wai-kam Ho. *Chinese Art under the Mongols. The Yüan Dynasty, 1279–1368.* Exh. cat. Cleveland: Cleveland Museum of Art, 1968.

Leidy and Thurman 1998
Leidy, Denise Patry, and Robert A. F. Thurman. *Mandala: The Architecture of Enlightenment.* Exh. cat. New York: Asia Society; New York: Tibet House; and Boston: Shambhala, 1998.

Lin 1990
Lin Xiaoping. "The Blue of Jingtai: The Samuel P. Avery, Jr., Collection of Chinese Cloisonné in The Brooklyn Museum." *Orientations* 21, no. 7 (July 1990): 30–38.

Lorber 2001
Lorber, Martin. "Japanese Buddhist Paintings in New York Museums." *Bulletin of the International Asian Art Fair.* New York: 2001.

Los Angeles County Museum of Art 1950
The Art of Greater India. Los Angeles: Los Angeles County Museum of Art, 1950.

Matsuoka 1930
Matsuoka, Asa. "Two Great Masterpieces in the Brooklyn Museum." *Brooklyn Museum Quarterly* 17, no. 4 (October 1930): 130–32.

Mayuyama 1966
Mayuyama Junkichi, ed. *Ōbei shūzō Nihon bijutsu zuroku/Japanese Art in the West.* Tokyo: Mayuyama Ryūsendō, 1966.

Medley 1986
Medley, Margaret. *The Chinese Potter: A Practical History of Chinese Ceramics.* Oxford: Phaidon, 1976. Reprint, Ithaca, N.Y.: Cornell University Press, 1986 (page references are to reprint edition).

Middleton 1996
Middleton, Andrew. *Rugs and Carpets: Techniques, Traditions, and Designs.* London: Mitchell Beazley, 1996.

Mirviss 1995
Mirviss, Joan B. *A Celebration of Twenty Years: Eleven Japanese Print Masterpieces.* New York: Joan B. Mirviss, 1995.

Moes 1985
Moes, Robert. *Mingei: Japanese Folk Art from The Brooklyn Museum Collection.* Exh. cat. Brooklyn: The Brooklyn Museum and New York: Universe, 1985.

Moes 1987
———. *Korean Art from The Brooklyn Museum Collection*. Exh. cat. Brooklyn: The Brooklyn Museum and New York: Universe, 1987.

Murase 1971
Murase, Miyeko. *Byobu: Japanese Screens from New York Collections*. Exh. cat. New York: Asia Society, distributed by New York Graphic Society, 1971.

Murase 1990
———. *Masterpieces of Japanese Screen Painting: The American Collections*. New York: George Braziller, 1990.

Nagata 1997
Nagata Seiji, ed. *Nyūyōku/Nyūjājī ukiyo-e korekushon ten: Burukkurin Bijutsukan, Metoroporitan Bijutsukan, Nyūyōku Kōritsu Toshokan, Nyuāku Bijutsukan/The New York and New Jersey Ukiyo-e Collection: The Brooklyn Museum of Art, The Metropolitan Museum of Art, The New York Public Library, The Newark Museum*. Exh. cat. Osaka: The Sankei Shinbun, 1997.

Narazaki 1960
Narazaki Muneshige. "On a Newly Discovered Picture Scroll of 'Courtesans and Their Life' and Its Illustrative Pictures in the Hakubyo Style." *Kokka*, no. 821 (August 1960): 305–11.

Newman 1984
Newman, Richard. *The Stone Sculpture of India: A Study of the Materials Used by Indian Sculptors from Ca. 2nd Century B.C. to the 16th Century*. Cambridge: Center for Conservation and Technical Studies, Harvard University Museum Art Museums, 1984.

Okudaira 1982
Okudaira Hideo. *Otogi zōshi emaki* (Illustrated narrative scrolls of late medieval Japan). Tokyo: Kadokawa Shoten, 1982.

Osaka City Museum 1942
Dai 6-kai meihō tenrankai zuroku (The 6th exhibition of masterpieces). Exh. cat. Osaka: Osaka City Museum, 1942.

Osaka 1992
Kōrai seiji eno izanai/An Introduction to Koryō Celadon. Exh. cat. Osaka: Museum of Oriental Ceramics and Osaka: Association for the Advancement of Fine Arts, 1992.

Ōta Memorial Museum of Art 1999
Burukkurin Bijutsukan shozō ukiyo-e meihin-ten/Masterpieces of Ukiyo-e from the Brooklyn Museum of Art. Exh. cat. Tokyo: Ōta Memorial Museum of Art et al. and Osaka: The Sankei Shinbun, 1999.

Paine and Soper 1955
Paine, Robert T., and Alexander Soper. *Art and Architecture of Japan*. Baltimore: Penguin Books, 1955.

Pal 1969
Pal, Pratapaditya. *Art of Tibet*. Exh. cat. New York: Asia Society, 1969.

Pal 1973–74
———. "A Brahmanical Triad from Kashmir and Some Related Icons." *Archives of Asian Art* 27 (1973–74): 33–45.

Pal 1978a
———. *The Arts of Nepal. Part II: Painting*. Leiden: E. J. Brill, 1978.

Pal 1978b
———. *The Ideal Image: The Gupta Sculptural Tradition and Its Influence*. Exh. cat. New York: Asia Society, in association with Weatherhill, 1978.

Pal 1978c
———. *The Sensuous Immortals: A Selection of Sculptures from the Pan-Asian Collection*. Exh. cat. Los Angeles: Los Angeles Museum of Art and Cambridge: MIT Press, 1978.

Pal 1983
———. *Court Paintings of India: 16th–19th Centuries*. New York: Navin Kumar, 1983.

Pal 1984
———, ed. *Light of Asia: Buddha Sakyamuni in Asian Art*. Exh. cat. Los Angeles: Los Angeles County Museum of Art, 1984.

Pal 1989
——— et al. *Romance of the Taj Mahal*. Exh. cat. Los Angeles: Los Angeles County Museum of Art and London: Thames and Hudson, 1989.

Pal 1997
———. "Preface." In Singer and Denwood 1997, 8–13.

Poster 1973
Poster, Amy G. *Figures in Clay: India Terracottas from the Bertram H. Schaffner Collection*. Exh. cat. Brooklyn: The Brooklyn Museum, 1973.

Poster 1982
———. "Art of the Himalayan Region." *Apollo* 115, no. 242 (April 1982): 260–63.

Poster 1986
———. *From Indian Earth: 4,000 Years of Terracotta Art*. Exh. cat. Brooklyn: The Brooklyn Museum, 1986.

Poster 1987
———. "Indian and Southeast Asian Art." In Ferber 1987, 145–86.

Poster 1989
———. "Religious Arts of Medieval Japan in The Brooklyn Museum." *Orientations* 20, no. 7 (July 1989): 28–37.

Poster 1994
———. *Realms of Heroism: Indian Paintings from The Brooklyn Museum*. Exh. cat. Brooklyn: The Brooklyn Museum, 1994.

Poster 1995
———. "The Heroic Ideal in Indian Painting." *Orientations* 26, no. 4 (April 1995): 63–70.

Poster 1996
———. "The First Century of the Asian Art Department." *Arts of Asia* 26, no. 6 (November–December 1996): 61–79.

Poster 1999
———. "Ukiyo-e and Asian Art at the Brooklyn Museum of Art." In Ōta Memorial Museum of Art 1999, 14–19.

Ramamrutham 1989
Ramamrutham, Usha. "Lacquer: A Panorama of Asian Decorative Arts." *Orientations* 20, no. 4 (April 1989): 74–79.

Rawson 1990
Rawson, Jessica. *Western Zhou Ritual Bronzes from the Arthur M. Sackler Collection*. Vol. IIa. Washington, D.C.: The Arthur M. Sackler Foundation, 1990.

Ray 2002
Ray, Simon. *Indian and Islamic Works of Art.* London: Simon Ray, 2002.

Rice 1965
Rice, Talbot. *Islamic Art.* New York: Praeger, 1965.

Rossi and Rossi 1996
Rossi, Anna Maria, and Fabio Rossi. *Early Tibetan Manuscript Covers: 12th–15th Centuries.* Texts by David Weldon, et al. Exh. cat. for *Guardians of the Sacred Work,* New York: Barbara Mathes Gallery. London: Rossi & Rossi, 1996.

Rubin 1975
Rubin, Ida Ely, ed. *The Guennol Collection: Volume I.* New York: The Metropolitan Museum of Art, 1975.

Sadō Shiryōkan 1982
Dai 57-kai shunki tokubetsu ten: Chano yu to Kyōyaki II – Ninnami, Hozen o chushin ni (The 57th special spring exhibition: Tea ceremony and Kyoto ceramics – Centering on Ninnami and Hozen). Exh. cat. Tokyo: Sadō Shiryōkan, 1982.

Satō 1993
Satō Yasuhiro. *Yuna-zu: Shisen no dorama* (A Picture of Bathhouse Women: A Dream of Gaze). E wa kataru/Cultural Memory in Arts, vol. 11. Tokyo: Heibonsha, 1993.

Savelle 1957
Savelle, Max. *History of World Civilization.* New York: Henry Holt and Company, 1957.

Schroeder 1981
Schroeder, Ulrich von. *Indo-Tibetan Bronzes.* Hong Kong: Visual Dharma Productions, 1981.

Seyller 1993
Seyller, John. "A Dated *Hamzanama* Painting." *Artibus Asiae* 53, no. 3–4 (1993): 502–5.

Seyller 2002
———. *The Adventures of Hamza: Painting and Storytelling in Mughal India.* Exh. cat. Washington, D.C.: Freer Gallery of Art and Arthur M. Sackler Gallery, Smithsonian Institution, in association with London: Azimuth Editions, 2002.

Shimizu and Wheelwright 1976
Shimizu, Yoshiaki, and Carolyn Wheelwright, eds. *Japanese Ink Paintings from American Collections: An Exhibition in Honor of Shujiro Shimada.* Exh. cat. Princeton: Art Museum, Princeton University, distributed by Princeton University Press, 1976.

Shibundō 2000
Smoking Tools. Art of Japan. Vol. 9. Tokyo: Shibundō, 2000.

Shinto 1970
Shinto Tōru, ed. *Hakubyō emaki* (Hakubyō handscrolls). Nihon no bijutsu (Japanese art), vol. 48. Tokyo: Shibundō, 1970.

Simpson 1979
Simpson, Marianna Shreve. *The Illustration of an Epic: The Earliest Shahnameh Manuscripts.* New York: Garland Publishing, 1979.

Singer 1998
Singer, Robert T. *Edo: Art in Japan 1615–1868.* Exh. cat. Washington, D.C.: National Gallery of Art, in collaboration with Agency for Cultural Affairs, Government of Japan, and The Japan Foundation, 1998.

Singer and Denwood 1997
Singer, Jane Casey, and Philip Denwood, eds. *Tibetan Art: Towards a Definition of Style.* London: Laurence King, in association with Alan Marcuson, 1997.

Smith and Poster 1986
Smith, Henry, II, and Amy G. Poster. *Hiroshige: One Hundred Famous Views of Edo.* New York: George Braziller, 1986.

Smith College Museum of Art 1957
Neolithic to Ming: Chinese Objects [in] the Myron S. Falk Collection. Exh. cat. Northampton, Mass.: Smith College Museum of Art, 1957.

Smith College Museum of Art 1975
One Hundred: An Exhibition to Celebrate the Centennial Year of Smith College. Northampton, Mass.: Smith College Museum of Art, 1975.

Song 1996
Song, Houmei. "Wild Geese and Reeds (*Luyan*) Painting of the Ming Dynasty." *Oriental Art* 42, no. 1 (Spring 1996): 30–42.

Soper 1971
Soper, Alexander. "Movable Feasts." *Artnews* 69, no. 10 (February 1971): 40–43, 68, 69.

Soustiel 1985
Soustiel, Jean. *La Céramique islamique: La Guide du Connoisseur.* Fribourg: Office du Livre and Paris: Vilo, 1985.

Spelman 1977
Spelman, Ruth. *The Arts of China: A Retrospective.* Exh. cat. Greenvale, N.Y.: Art Gallery, School of the Arts, C. W. Post Center, Long Island University, 1977.

Stanley-Baker 1992
Stanley-Baker, Joan. *The Transmission of Chinese Idealist Painting to Japan: Notes on the Early Phase (1661–1799).* Michigan Papers in Japanese Studies, no. 21. Ann Arbor: Center for Japanese Studies, University of Michigan, 1992.

Stchoukine 1964
Stchoukine, Ivan. *Les Peintures des manuscrits de Shah Abbas Ier à la fin des Safavis.* Bibliothèque Archéologique et Historique, vol. 76. Paris: Librairie Orientaliste, P. Geuthner, 1964.

Stone 1994
Stone, Elizabeth Rosen. *The Buddhist Art of Nagarjunakonda.* Delhi: Motilal Banarsidass Publishers, 1994.

Takeda H. 1977
Takeda Hisao et al., eds. *Fūzoku-ga: Yūraku, tagasode* (Genre painting: Entertainment and kimono). Nihon byōbu-e shūsei (Japanese screen collections), vol. 14. Tokyo: Kōdansha, 1977.

Takeda T. 1967
Takeda Tsuneo. *Kinsei shoki fūzoku-ga* (Early premodern genre painting). Nihon no bijutsu (Japanese art), vol. 20. Tokyo: Shibundō, 1967.

Tōbu Museum of Art 1995
Dai Sharaku-ten/Sharaku Exhibition. Exh. cat. Tokyo: Tōbu Museum of Art, NHK (Japan Broadcasting Company), and NHK Promotions Company, 1995.

Tokugawa Museum of Art 1997
Kabuku bi no sekai – E wa kataru: Itan to kyoraku no ukiyo/Early Seventeenth-Century Genre Paintings: The World of Lively Entertainment. Exh. cat. Nagoya: The Tokugawa Museum of Art, 1997.

Tokyo Bijutsu Gakkō 1933
Catalogue of Art Treasures of Ten Great Temples of Nara, Volume Fifteen: The Kofukuji Temple, Part 2. Tokyo: Tokyo Bijutsu Gakkō, 1933.

Tokyo National Museum 1985
Tokubetsu-ten: Nihon no tōji/Special Exhibition: Japanese Ceramics. Exh. cat. Tokyo: Tokyo National Museum, 1985.

Travelstead 1982
Travelstead, Brooke. "An Ornamental Ceramic Globe from the Ottoman Period." *Apollo* 115, no. 242 (April 1982): 237.

Trubner 1957
Trubner, Henry. *The Arts of the T'ang Dynasty.* Exh. cat. Los Angeles: Los Angeles County Museum of Art, 1957.

Varley 1977
Varley, H. Paul. *Japanese Culture: A Short History.* New York: Praeger, 1977.

Varnedoe 1989
Varnedoe, Kirk. *A Fine Disregard: What Makes Modern Art Modern.* New York: Harry N. Abrams, 1989.

Volov 1966
Volov (Golombek), Lisa. "The Plaited Kufic on Samanid Epigraphic Pottery." *Ars Orientalis* 6 (1966): 107–33.

Watt and Wardwell 1997
Watt, James C. Y., and Anne E. Wardwell. *When Silk Was Gold: Central Asian and Chinese Textiles.* Exh. cat. New York: The Metropolitan Museum of Art, in cooperation with Cleveland Museum of Art, 1997.

Weimann 1983
Weimann, Christopher. "Techniques of Marbling and Early Indian Paintings." *Fine Print* (October 1983): 135–37. Reprinted in *Ink and Gall* 5, no. 2 (Winter 1991): 16–23.

Welch 1979
Welch, Anthony. *Calligraphy and the Arts of the Muslim World.* Exh. cat. New York: Asia Society and Austin: University of Texas Press, 1979.

Woo 1999
Woo, Hyunsoo. "Brooklyn e Soomshi nun Hankookmi ui Soomkyol (Korean Art Collection of the Brooklyn Museum of Art)." *Wolgan misool (The Monthly Art Magazine)* 2, no. 1 (January 1999): 118–23.

Yawata 1975
Yawata Yotaro. "Nihon to Amerika ni wakareta isoo no shoki suzoku-zu byobu" (A screen separated from Japan to the United States). *Geijutsu Shinchō* (November 1970).

Yoshinaga 1996
Yoshinaga, Miyako. "Modern and Contemporary Japanese Ceramics." *Arts of Asia* 26, no. 6 (November–December 1996): 92–99.

Yuan 2000
Yuan, Frances. "Chinese Art, the Wonder Cabinet, and the Guennol Collection." *Orientations* 31, no. 3 (March 2000): 84–89.

Yuan 2001
———. "Transition and Development: A Selection of Early Chinese Bronzes at the Brooklyn Museum of Art." *Orientations* 32, no. 2 (March 2001): 103–7.

Index

Page numbers in italics refer to illustrations.